S0-ABA-240

GREGG SHORTHAND FOR COLLEGES Volume One

Diamond Jubilee Series

Second Edition

Louis A. Leslie
Coauthor Diamond Jubilee Series of Gregg Shorthand

Charles E. Zoubek
Coauthor Diamond Jubilee Series of Gregg Shorthand

A. James Lemaster
Assistant Professor of Education
Baruch College, City University of New York

Russell J. Hosler
Professor of Education
University of Wisconsin

Shorthand written by
Charles Rader

GREGG SHORTHAND FOR COLLEGES Volume One

Diamond Jubilee Series

Second Edition

Gregg Division | McGraw-Hill Book Company

New York | St. Louis | Dallas | San Francisco
Düsseldorf | Johannesburg | Kuala Lumpur
London | Mexico | Montreal | New Delhi | Panama
Rio de Janeiro | Singapore | Sydney | Toronto

Art Director	Frank Medina
Designer	Barbara Bert
Shorthand Production Supervisor	Charles Rader
Editorial Staff	Jerome Edelman, Mary Buchanan, Kathy Flynn
Photographer	Sebastian Milito
Compositor	King Typographic Service
Printer	R. R. Donnelley & Sons Company

Library of Congress Cataloging in Publication Data

Main entry under title:

Gregg shorthand for colleges.

(Diamond jubilee series)

First ed. by L. A. Leslie, C. E. Zoubek, and R. J. Hosler.

1. Shorthand—Gregg. I. Leslie, Louis A., date.
II. Leslie, Louis A., date. Gregg shorthand for colleges.

Z56.G833G74 653'.427 72-10140

ISBN 0-07-037401-5 (v. 1)

ISBN 0-07-037406-6 (v. 2)

GREGG SHORTHAND FOR COLLEGES, Volume One

Diamond Jubilee Series

Second Edition

890 DODO 2109876

Preface

Gregg Shorthand, the System of Millions

Gregg Shorthand, which was first published on May 28, 1888, by John Robert Gregg, its inventor, is today the world's most widely used system of shorthand. It is used by millions of writers throughout the world not only in English but in many foreign languages as well. To many people, the terms "shorthand" and "Gregg" are synonymous.

Gregg Shorthand is a vocational tool that hundreds of thousands of stenographers and secretaries use to obtain interesting and lucrative positions in business, in government, and in industry. It is also a personal tool that many business and professional men and women use to relieve them of the burden of writing cumbersome longhand when they make notes, compose important letters and memorandums, and draft speeches and reports.

The success of any system of shorthand rests on the merits of its alphabet. The Gregg alphabet is the most efficient shorthand alphabet ever devised in more than 2,000 years of shorthand history. The fact that the Gregg alphabet, virtually without change, has been the basis of Gregg Shorthand since 1888 is indeed a tribute to the genius of John Robert Gregg.

Gregg Shorthand for Colleges, Diamond Jubilee Series, Second Edition

To meet the needs of private business schools, colleges, junior colleges, community colleges, and other post-high school institutions, *Gregg Shorthand, Diamond Jubilee Series,* has been made available in a college edition. This edition provides shorthand instructional materials that are different from those used in high schools, materials that are more challenging and that are geared to the interests of the more mature college student.

OBJECTIVES

The major objectives of this second edition are these:

1 To teach the student to read and write Gregg Shorthand rapidly and accurately in the shortest possible time.

2 To develop and improve the student's grasp—concurrently with the teaching of shorthand—of the nonshorthand elements of transcription, which include vocabulary development, spelling, punctuation, grammar, and typing style.

The features of this second edition that are designed to help achieve these objectives are described later in this preface.

Format and Organization

In this second edition, no word-building principles or outlines have been changed. The organization of the lessons and the order of presentation of shorthand principles are the same as those of the first edition.

However, a significant change has been made in the format. The shorthand practice material is presented in two columns that are approximately the width of the columns of the student's shorthand notebook. The shorter lines make reading easier, for the eye does not have to travel so far from the end of one line to the beginning of the next. The new format also makes possible the highlighting of the words from the Reading and Writing Practice that are singled out for spelling attention. These words are placed in the margins rather than in the body of the shorthand.

Like the first edition, the second edition is divided into three parts as follows:

Part 1: Principles—Chapters 1-8 Each chapter contains six lessons. The first five lessons of each chapter are devoted to the presentation of principles, and the sixth lesson is a recall. The last group of new principles is presented in Lesson 47.

Part 2: Reinforcement—Chapter 9 Chapter 9 contains eight lessons, each of which reviews intensively the principles presented in one of the eight chapters in Part 1.

Part 3: Shorthand and Transcription Skill Building—Chapter 10 This chapter consists of fourteen lessons, each of which is designed to strengthen the student's grasp of a major principle of Gregg Shorthand. In addition, each lesson continues to develop the student's vocabulary and to improve his ability to spell, to punctuate, and to apply rules of grammar correctly.

TRANSCRIPTION SKILLS

This second edition continues to place strong emphasis on the nonshorthand elements of transcription, which are taught concurrently with shorthand. It retains all the helpful transcription drills of the first edition, with slight, but effective, modifications. These include:

Business Vocabulary Builders Beginning with Chapter 3, each lesson contains a Business Vocabulary Builder consisting of several words or expressions and their definitions. These words and expressions are selected from the Reading and Writing Practice of the lesson. The Business Vocabulary Builders help to overcome a major transcription problem—a limited vocabulary.

Spelling—Marginal Reminders Beginning with Chapter 4, words are singled out from the Reading and Writing Practice for special spelling attention. These words appear in a second color in the shorthand and in print type in the margin of the shorthand, correctly divided.

Spelling—Families An effective device for improving spelling is the study of words in related groups, or spelling families. Spelling families are provided in a number of lessons, beginning with Lesson 45.

Similar-Words Drills These drills teach the student the differences in meaning between similar words that transcribers often confuse, for example, *their-there, accept-except.*

Punctuation Beginning with Lesson 31, nine frequent usages of the comma are introduced. Only one comma usage is presented in a lesson. The commas appear in a circle in the shorthand, and the reason for the use of the comma is printed above the circle.

Common Prefixes An understanding of the meaning of common English prefixes enables students to improve their command of words. Several of the lessons contain common prefixes, beginning with Lesson 56.

Grammar Checkup In a number of lessons, drills are provided on rules of grammar that transcribers often apply incorrectly.

Transcription Quiz Beginning with Lesson 57, each lesson contains a Transcription Quiz consisting of a letter in which the student must supply the internal punctuation. This quiz provides him with the opportunity to test his mastery of the punctuation rules presented in earlier lessons.

OTHER FEATURES

Shorthand Spelling Helps Each time a new shorthand letter or abbreviating device is presented, the shorthand spelling is given. Formerly, this information had to be provided by the teacher.

Chapter Openings Each chapter opens with a beautifully illustrated introduction that not only shows the student a vivid picture of the life and duties of a secretary but also inspires and encourages him in his efforts to acquire the necessary qualifications.

Student Helps The student is given step-by-step suggestions on how to handle each new phase of his shorthand study when it is first introduced.

Reading Scoreboards At various points in the text, the student is given an opportunity to determine his shorthand reading speed by means of a scoreboard. The scoreboard enables him to calculate the number of words a minute he is reading. By comparing his reading speed from scoreboard to scoreboard, he sees some indication of his shorthand reading growth.

Check Lists To keep the student constantly reminded of the importance of good practice procedures, an occasional check list is provided. These check lists deal with writing shorthand, reading shorthand, homework, proportion, etc.

Charts and Lists The last lesson in each of the eight chapters in Part 1 contains a recall chart that reviews all the principles of the chapter as well as the principles of previous chapters.

On the inside back cover of this book is a chart of the brief forms in the order of their presentation in the text, as well as a list of commonly used phrases.

The authors and publishers wish to express their gratitude to the many teachers who shared with them their experiences in teaching the first edition of Gregg Shorthand for Colleges, Diamond Jubilee Series.

This second edition of Gregg Shorthand for Colleges, DJS, Volume One, is presented with the confidence that it will enable college shorthand teachers to do an even more effective job of training rapid and accurate shorthand writers and transcribers.

The Publishers

Contents

Shorthand Practice Procedures

The rate at which your shorthand skill develops will depend largely on two factors: (1) The amount of time you devote to practice. (2) The efficiency with which you practice. The person who practices efficiently will derive more benefit from an hour's practice than another who may spend several hours on his practice but follows no plan.

By following the procedures suggested here, you will derive the maximum benefit from your investment in practice time.

READING WORD LISTS

Each principle of Gregg Shorthand that you study is accompanied by a list of illustrations in shorthand and in type. Practice each list in this way:

1 With the type key to the shorthand exposed, pronounce and spell aloud—if possible—each word and shorthand outline in the list, thus: *say, s-a; see, s-e.* Reading aloud will help to impress the shorthand outlines on your mind. Read all the shorthand words in the list in this way—with the type exposed—until you feel you can read the shorthand outlines *without* referring to the key.

2 With a card or piece of paper, cover up the type key to the first column of the list. Then read aloud from the shorthand, thus: *s-a, say; s-e, see.*

3 If the spelling of a shorthand outline does not immediately give you the meaning, move your card or piece of paper aside and refer to the type key. Do not spend more than a few seconds trying to decipher an outline.

4 Follow this procedure with the remaining columns of words in the list.

5 After you have read all the words in the list from the shorthand, reread the entire list once or twice again.

◈ Note: In reading brief forms and phrases, which first occur in Lesson 3, you need not spell the shorthand outlines.

The student studies the word lists by placing a card or a slip of paper over the type key and reading the shorthand words aloud.

Photographs: Syd Karson

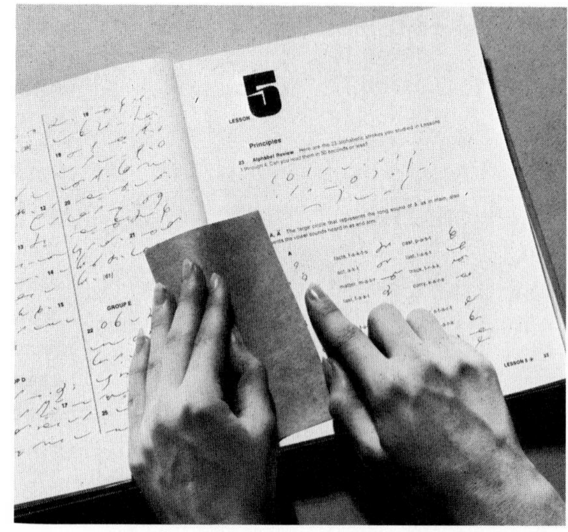

READING SENTENCES, LETTERS, AND ARTICLES

Each lesson contains a Reading Practice (Lessons 1-6) or a Reading and Writing Practice (Lessons 7-70).

Sentences, letters, or articles are written in shorthand. Reading these sentences, letters, and articles will help to impress the shorthand principles on your mind and enable you to develop a large shorthand vocabulary rapidly.

Two procedures for reading shorthand are outlined here—the first for those students who have been supplied with the *Student's Transcript of Gregg Shorthand For Colleges, Volume One;* the second for those students who will work without the *Student's Transcript.*

Procedure 1: With Student's Transcript

1 Place your *Student's Transcript* to the right of your textbook and open it to the transcript of the Reading Practice or Reading and Writing Practice you are about to read.

2 Place your left index finger under the shorthand outline that you are about to read and your right index finger under the corresponding word in the *Student's Transcript.*

Refer to your Transcript whenever you cannot read an outline. Keep your left index finger anchored in the shorthand; the right index finger on the corresponding place in the Transcript.

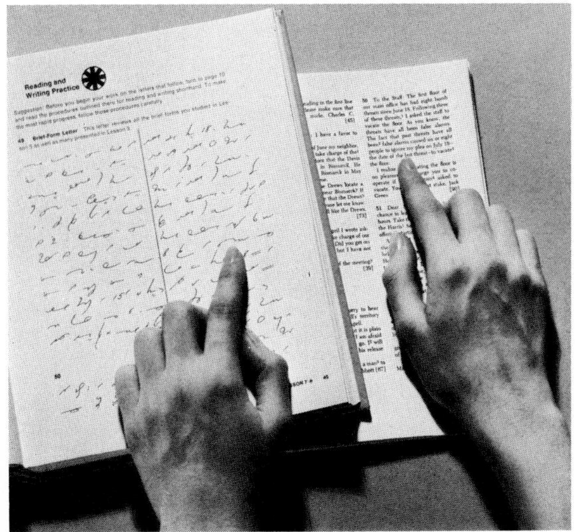

3 Read the shorthand outlines aloud until you come to an outline that you cannot read. Spell the outline. If the spelling does not immediately give you the meaning, anchor your left index finger on the outline and look in the transcript, where your right index finger is resting near the point at which you are reading.

4 Determine the meaning of the outline you cannot read and place your right index finger on it.

5 Return to the shorthand from which you are reading—your left index finger has kept your place for you—and continue reading.

6 If time permits, reread the material aloud a second time, once again spelling any outline you cannot read and referring to the transcript when the spelling does not immediately give you the meaning.

By following this procedure, you will not lose any time finding your place in the shorthand and in the transcript when you cannot read an outline.

Procedure 2: Without Student's Transcript

1 Before you start your work on a Reading Practice or Reading and Writing Practice, have a blank card or a sheet of paper and a pencil handy.

2 Read the shorthand outlines aloud.

3 When you come to an outline that you cannot read, spell it. If the spelling does not immediately give you the meaning of the outline, write the outline on your card or sheet of paper (or encircle it in your book if it is your personal property) and continue reading. Do not spend more than a few seconds trying to decipher the outline.

4 After you have gone through all the material in this way, repeat the procedure if time permits. On the second reading you may be able to read some of the outlines that escaped you the first time. When that happens, cross those outlines off your sheet or card.

5 Finally—and very important—at the earliest opportunity ask your teacher or a classmate the meaning of the outlines you could not read.

During the early stages of your shorthand study, your reading rate may not be very rapid, but this is only natural as you are, in a sense, learning to read a new language. If you read each lesson faithfully, following the procedures just suggested, your shorthand reading rate will increase almost from day to day.

WRITING THE READING AND WRITING PRACTICE

After you have read the Reading and Writing Practice of a lesson, you should make a shorthand copy of it. Before you do any writing, however, you should give some thought to the tools of your trade—your notebook and your writing instrument.

Your Notebook The best notebook for shorthand writing is one that measures 6 x 9 inches and has a vertical rule down the middle of each sheet. If the notebook has a spiral binding, so much the better, as the spiral binding enables you to keep the pages flat at all times. The paper, of course, should take ink well.

Your Writing Instrument If it is at all possible use a fountain pen or a good ball-point pen for your shorthand writing. Why use a pen for shorthand writing rather than a pencil? It requires less effort to write with a pen; consequently, you can write for long periods of time without fatigue. On the other hand, the point of a pencil soon becomes blunt, and the blunter it gets, the more effort you have to expend as you write with it. Pen-written notes remain readable almost indefinitely; pencil notes soon become blurred and hard to read. Pen-written notes are also easier to read under artificial light.

Having selected your writing tools, you should follow these steps in working with each Reading and Writing Practice:

1 Read the material you are going to copy, following the suggestions given under the heading, "Reading Sentences, Letters, and Articles," on page 11. Always read the Reading and Writing Practice before you copy it.

2 Read a convenient group of words from the printed shorthand and then write that group. If possible, say each outline aloud as you write it. Keep your place in the shorthand with your left index finger if you are right-handed; with your right index finger if you are left-handed.

* * *

Quite naturally, your early writing efforts may not be very rapid, nor will your shorthand outlines look as pretty as those in your book. With regular practice, however, you will soon become so proud of your shorthand notes that you won't want to write any more longhand!

The student reads the Reading and Writing Practice, writing on the card any outlines that she cannot read after spelling them.

Photographs: Syd Karson

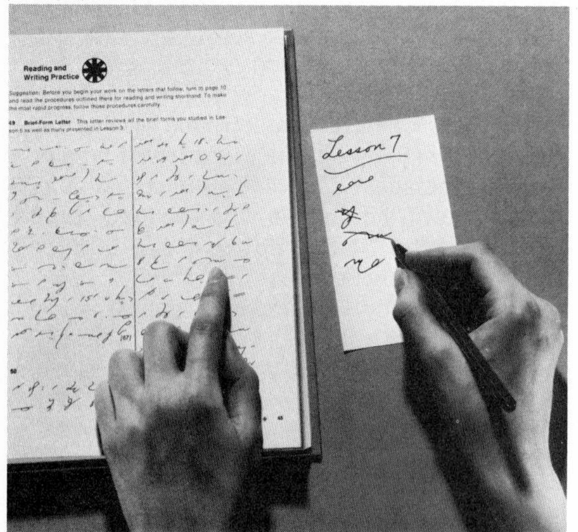

When copying, the student reads a convenient group of words aloud and then writes that group in her notebook. Notice how she keeps her place in the shorthand with her left index finger.

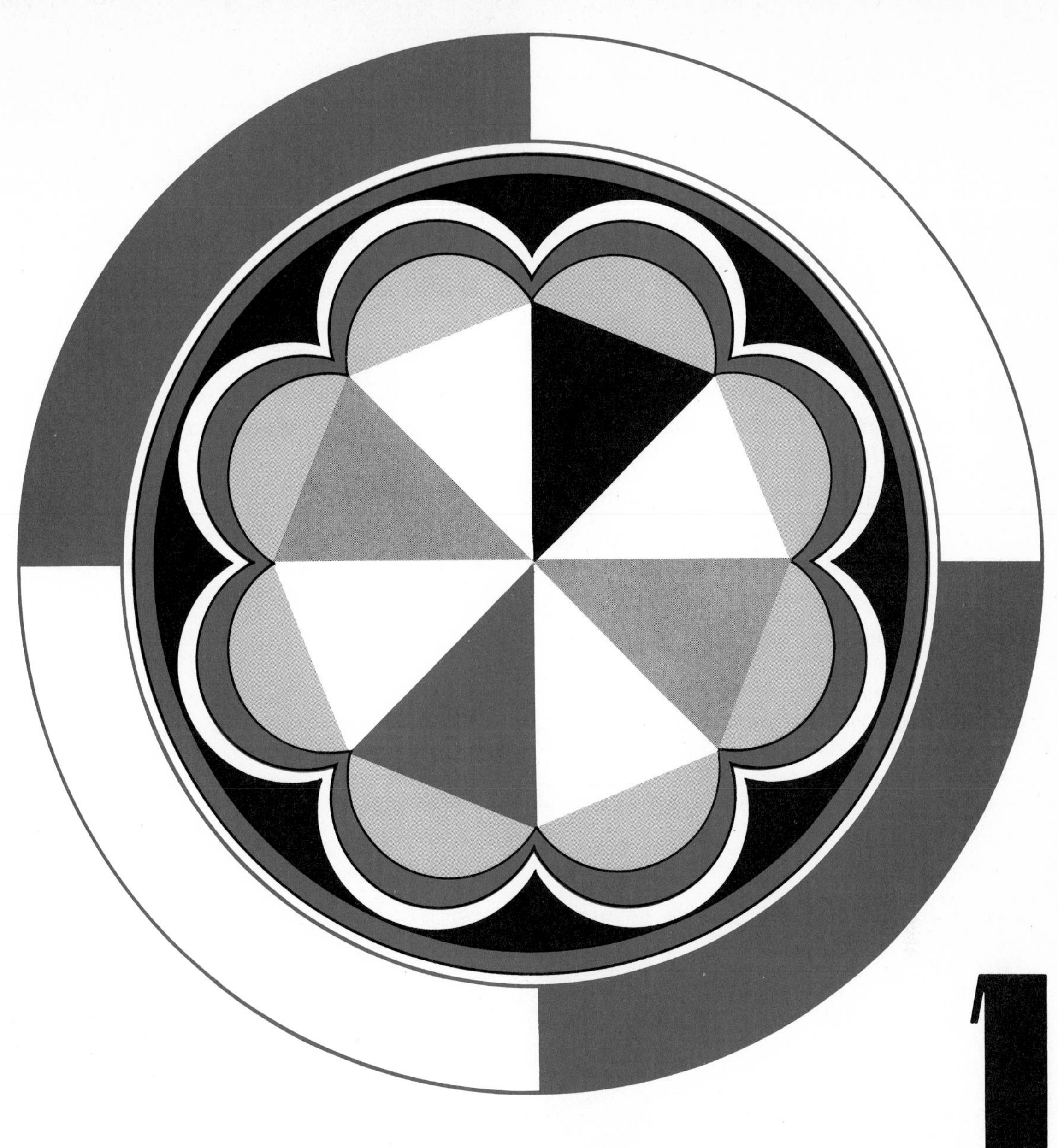

1
PRINCIPLES

Chapter 1 Shorthand—a Skill for Today and Tomorrow

Open to the help-wanted section of almost any newspaper in the country, and you will find help-wanted ads for secretaries. In the Sunday editions of newspapers in some of the larger cities, you will find hundreds of ads that read "Help Wanted—Good Shorthand Skills Required." Employment agencies have thousands of desirable stenographic openings just waiting for competent people to claim them. The demand for well-trained secretaries who can take dictation and transcribe rapidly and accurately is tremendous, and all indications are that this demand will increase in the years ahead.

While automation has eliminated many types of office jobs, it has not affected the demand for persons with stenographic skills. True, the spoken word can be recorded on many different types of electronic devices, but these devices will never replace competent shorthand writers. A major reason for this fact is that shorthand is a convenient tool. All that the shorthand writer requires is a piece of paper and a pen or pencil, and

he can write shorthand anywhere and at any time. He does not need a special machine or recorder that requires batteries or an electric outlet.

Businessmen prefer to dictate to a secretary for a number of reasons. For one thing, they like to dictate to a live person rather than to an inanimate machine. For another, they can easily make changes or corrections in their dictation by simply saying, "Scratch that out" or "Let's change that to . . . "—and the correction or change is quickly made in the secretary's notes. Such changes and corrections are not so simple on mechanical equipment. Moreover, the secretary can be a font of information that is of value to the dictator as he dictates.

Shorthand, of course, is a must in a secretarial position, but it is also valuable as a personal tool. The shorthand writer can use his skill to make notes on lectures and discussions in college classes. Once he has learned Gregg Shorthand well, he will have a lifelong skill. Thousands of mature women who left their jobs years ago to marry and perhaps raise a family are reentering the secretarial field every year. Many of them are doing so without any special retraining; others require simply a brief refresher course to help them regain their former skill.

You have made a wise decision to study shorthand. Not only will it enable you to obtain an interesting and profitable position upon the completion of your course, but it will also be a source of "employment insurance" for you during your entire lifetime.

LESSON 1

GREGG SHORTHAND IS EASY TO LEARN

Is there the slightest doubt in your mind whether you can learn to write Gregg Shorthand? If there is, dismiss it! If you can write longhand—and of course you can!—you can learn to write Gregg Shorthand. It is as simple as that. The strokes you will write in Gregg Shorthand are the same strokes that you are accustomed to writing in longhand.

Actually, you will find Gregg Shorthand easier to learn than longhand. If you are skeptical, the following illustration should convince you of the truth of that statement.

In longhand there are many ways to write the sound of *f*. Here are six of them:

What's more, in many words the sound of *f* is expressed by combinations of other letters in the alphabet, for example, *ph,* as in *phase; gh,* as in *rough.*

In Gregg Shorthand there is one way—and only one way—to express the sound of *f,* as you will learn later in this lesson.

With Gregg Shorthand you can reach almost any speed goal that you set for yourself. All it takes is faithful, intelligent practice.

Principles

GROUP A

1 **S-Z** The first shorthand stroke you will learn is *s,* one of the most frequently used letters in the English language. The shorthand *s* is a tiny downward curve that resembles the longhand comma in shape.

Because in English *s* often has the sound of *z,* as in *saves,* the same tiny downward curve is used to express *z.*

S-Z

2 A The next stroke you will learn is the shorthand *a,* which is simply the longhand *a* with the final connecting stroke omitted. The circle may be written in either direction.

A

3 Omission of Silent Letters In English, many words contain letters that are not pronounced. In shorthand, these silent letters are omitted; only the sounds that you actually hear are written. *Example:* the word *say* would be written *s-a;* the *y* would not be written because it is not pronounced. The word *face* would be written *f-a-s;* the *e* would be omitted because it is silent, and the *c* would be represented by the shorthand *s* because it is pronounced *s.*

In the following words, what letters would not be written because they are not pronounced?

save	steam	snow	hole
day	dough	main	right

4 S-A Words With the strokes for *s* and *a,* you can form the shorthand outlines for two words:

say, s-a   ace, a-s

◈ Notice that the *c* in *ace* is represented by the shorthand *s* because it has the *s* sound.

5 F, V The shorthand stroke for *f* is a downward curve the same shape as *s,* but it is somewhat larger—about half the height of the space between the lines of your shorthand notebook.

The shorthand stroke for *v* is also a downward curve the same shape as *s* and *f,* but it is very large—almost the full height of the space between the lines of your shorthand notebook. Notice the difference in the sizes of *s, f, v.*

S   F   V

F

safe, s-a-f   face, f-a-s   safes, s-a-f-s

V

save, s-a-v   vase, v-a-s   saves, s-a-v-s

◈ Notice that the final *s* in *saves* has the *z* sound, which is represented by the *s* stroke.

6 E The stroke for *e* is a tiny circle. It is simply the longhand *e* with the two connecting strokes omitted. The circle may be written in either direction.

E

◈ Notice the difference in the sizes of *a* and *e*.

A   E

see, s-e   sees, s-e-s   ease, e-s

fee, f-e   fees, f-e-s   easy, e-s-e

◈ Notice that the *y* in *easy* is pronounced *e;* therefore, it is represented by the *e* circle.

Suggestion: At this point take a few minutes to read the procedures outlined for practicing word lists on page 10. To derive the greatest benefit from your practice, follow those procedures carefully.

GROUP B

7 N, M The shorthand stroke for *n* is a very short forward straight line. The shorthand stroke for *m* is a longer forward straight line.

N   M

N

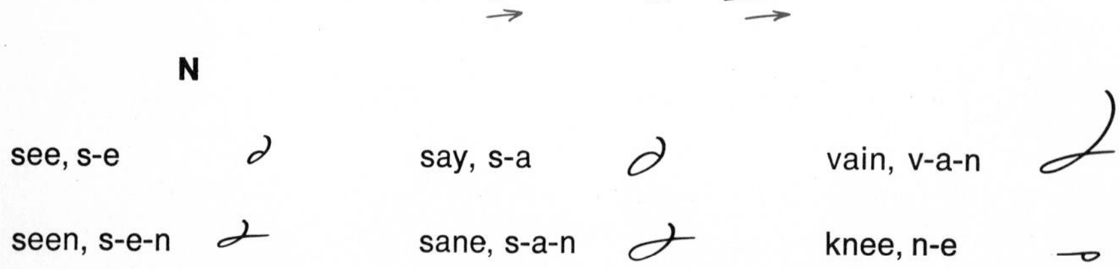

see, s-e   say, s-a   vain, v-a-n

seen, s-e-n   sane, s-a-n   knee, n-e

◈ Notice that the *k* in *knee* is not written because it is not pronounced.

M

may, m-a   mean, m-e-n   seem, s-e-m

main, m-a-n   aim, a-m   same, s-a-m

me, m-e   name, n-a-m   fame, f-a-m

8 T, D The shorthand stroke for *t* is a short upward straight line. The shorthand stroke for *d* is a longer upward straight line.

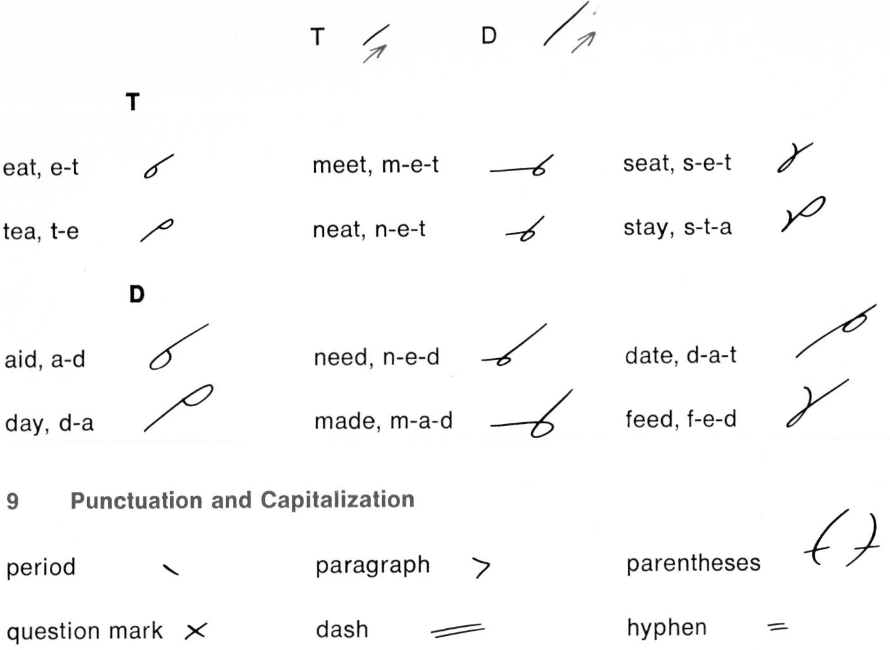

The regular longhand forms are used for all other punctuation marks.

Capitalization is indicated by two upward dashes placed underneath the word to be capitalized.

With the Gregg Shorthand strokes you have already learned, you can, with the help of an occasional longhand word, read complete sentences.

Read the following sentences, spelling each shorthand outline aloud as you read it, thus: *N-a-t, Nate; s-a-v-d, saved; m-a, May.* If you cannot read a shorthand outline after you have spelled it, refer to the key.

GROUP A

1 ... 15 for a ... with ... .

2 The ... paid ... a ... .

3 Can ... ?

4 ... office ...

GROUP C

GROUP B

[77]

GROUP A

1 Nate saved May 15 for a date with me. 2 The Navy paid me a fee. 3 Can Dave eat meat? 4 Dave's office faced East Main Street. 5 Dean may meet me at eight.

GROUP B

6 The Navy team made a safety. 7 Fay need not feed me on our date. 8 Dave's team faced Navy. 9 Fay heard Amy say, "Save me." 10 Dave may stay to aid me. 11 Amy made me save the fee.

GROUP C

12 Can Dean meet me on East Main at five? 13 Fay is mean and vain. 14 Dave's deed is in Fay's safe. 15 Mr. Mead stayed all day. 16 Mae made tea for Mr. Mead.

LESSON 

Principles

10 Alphabet Review In Lesson 1 you studied the following nine strokes. How fast can you read them?

11 O, R, L In this paragraph you will learn how to write *o, r,* and *l* in shorthand.

The shorthand stroke for *o* is a small deep hook.

The shorthand stroke for *r* is a short forward curve.

The shorthand stroke for *l* is a longer forward curve about three times as long as the stroke for *r.*

◈ Notice how these shorthand strokes are derived from the longhand forms.

O R L

O

toe, t-o	so, s-o	own, o-n
dough, d-o	foe, f-o	tone, t-o-n
no, n-o	phone, f-o-n	stone, s-t-o-n
snow, s-n-o	vote, v-o-t	dome, d-o-m

◈ Notice that in the words in the third column, the *o* is placed on its side. By writing o on its side before *n* and *m* in these and similar words, we obtain smoother, more easily written joinings.

R

ear, e-r	mere, m-e-r	fear, f-e-r
near, n-e-r	dear, d-e-r	fare, f-a-r

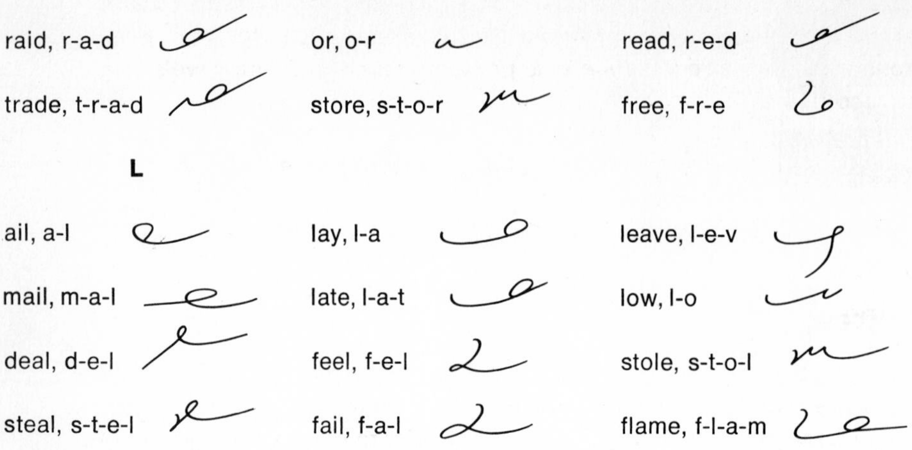

raid, r-a-d — or, o-r — read, r-e-d

trade, t-r-a-d — store, s-t-o-r — free, f-r-e

L

ail, a-l — lay, l-a — leave, l-e-v

mail, m-a-l — late, l-a-t — low, l-o

deal, d-e-l — feel, f-e-l — stole, s-t-o-l

steal, s-t-e-l — fail, f-a-l — flame, f-l-a-m

◈ Notice that *fr,* as in *free,* and *fl,* as in *flame,* are written with one sweep of the pen, with no stop between the *f* and the *r* or *l.*

free — flame

12 H, -ing The letter *h* is simply a dot placed above the vowel. With few exceptions, *h* occurs at the beginning of a word.

Ing, which almost always occurs at the end of a word, is also represented by a dot.

H

he, h-e — whole, h-o-l — home, h-o-m

-ing

hearing, h-e-r-ing — heating, h-e-t-ing — heeding, h-e-d-ing

13 Long ī The shorthand stroke for the long sound of *ī,* as in *high,* is a large broken circle. It may be written in either direction.

I

high, h-ī — sign, s-ī-n — life, l-ī-f

my, m-ī — side, s-ī-d — right, (write), r-ī-t

might, m-ī-t — line, l-ī-n — tire, t-ī-r

14 Omission of Minor Vowels Many words in the English language contain vowels that are sounded only slightly or are slurred. For example, the word *even* is really pronounced *e-vn;* the word *meter* is pronounced *met-r.* These vowels may be omitted in shorthand.

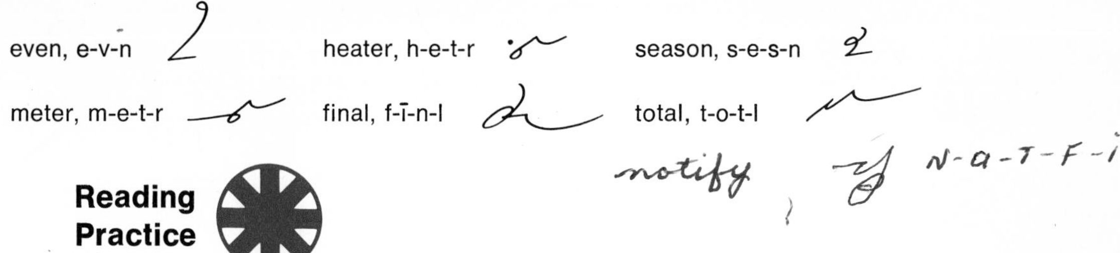

Reading Practice

With the aid of a few words in longhand, you can now read the following sentences. Spell each shorthand word aloud as you read it and refer to the key when you cannot read a word.

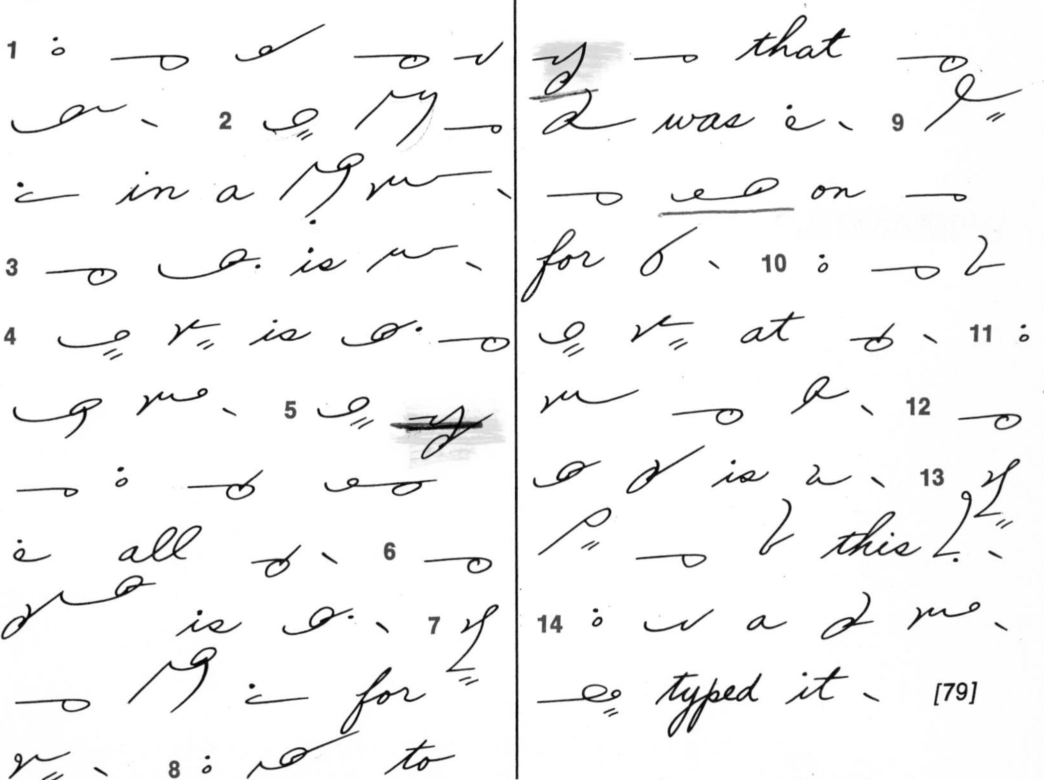

1 He may read my note later. 2 Ray drove me home in a driving storm. 3 My lining is torn. 4 Lee Stone is writing my life story. 5 Ray notified me he might remain here all night. 6 My sideline is writing. 7 Steven may drive home for Easter. 8 He tried to notify me that my file was here. 9 Dale may rely on me for aid. 10 He may phone Ray Stone at night. 11 He stole my tire. 12 My right side is sore. 13 Steven Day may vote this evening. 14 He wrote a fine story. Mary typed it.

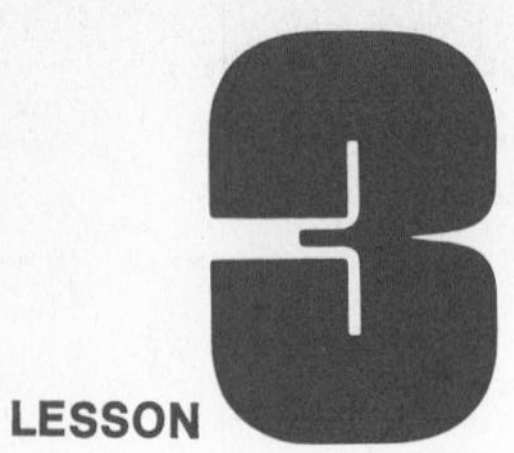

LESSON 3

Principles

15 **Alphabet Review** Here are the 14 strokes you studied in Lessons 1 and 2. How rapidly can you identify them?

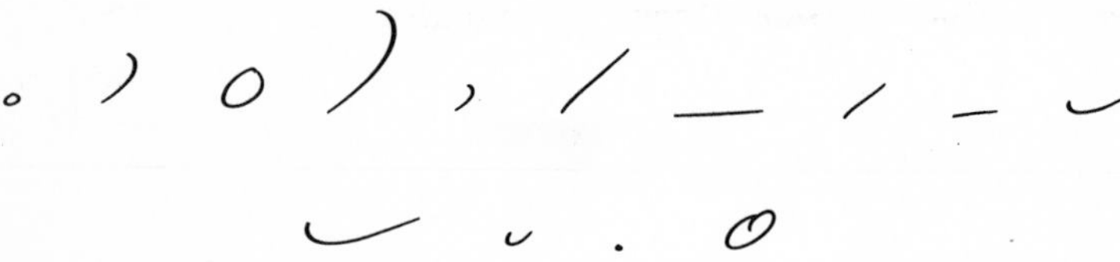

16 **Brief Forms** There are many words in the English language that are used over and over again. As an aid to rapid shorthand writing, special abbreviations, called "brief forms," are provided for many of these common words. For example, we write *m-r* for *Mister; v,* for *have.*

This process of abbreviation is common practice in longhand, too. You are, of course, familiar with such abbreviations as *Ave.* for *Avenue; memo* for *memorandum; Sat.* for *Saturday,* etc.

Because the brief forms occur so frequently, make a special effort to learn them well.

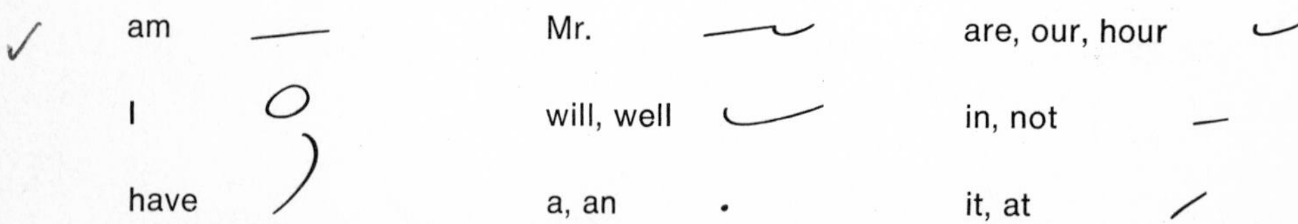

am	Mr.	are, our, hour
I	will, well	in, not
have	a, an	it, at

◈ Notice that a number of the brief forms have two or more meanings. When you are transcribing material you have taken from dictation, context will help you select the correct meaning of a brief form.

17 **Phrasing** The use of brief forms for common words enables us to save writing time. Another device for saving writing time is called "phrasing," or the

writing of two or more shorthand outlines together. Here are a number of phrases built with the brief forms you have just studied.

I have		I have not		I am	
I will		he will		in our	
I will have		he will not		are not	

18 Left S-Z In Lesson 1 you learned one stroke for *s* and *z*. Another stroke for *s* and *z* is also used in order to provide an easy joining in any combination of strokes —a backward comma, which is also written downward. For convenience, it is called the "left *s*."

At this point you need not try to decide which *s* stroke to use in any given word; this will become clear to you as your study of shorthand progresses.

S-Z

days, d-a-s		most, m-o-s-t		writes, r-ī-t-s	
raise, r-a-s		least, l-e-s-t		mails, m-a-l-s	
dates, d-a-t-s		ties, t-ī-s		seal, s-e-l	
homes, h-o-m-s		names, n-a-m-s		sale, s-a-l	

19 P, B The shorthand stroke for *p* is a downward curve the same shape as the left *s*, except that it is larger—approximately half the height of the space between the lines in your shorthand notebook.

The shorthand stroke for *b* is also a downward curve the same shape as the left *s* and *p*, except that it is *much* larger—approximately the full height of the space between the lines in your shorthand notebook.

◈ Notice the difference in the sizes of the left *s*, *p*, and *b*.

S P B

P

pay, p-a		please, p-l-e-s		open, o-p-n	
pays, p-a-s		plain, p-l-a-n		hope, h-o-p	
space, s-p-a-s		place, p-l-a-s		prepare, p-r-e-p-a-r	
spare, s-p-a-r		price, p-r-ī-s		paid, p-a-d	

B

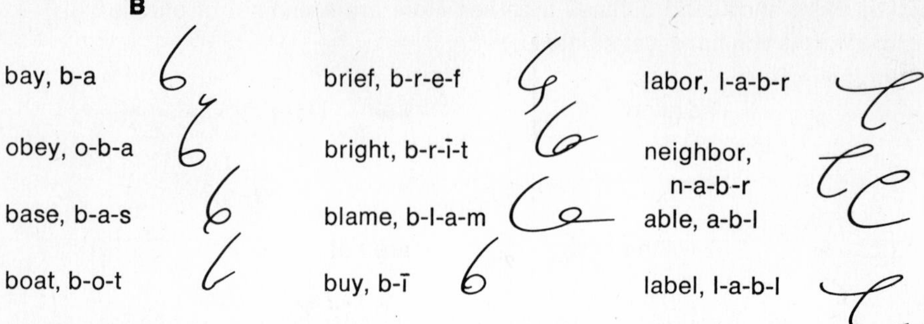

◈ Notice that the combinations *pr* as in *price; pl,* in *please; br,* in *bright;* and *bl,* as in *blame,* are written with one sweep of the pen without a pause between the *p* or *b* and the *r* or *l.*

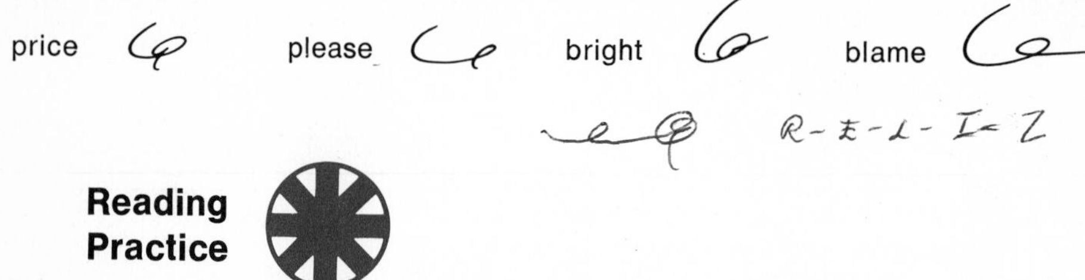

Reading Practice

You have already reached the point where you can read sentences written entirely in shorthand.

Suggestion: Before you start your work on this Reading Practice, read the practice procedures for reading shorthand on page 11. By following those procedures, you will obtain the most benefit from your reading.

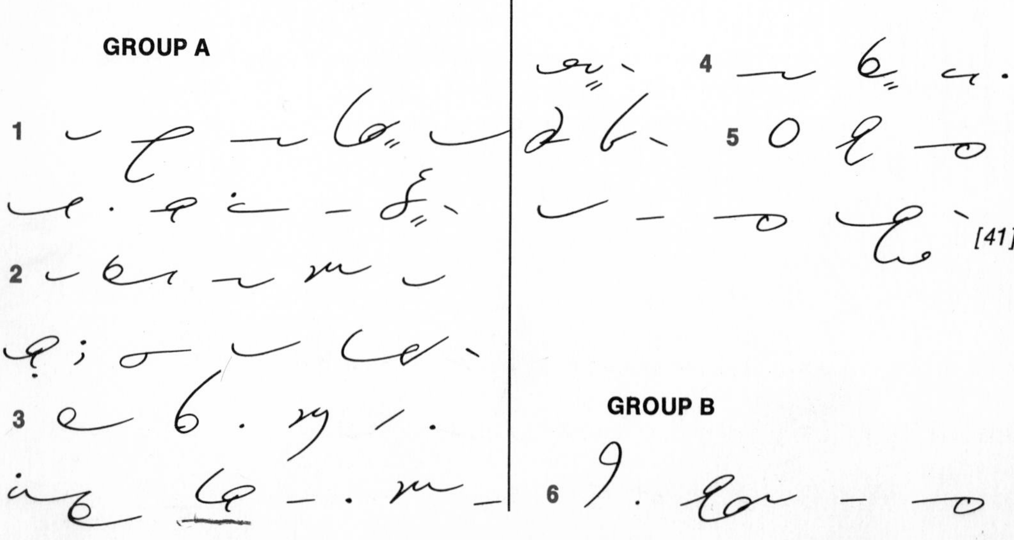

7

8

9

10

11

[64]

GROUP C

12

13

14

15

16

17

[50]

GROUP D

18

19

20

21

22

23

24

25

[60]

GROUP E

26

10

27

60

40

28

29

8

10

30

[56]

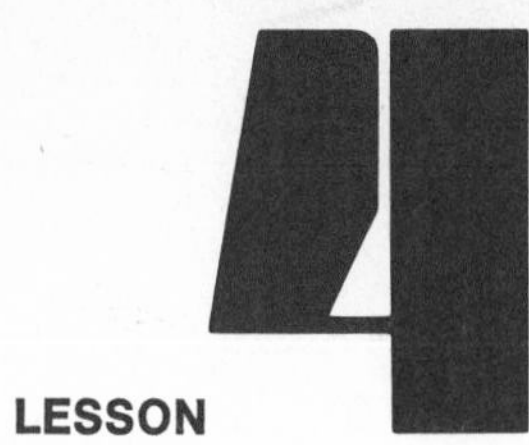

LESSON 4

Principles

20 Alphabet Review Here are the 17 shorthand strokes you studied in Lessons 1 through 3. How rapidly can you read them?

21 Sh, Ch, J The shorthand stroke for *sh* (called "ish") is a very short downward straight stroke.

The shorthand stroke for *ch* (called "chay") is a longer downward straight stroke approximately half the height of the space between the lines of your shorthand notebook.

The shorthand stroke for the sound of *j,* as in *jail* and *age,* is a long downward straight stroke almost the full height of the space between the lines in your shorthand notebook.

◈ Note carefully the difference in the sizes of these strokes.

Ish / Chay / J /

Ish

she, ish-e	showing, ish-o-ing	shine, ish-ī-n
show, ish-o	shade, ish-a-d	shaped, ish-a-p-t

Chay

each, e-chay	reaching, r-e-chay-ing	speech, s-p-e-chay
teach, t-e-chay	chairs, chay-a-r-s	cheap, chay-e-p

J

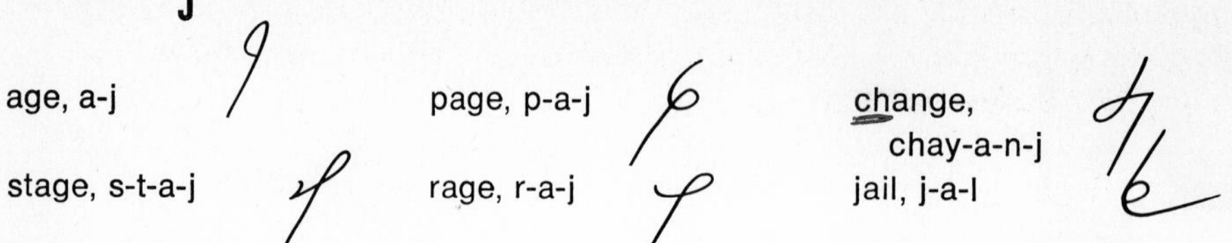

age, a-j — page, p-a-j — change, chay-a-n-j

stage, s-t-a-j — rage, r-a-j — jail, j-a-l

22 OO, K, G The shorthand stroke for the sound of *oo,* as in *to,* is a tiny upward hook.

The shorthand stroke for *k* is a short forward curve.

The shorthand stroke for the hard sound of *g,* as in *game,* is a much longer forward curve. It is called "gay."

OO K Gay

OO

to, (two, too), t-oo — fruit, f-r-oo-t — room, r-oo-m

do, d-oo — true, t-r-oo — ruler, r-oo-l-r

shoe, ish-oo — drew, d-r-oo — noon, n-oo-n

who, h-oo — pool, p-oo-l — moved, m-oo-v-d

◈ Notice that the *oo* is placed on its side when it follows *n* or *m,* as in *noon* and *moved.* By placing the *oo* on its side in these combinations rather than writing it upright, we obtain smooth joinings.

K

ache, a-k — came, k-a-m — keeping, k-e-p-ing

take, t-a-k — care, k-a-r — claims, k-l-a-m-s

make, m-a-k — like, l-ī-k — maker, m-a-k-r

Gay

gain, gay-a-n — go, gay-o — gale, gay-a-l

game, gay-a-m — goal, gay-o-l — grading, gay-r-a-d-ing

gave, gay-a-v — girl, gay-r-l — legal, l-e-gay-l

◈ Notice that *k-r,* as in *maker,* and *gay-l,* as in *legal,* are written with a smooth, wavelike motion. But *k-l,* as in *claim,* and *gay-r,* as in *grade,* are written with a hump between the *k* and the *l* and the *gay* and the *r.*

maker legal claim grade

Reading Practice

group gay-r-oo-p

locate L-O-K-A-T

The following sentences contain many illustrations of the new shorthand strokes you studied in Lesson 4. In addition, they review all the shorthand strokes, brief forms, and phrases you studied in Lessons 1 through 3.

Read the sentences aloud, spelling each shorthand outline that you cannot immediately read.

GROUP A

1

2

3

4

5

[71]

GROUP B

6

7

8

9

10

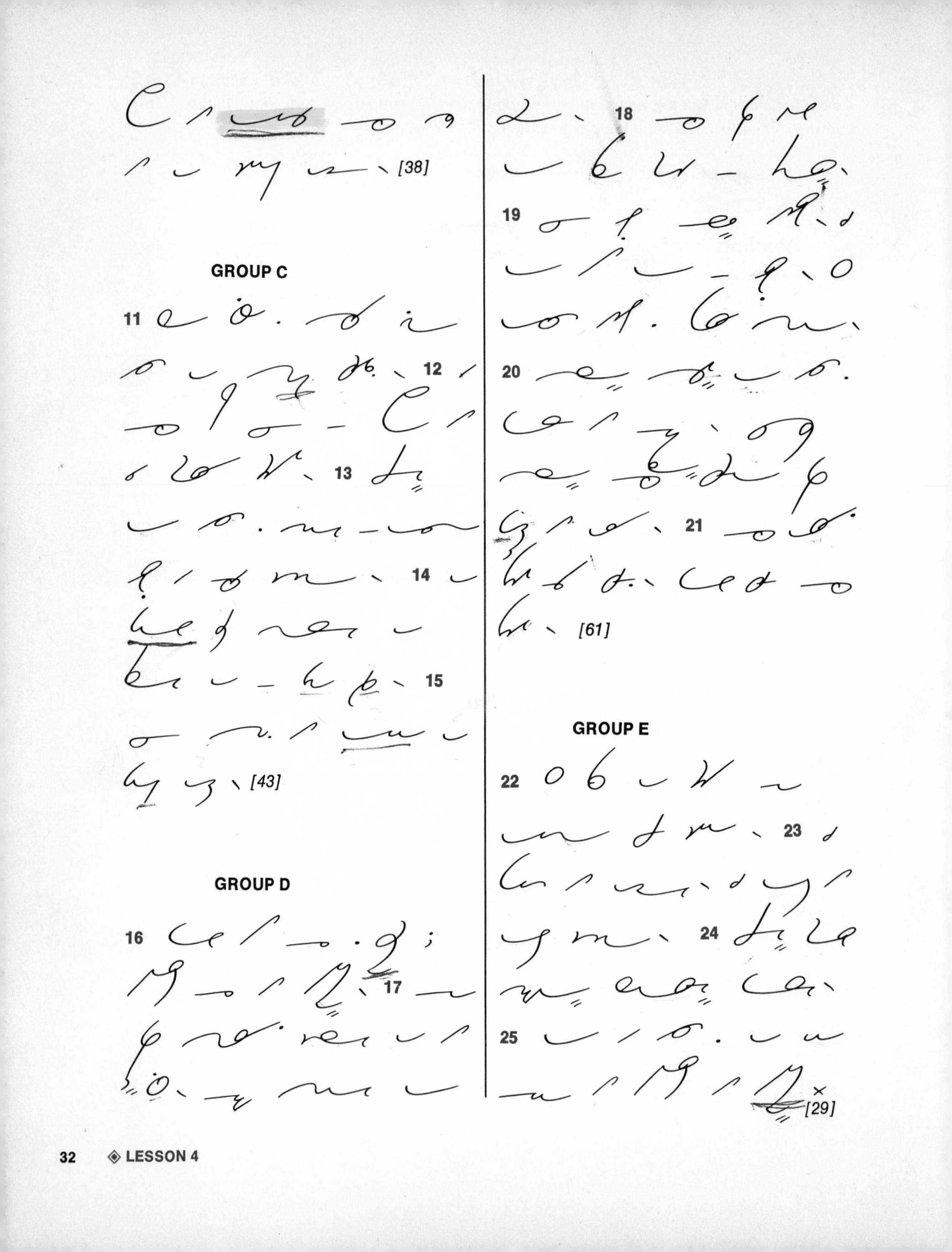

[38]

GROUP C

11

12

13

14

15

[43]

GROUP D

16

17

18

19

20

21

[61]

GROUP E

22

23

24

25

[29]

Principles

23 Alphabet Review Here are the 23 alphabetic strokes you studied in Lessons 1 through 4. Can you read them in 30 seconds or less?

24 A, Ä The large circle that represents the long sound of ā, as in *main,* also represents the vowel sounds heard in *as* and *arm.*

A

as, a-s	facts, f-a-k-t-s	past, p-a-s-t
has, h-a-s	act, a-k-t	last, l-a-s-t
had, h-a-d	matter, m-a-t-r	track, t-r-a-k
man, m-a-n	fast, f-a-s-t	carry, k-a-r-e

Ä

arm, a-r-m	far, f-a-r	start, s-t-a-r-t
harm, h-a-r-m	farm, f-a-r-m	park, p-a-r-k
charge, chay-a-r-j	car, k-a-r	mark, m-a-r-k
calm, k-a-m	large, l-a-r-j	dark, d-a-r-k

25 E, I, Obscure Vowel The tiny circle that represents the sound of ē, as in *eat,* also represents the vowel sounds heard in *let* and *if,* as well as the obscure vowel heard in *her, church.*

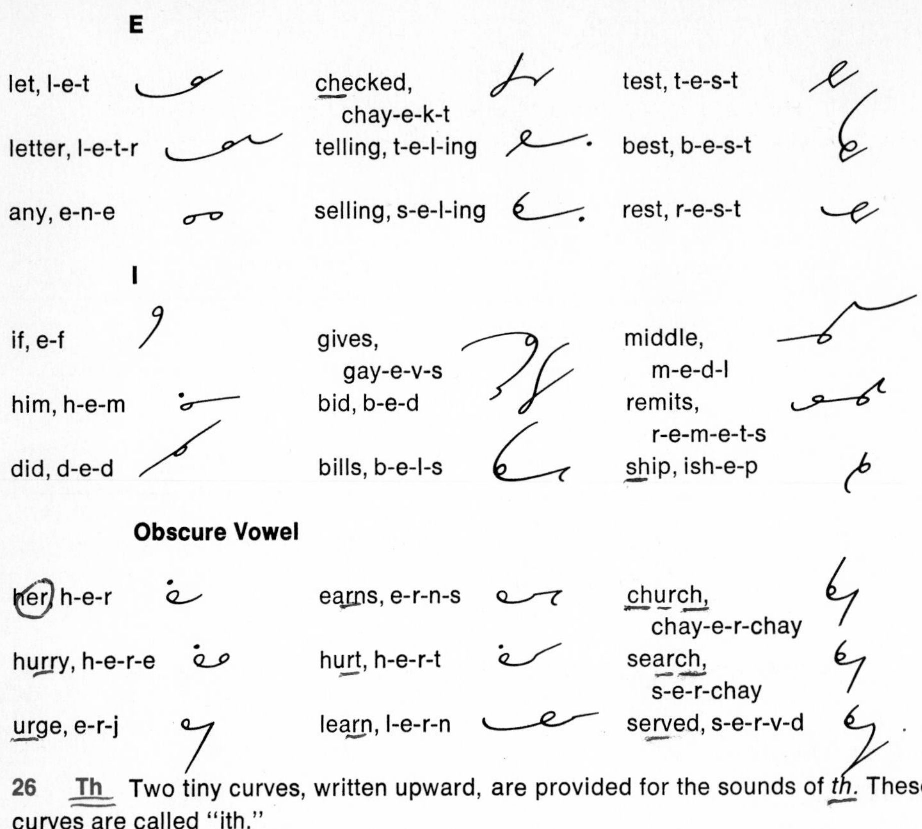

E

let, l-e-t | checked, chay-e-k-t | test, t-e-s-t
letter, l-e-t-r | telling, t-e-l-ing | best, b-e-s-t
any, e-n-e | selling, s-e-l-ing | rest, r-e-s-t

I

if, e-f | gives, gay-e-v-s | middle, m-e-d-l
him, h-e-m | bid, b-e-d | remits, r-e-m-e-t-s
did, d-e-d | bills, b-e-l-s | ship, ish-e-p

Obscure Vowel

her, h-e-r | earns, e-r-n-s | church, chay-e-r-chay
hurry, h-e-r-e | hurt, h-e-r-t | search, s-e-r-chay
urge, e-r-j | learn, l-e-r-n | served, s-e-r-v-d

26 Th Two tiny curves, written upward, are provided for the sounds of *th.* These curves are called "ith."

At this time you need not try to decide which *th* stroke to use in any given word; this will become clear to you as your study of Gregg Shorthand progresses.

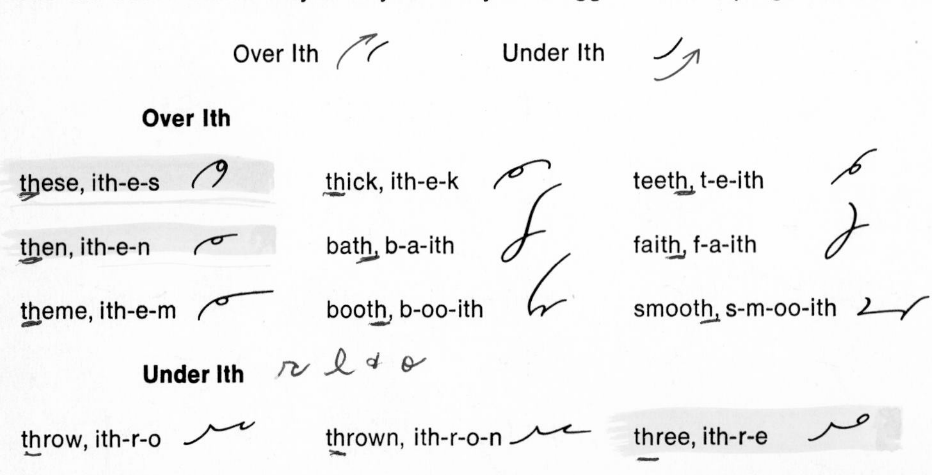

Over Ith Under Ith

Over Ith

these, ith-e-s | thick, ith-e-k | teeth, t-e-ith
then, ith-e-n | bath, b-a-ith | faith, f-a-ith
theme, ith-e-m | booth, b-oo-ith | smooth, s-m-oo-ith

Under Ith

throw, ith-r-o | thrown, ith-r-o-n | three, ith-r-e

though, ith-o	clothing, k-l-o-ith-ing	thorough, ith-e-r-o
health, h-e-l-ith	earth, e-r-ith	both, b-o-ith

27 Brief Forms Here is another group of brief forms for very frequently used words. Learn them well.

is, his	can	of
the	you, your	with
that	Mrs.	but

28 Common Phrases

at the	you are	it is
of the	with you, with your	with his
in that	I can	in his

◈ Notice that in the phrases in the third column, the left *s* is used for *is* and *his.*

Reading Practice

29 Brief-Form Letter This letter contains one or more illustrations of all the brief forms you studied in this lesson.

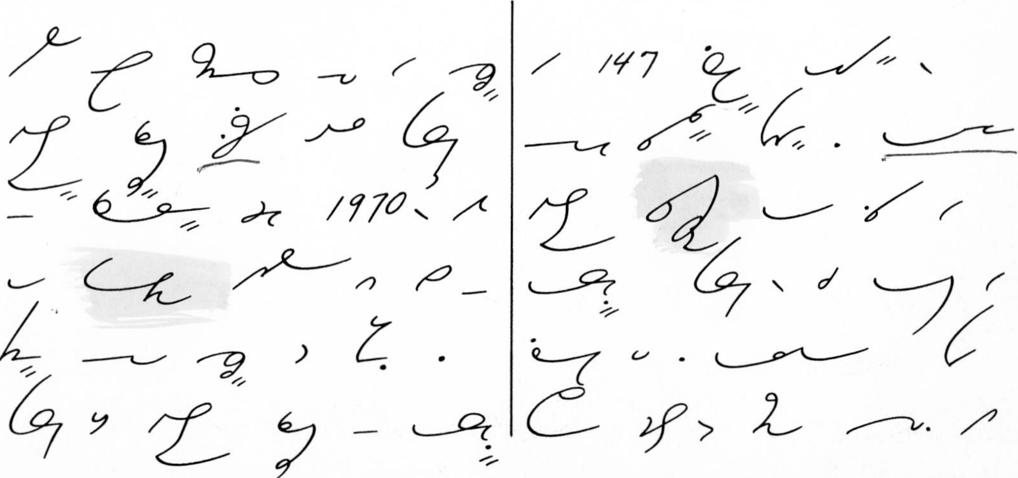

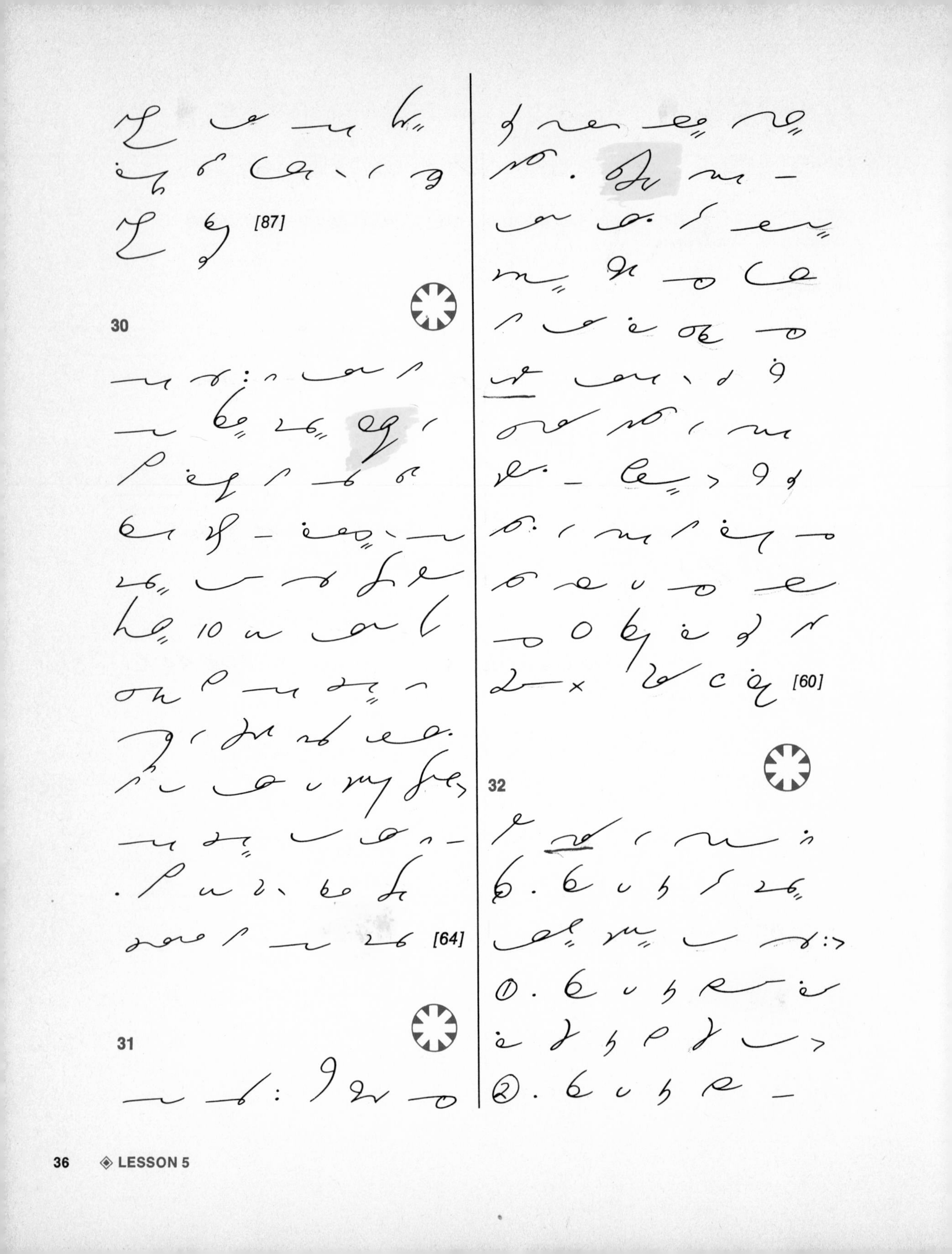

[87]

30

[64]

31

[60]

32

[76]

[66]

33

34

[49]

LESSON 6

RECALL

Lesson 6 is a "breather"; it contains no new shorthand principles for you to learn. In this lesson you will find an Alphabet Review, a simple explanation of the principles that govern the joining of the strokes you have studied thus far, a Recall Chart, and a Reading Practice.

35 Alphabet Review Here are the 25 shorthand strokes you studied in Lessons 1 through 5. Can you read them in 20 seconds or less?

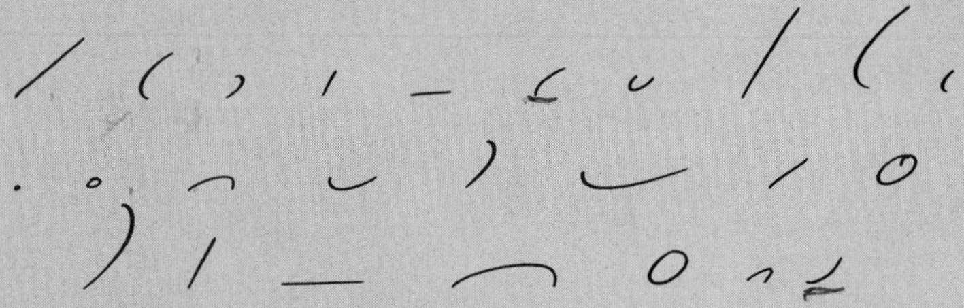

Principles of Joining

As a matter of interest, you might like to know the principles under which the words you have already learned are written. Notice the groups into which the joinings naturally fall.

36 Circles are written inside curves and outside angles.

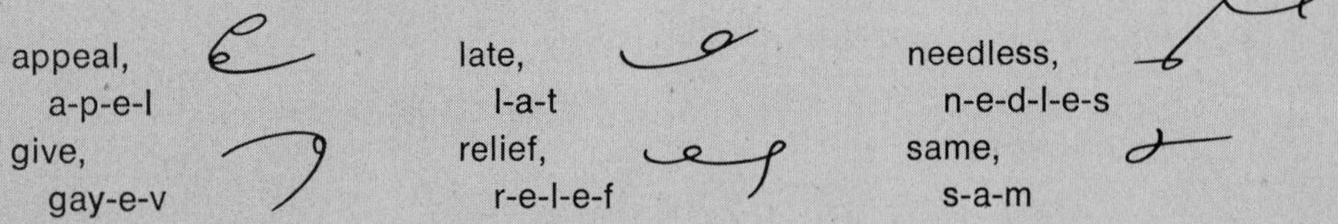

appeal, a-p-e-l
late, l-a-t
needless, n-e-d-l-e-s
give, gay-e-v
relief, r-e-l-e-f
same, s-a-m

37 Circles are written clockwise (in this direction) on a straight stroke or between two straight strokes in the same direction.

any, e-n-e
each, e-chay
date, d-a-t
age, a-j
mean, m-e-n
stayed, s-t-a-d

38 Between two curves written in opposite directions, the circle is written on the back of the first curve.

care, k-a-r — gear, gay-e-r — vapor, v-a-p-r

rack, r-a-k — leak, l-e-k — pave, p-a-v

39 The *o* hook is written on its side before *n, m* unless a downward stroke comes before the hook.

own, o-n — stone, s-t-o-n — loan, l-o-n

but

shown, ish-o-n — bone, b-o-n — zone, s-o-n

40 The *oo* hook is written on its side after *n, m*.

noon, n-oo-n — move, m-oo-v — moon, m-oo-n

41 The under *ith* is used when it is joined to *o, r, l;* in other cases, the over *ith* is used.

though, ith-o — through, ith-r-oo — health- h-e-l-ith

but

these, ith-e-s — thick, ith-e-k — then, ith-e-n

42 **Recall Chart** The following chart reviews all the shorthand devices you studied in Lessons 1 through 5.

Spell out each word aloud, thus: *ith-r-o, throw.* You need not spell the brief forms and phrases.

The chart contains 84 words and phrases. Can you read the entire chart in 9 minutes or less?

WORDS

1

2

3

4

5

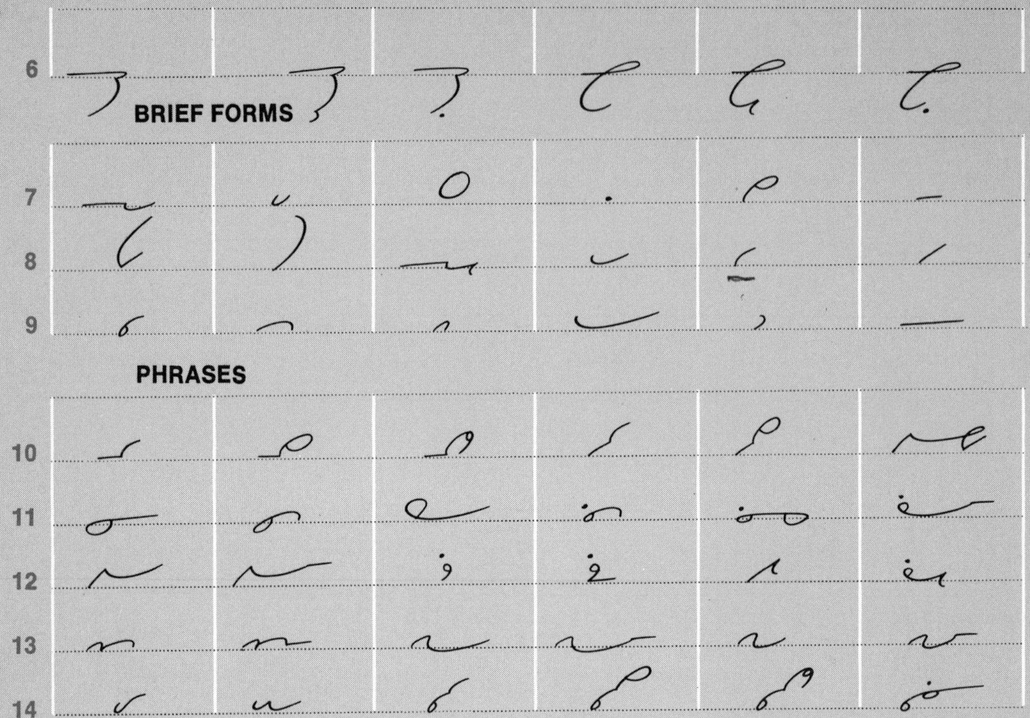

Reading Practice

43

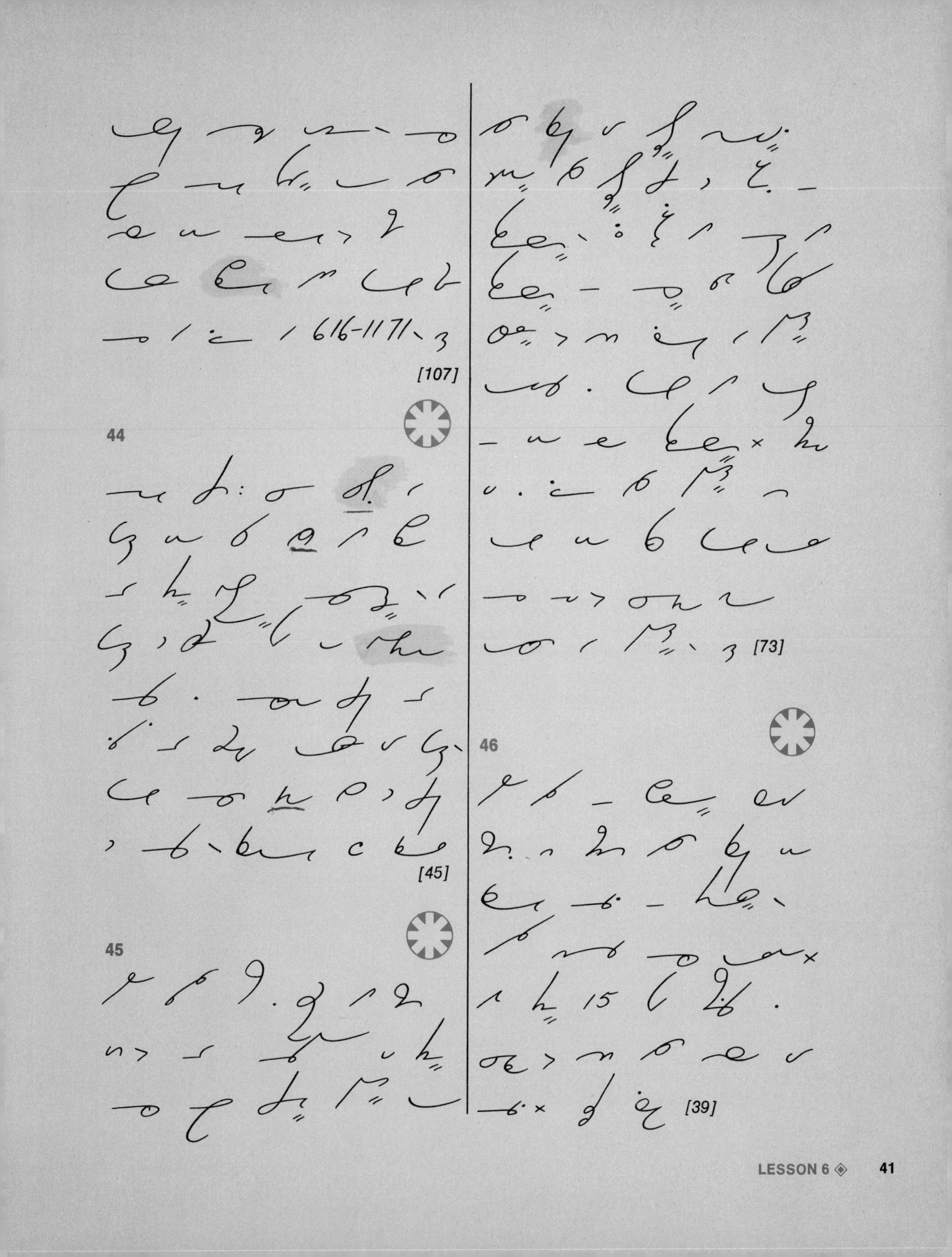

[107]

44

[45]

45

[73]

46

[39]

Chapter 2 Educational Background

When a businessman considers an applicant for a secretarial position, he is naturally interested in her basic skills. However, he is also interested in her educational background. He realizes that the more education and training she has, the more valuable she will be to him. Consequently, he is willing to pay considerably more to a college-educated and trained person than to one who has not continued her studies beyond high school.

Although a college degree is not an absolute necessity for secretarial employment, it gives applicants three decided advantages:

1. They command better starting salaries.
2. They usually work for higher-level executives.
3. They have opportunities for more rapid promotions to positions of greater responsibility.

You must realize, however, that college training in and of itself will not guarantee you success in business. You must prove that you have the ability to perform efficiently the tasks assigned to you by your employer. If you do not have this ability, even the most advanced degrees will be of no value to you.

College is often a proving ground that separates the leaders from the followers. If you are successful in your college work, the chances are excellent that you will be successful in the business world. You will bring to your job a higher level of skill, more maturity, and a more sophisticated attitude than the person with no college training. As a college-trained secretary, you will have a better command of the English language, a larger vocabulary, and a surer grasp of communications skills than will the person with no college training.

In addition, you will probably have a better understanding of business organization, economics, and finance—all of which will make you a more valuable employee and help you succeed in business.

Get as much education and training in college as you can. The time you spend in college is a good investment in your future. Not only will it make you a more valuable person; it will also put money in your pocket.

LESSON 7

Principles

47 O, Aw The small deep hook that represents *o,* as in *low,* also represents the sounds heard in *hot* and *draw.*

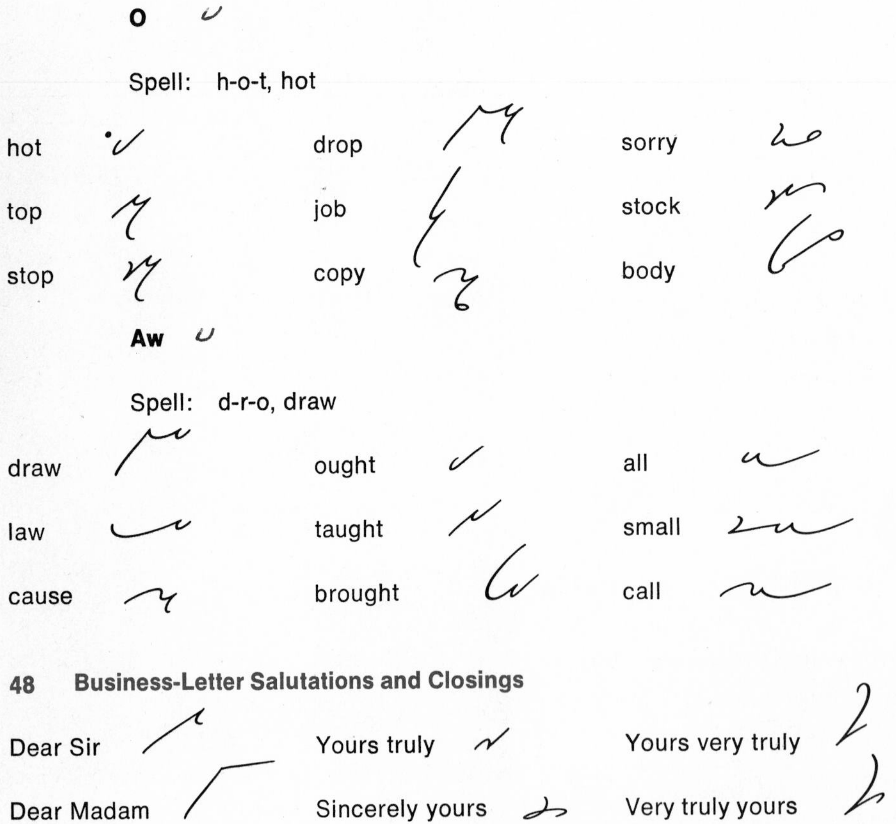

O

Spell: h-o-t, hot

hot	drop	sorry
top	job	stock
stop	copy	body

Aw

Spell: d-r-o, draw

draw	ought	all
law	taught	small
cause	brought	call

48 Business-Letter Salutations and Closings

Dear Sir	Yours truly	Yours very truly
Dear Madam	Sincerely yours	Very truly yours

◈ Note: While the expressions *Dear Sir, Dear Madam,* and *Yours truly* are considered too impersonal by experts in letter writing, they are still used by many businessmen. Therefore, special abbreviations are provided for them.

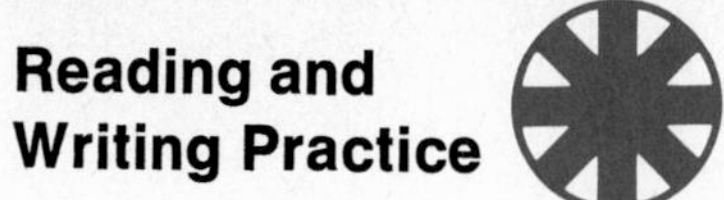

Reading and Writing Practice

Suggestion: Before you begin your work on the letters that follow, turn to page 11
ed there for reading and writing shorthand. To make
hose procedures carefully.

tter reviews all the brief forms you studied in Les-
in Lesson 3.

[67]

[90]

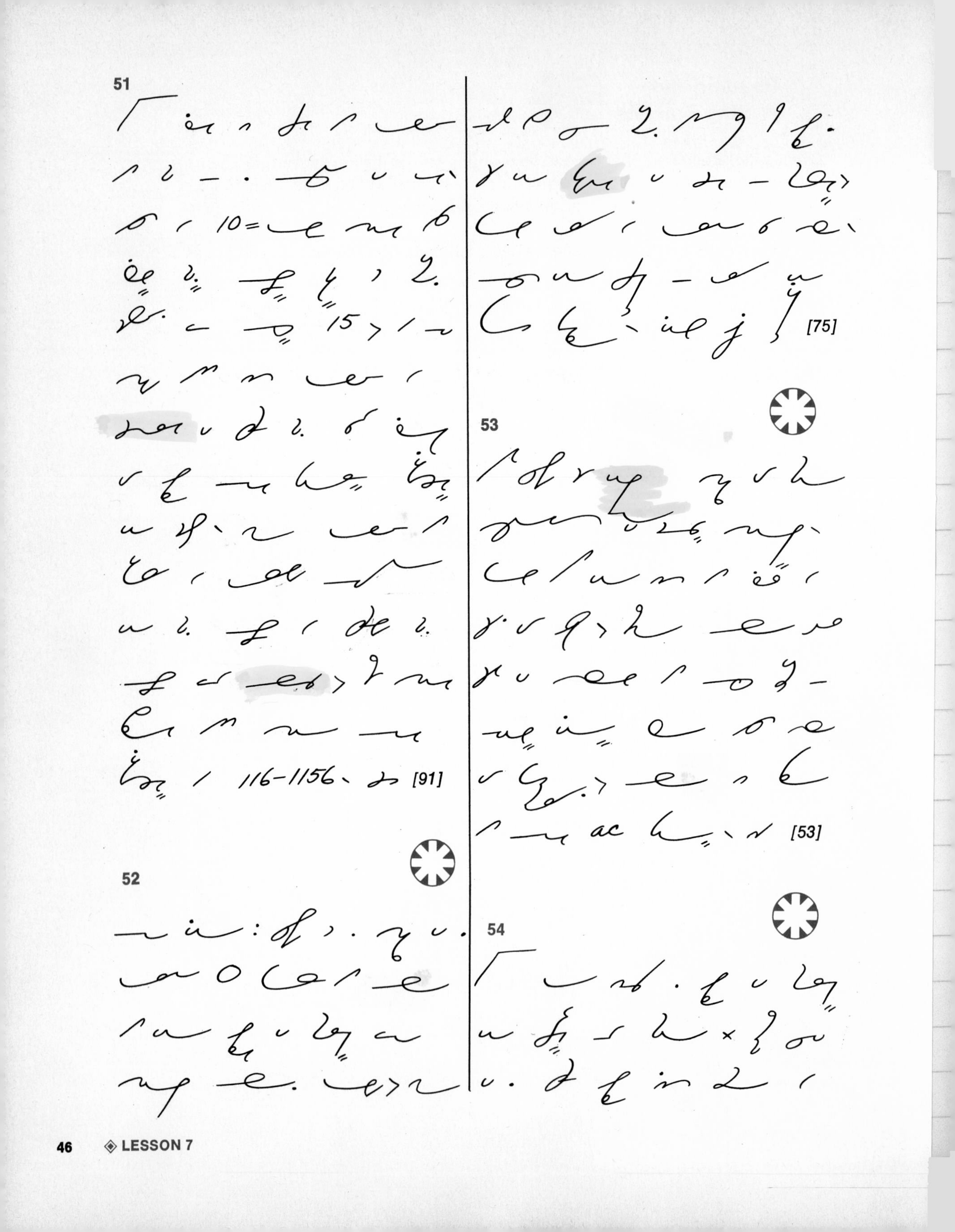

51

10 15

116-1156 [91]

52

[75]

53

[53]

54

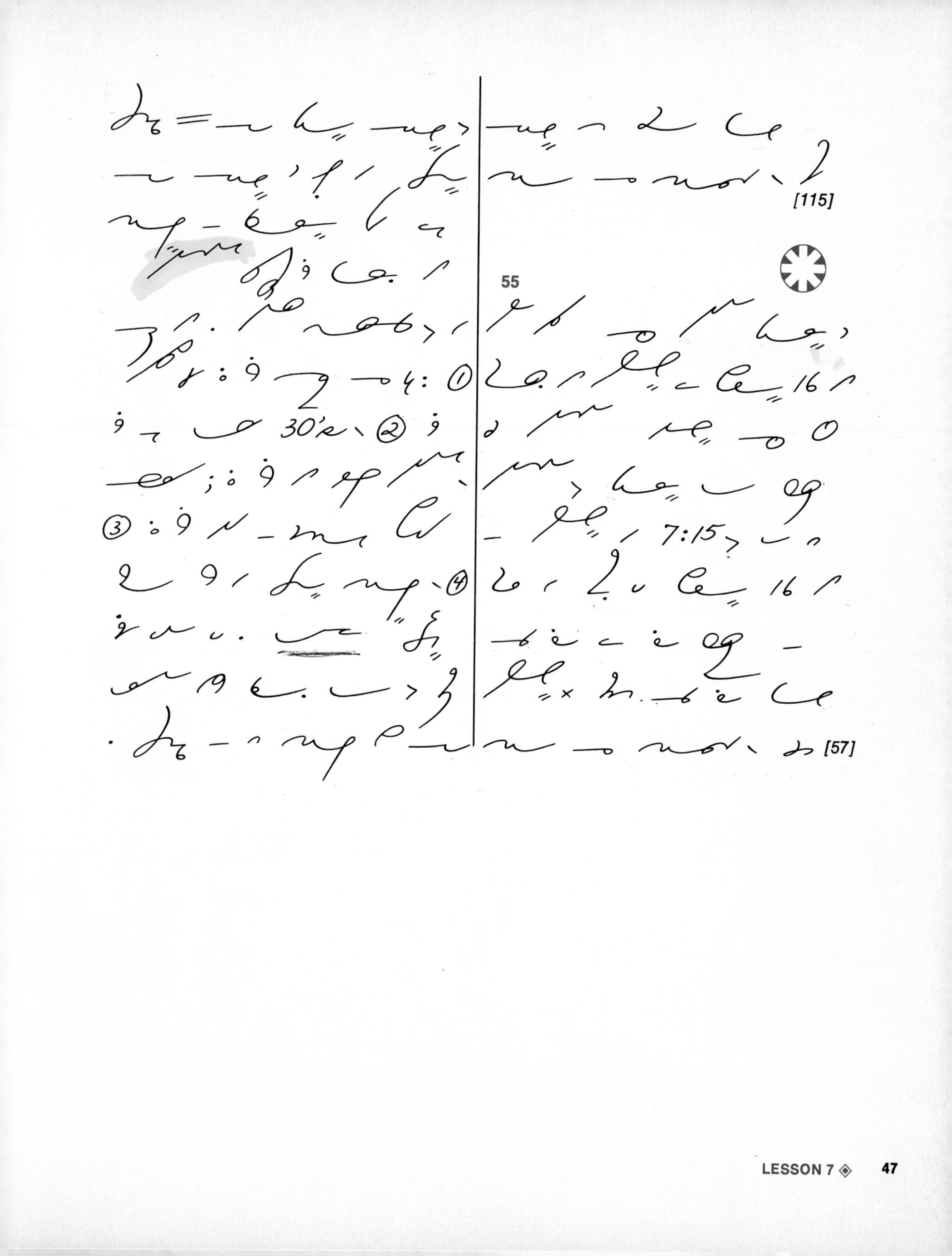

[115]

55

[57]

LESSON 

Principles

56 Brief Forms

shall	put	there (their)
which	be, by	this
for	would	good

57 Frequent Phrases

for the	which is	I would
for that	this is	I would not
for this	there is	he would
for me	by the	he would not
for my	by that	I shall

58 Word Ending -ly

The common word ending *-ly* is represented by the *e* circle.

Spell: n-e-r-lē, nearly

nearly	properly	plainly
merely	briefly	totally
fairly	mainly	highly
only	rarely	daily

◈ Notice that in *highly* the small circle for *-ly* is written inside the large circle; that in *daily,* it is added to the other side of the *d* after the *a* has been written.

59 Amounts and Quantities In business you will often take dictation in which amounts and quantities are used. Here are some devices that will enable you to write them rapidly.

300	$12	8 o'clock
6,000	$3,000	$4.50
800,000	$600,000	6 percent

◈ Notice that the *n* for *hundred* and the *th* for *thousand* are placed *underneath* the figure.

Reading and Writing Practice

60 Brief-Form Letter

[102]

61

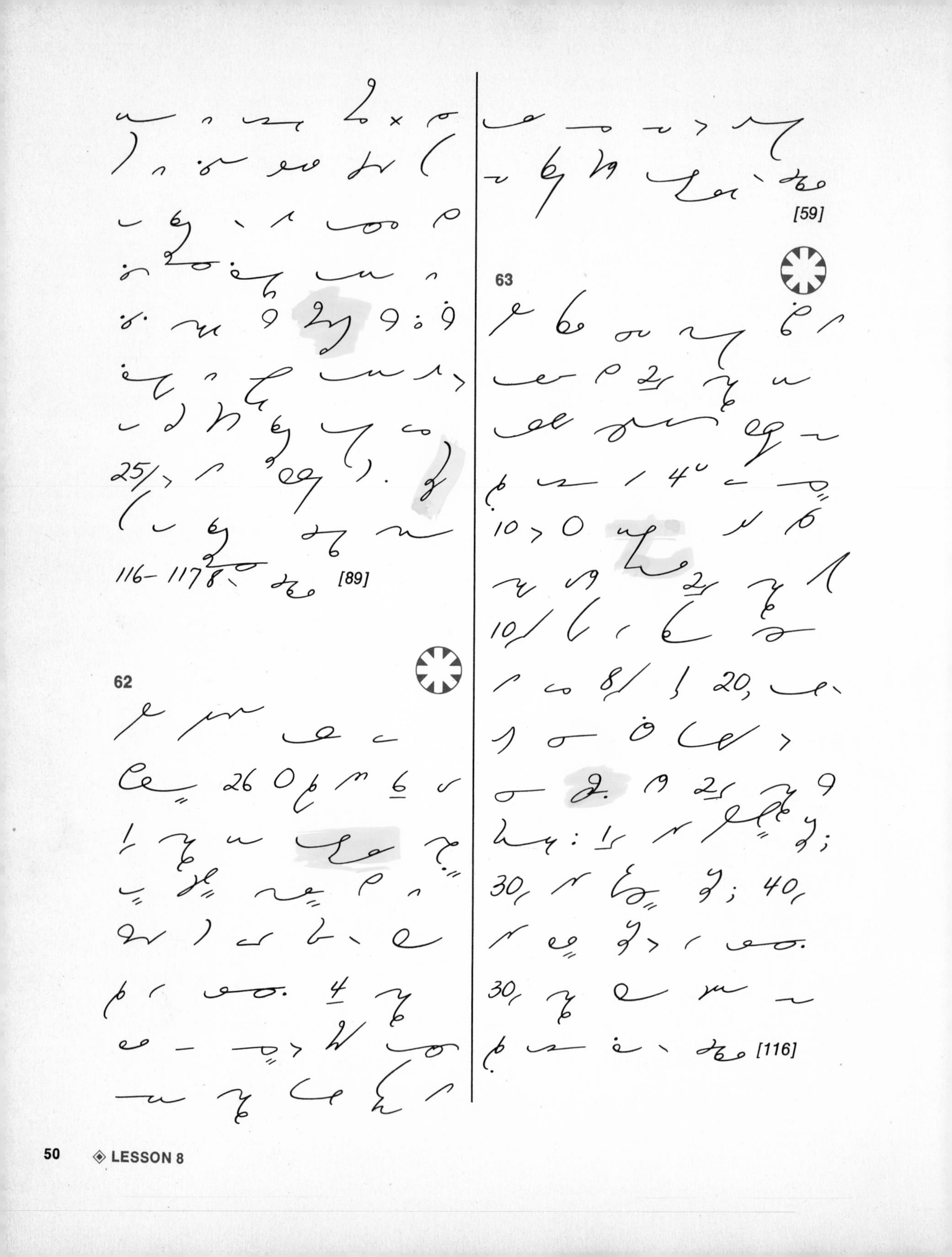

[89]

62

[59]

63

[116]

64

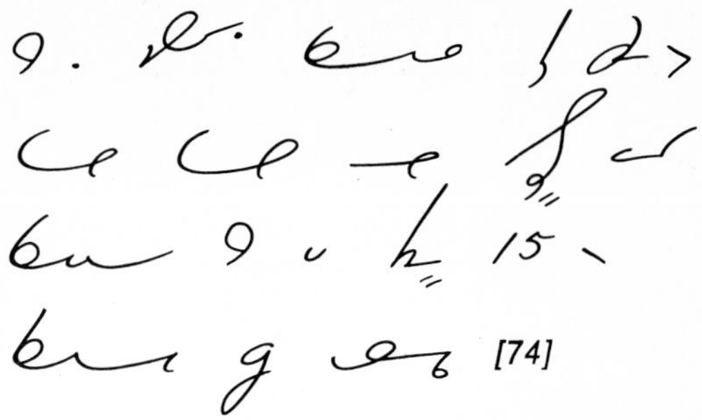

[61]

65

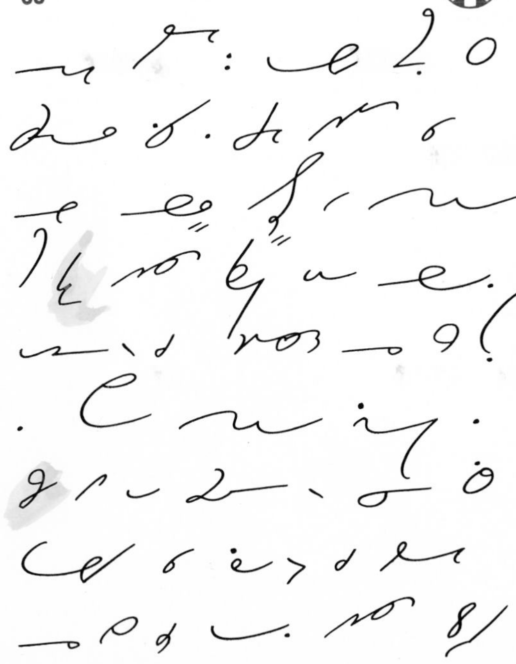

[74]

66

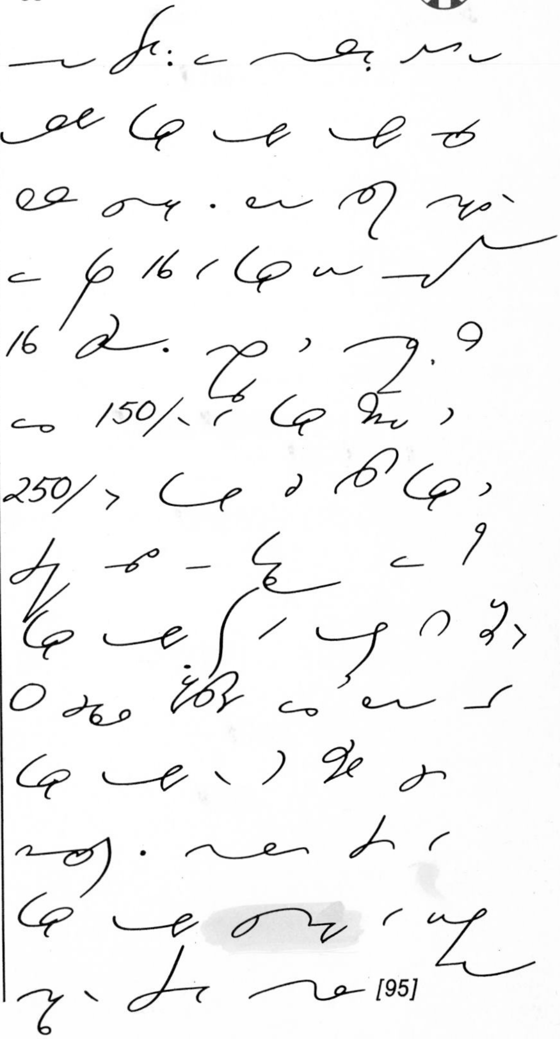

[95]

Principles

67 Word Ending -tion The word ending *-tion* (sometimes spelled *-sion, -cian,* or *-shion*) is represented by *ish.*

Spell: a-k-shun, action

action	occasion	nations
faction	collection	national
position	physician	nationally
portion	fashion	cautioned

68 Word Endings -cient, -ciency The word ending *-cient* is represented by *ish-t; -ciency,* by *ish-s-e.*

Spell: p-a-shun-t, patient; e-f-e-shun-s-e, efficiency

patient	efficient	proficient
patiently	efficiency	proficiency

69 Word Ending -tial The word ending *-tial* (or *-cial*) is represented by *ish.*

Spell: s-o-shul, social

social	special	initial
official	specially	initialed
financial	partial	initially

70 T for To in Phrases In phrases, *to* is represented by *t* when it is followed by a downstroke.

to be	to change	to buy
to have	to charge	to fill
to plan	to show	to see
to pay	to share	to say

◈ Notice that the left *s* is used in *see* and *say* when these words occur in phrases.

Reading and Writing Practice

71 Brief-Form Review Letter

[129]

72

[97]

[120]

73

74

[104]

75

[75]

STUDY-HABIT CHECK LIST

No doubt as a conscientious student you do your home assignments faithfully. Do you, however, derive the greatest benefit from the time you devote to practice?

You do if you practice in a quiet place that enables you to concentrate.

You don't if you practice with one eye on the television and the other on your practice work!

You do if, once you have started your assignment, you do not leave your desk or table until you have completed it.

You don't if you interrupt your practice from time to time to call a friend or raid the refrigerator!

LESSON 10

Principles

76 Nd The shorthand strokes for *n-d* are joined without an angle to form the *nd* blend, as in *signed.*

Nd

Compare: sign signed

Spell: s-ī-end, signed; l-a-end, land

land	trained	kind
planned	strained	mind
friend	find	spend

77 Nt The stroke for *nd* also represents *nt,* as in *sent.*

Spell: s-e-ent, sent; ent-oo, into

sent	rented	agent
event	painted	into
prevent	parent	entirely

78 Ses The sound of *ses,* as in *senses,* is represented by joining the two forms of *s.* The similar sounds of *sis,* as in *sister,* and *sus,* as in *versus,* are represented in the same way.

Compare: sense senses

face faces

Spell: s-e-n-sez, senses

places	losses	passes
causes	necessary	sister
addresses	offices	basis
promises	cases	versus

Reading and Writing Practice

79 Brief-Form Review Letter

[88]

80

[95]

81

15

[114]

82

350

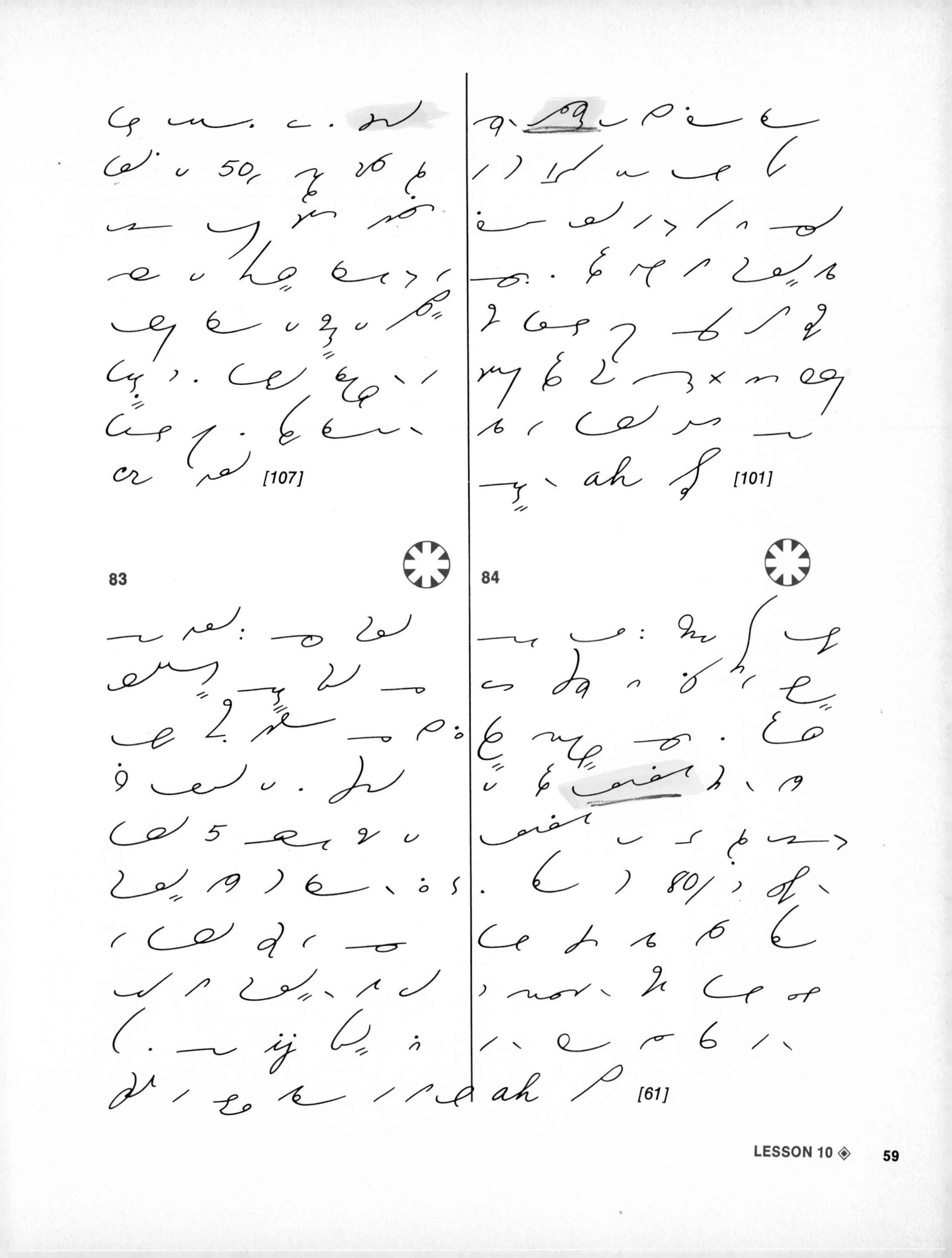

[107]

[101]

83

[61]

84

LESSON 11

Principles

85 Brief Forms Here is another set of brief forms for common words.

should | was | and
could | when | they
send | from | them

◈ Note: *Them* is a combination of the over *ith* and *m* joined without an angle.

86 Rd The combination *rd* is represented by writing *r* with an upward turn at the finish.

Compare: store stored

Spell: s-t-o-ärd, stored; h-e-ärd, heard

stored | tired | hard
hired | record | harder
appeared | toward | guarded

87 Ld The combination *ld* is represented by writing the *l* with an upward turn at the finish.

Compare: fail failed

Spell: o-eld, old; n-a-eld, nailed

old | mailed | folder

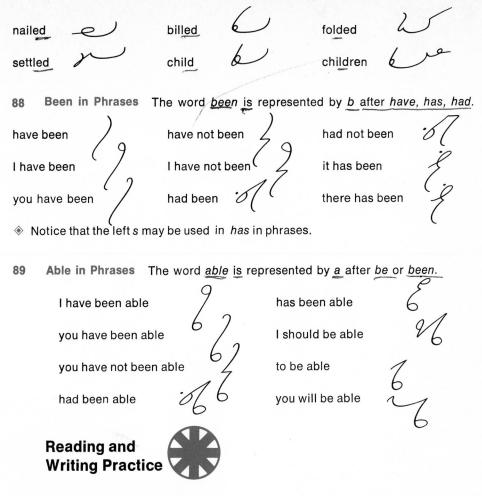

nailed billed folded

settled child children

88 Been in Phrases The word *been* is represented by *b* after *have, has, had.*

have been | have not been | had not been

I have been | I have not been | it has been

you have been | had been | there has been

◈ Notice that the left *s* may be used in *has* in phrases.

89 Able in Phrases The word *able* is represented by *a* after *be* or *been.*

I have been able | has been able

you have been able | I should be able

you have not been able | to be able

had been able | you will be able

Reading and Writing Practice

90 Brief-Form Letter The following letter contains at least one illustration of every brief form in paragraph 85.

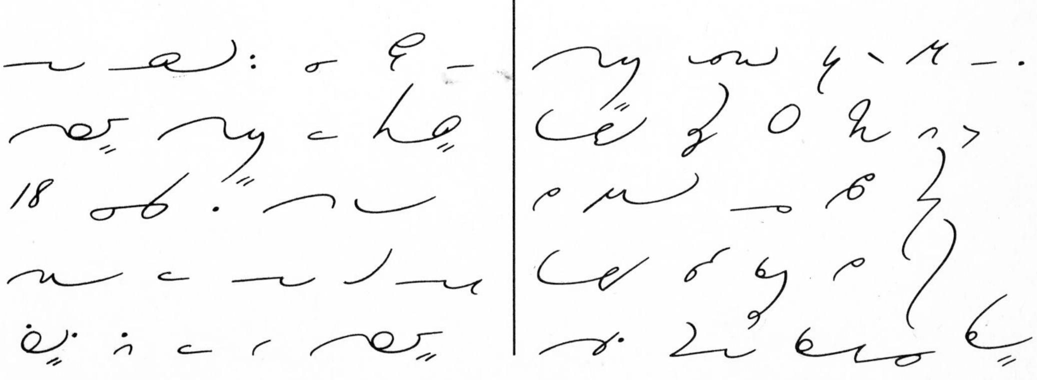

15

[113]

[98]

91

92

1972

18

[89]

93

[78]

94

[126]

LESSON 12

RECALL

Lesson 12 is a "breather"; it presents no new principles for you to learn. It reviews the shorthand strokes you learned in Lessons 1-11.

Principles of Joining

The following principles deal with the joinings of the two forms of *s*.

95 At the beginning and ends of words, the comma *s* is used before and after *f, v, k, gay;* the left *s,* before and after *p, b, r, l.*

saves  sips  series

seeks  globes  rags

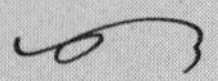

96 The comma *s* is used before *t, d, n, m, o;* the left *s* is used after those strokes.

stones 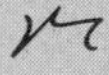 solos 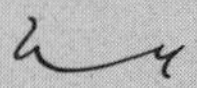 needs

97 The comma *s* is used before and after *ish, chay, j.*

sessions  reaches  stages

98 The comma *s* is used in words consisting of *s* and a circle vowel or *s* and *ith* and a circle vowel.

say these seethe

99 Gregg Shorthand is equally legible whether it is written on ruled or unruled paper; consequently, you need not worry about the exact placement of your outlines on the printed lines in your notebook. The main purpose that the printed lines in your notebook serve is to keep you from wandering uphill and downhill as you write.

However, so that all outlines may be uniformly placed in the shorthand books from which you study, this general rule has been followed:

The base of the first consonant of a word is placed on the line of writing. When *s* comes before a downstroke, however, the downstroke is placed on the line of writing.

name safe pace

dealer chief space

100 Recall Chart The following chart contains all the brief forms presented in Chapter 2 and one or more illustrations of all the shorthand devices you studied in Chapters 1 and 2.

Can you read it in 6 minutes or less?

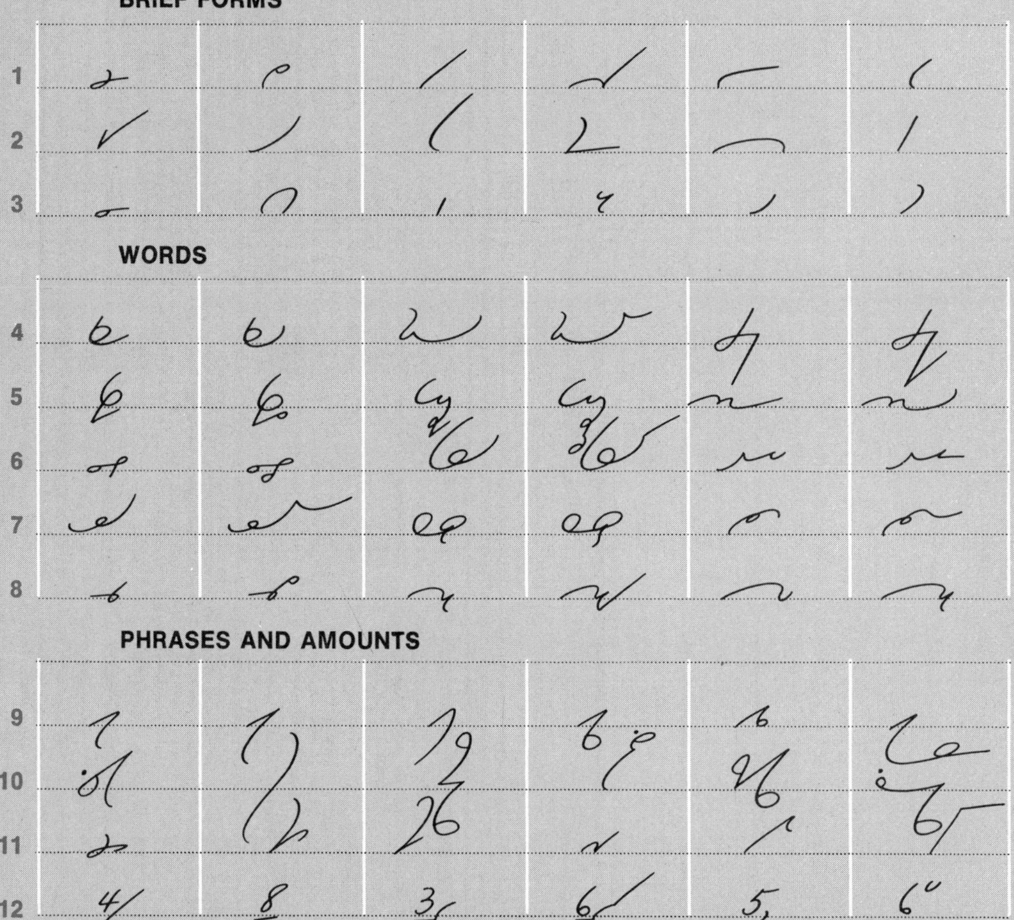

Reading and Writing Practice

101 Brief-Form Review Letter

[116]

102

[83]

103

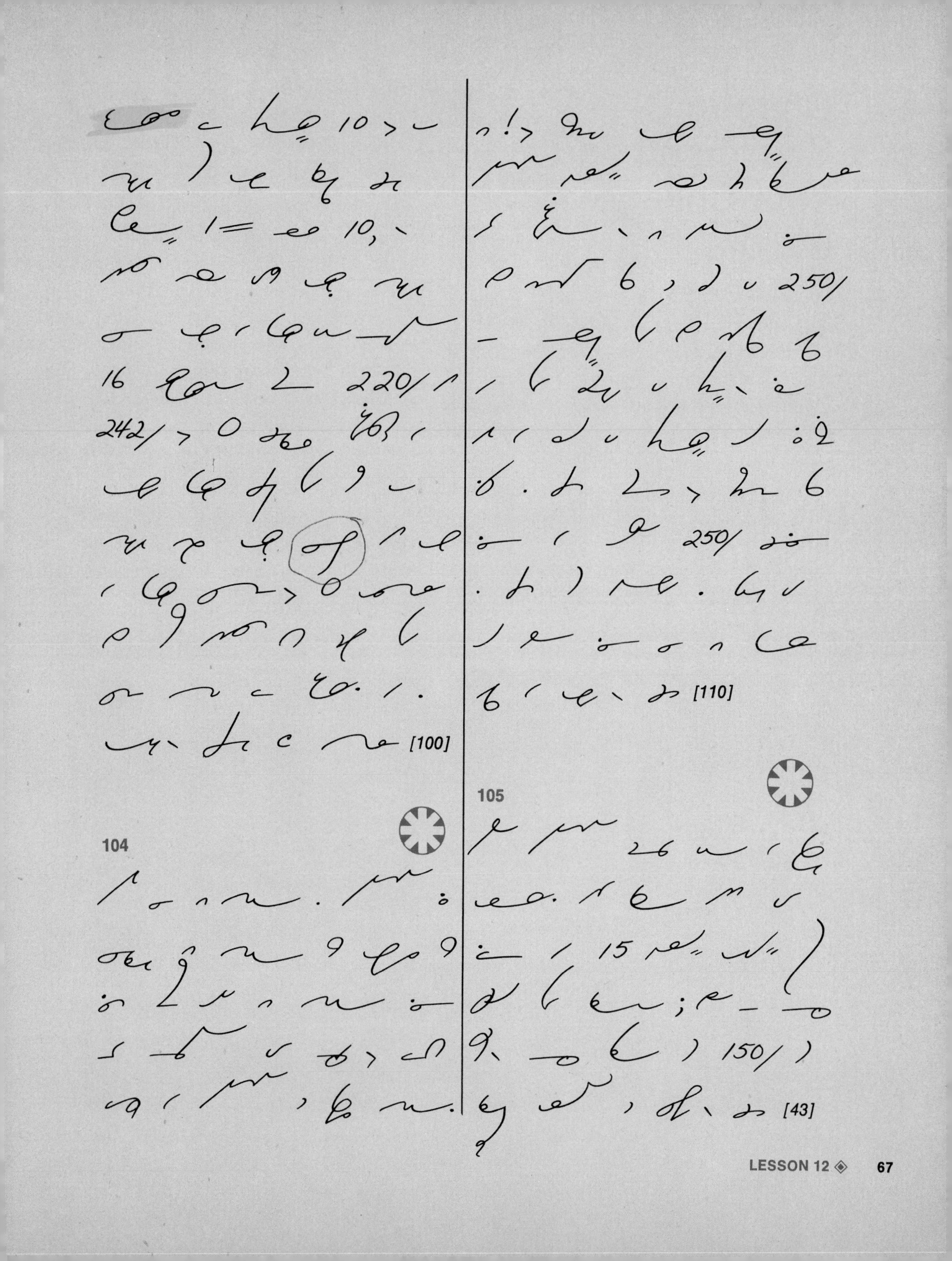

[100]

104

[110]

105

[43]

Chapter 3 Shorthand and Your College Major

People study shorthand for many reasons, but college students do so for very special reasons. The primary reason for many is that they want to obtain desirable, well-paying secretarial positions in business or government, and they know that college-trained secretaries are in great demand.

Others who do not plan to make a career of secretarial work realize that being able to list shorthand skills among their achievements will help them get a foothold in their chosen fields that would otherwise be denied them. Shorthand provides the "extra" that puts the liberal arts major well ahead of his classmates who have no specific skills to offer when they look for that first job.

If you have chosen journalism as your career, consider how helpful shorthand will be to you in making notes of interviews and in recording important events that you witness. If you have decided to major in history, government, or political science, again shorthand will be of great value to you. Business often prefers shorthand training for those who work in research. But how do you "market" this particular skill in a business or government organization?

Even if your grades are above average, you will not find it easy to obtain the job you want unless you bring an extra skill to it. Shorthand is that skill.

H. Armstrong Roberts

United Press International Photo

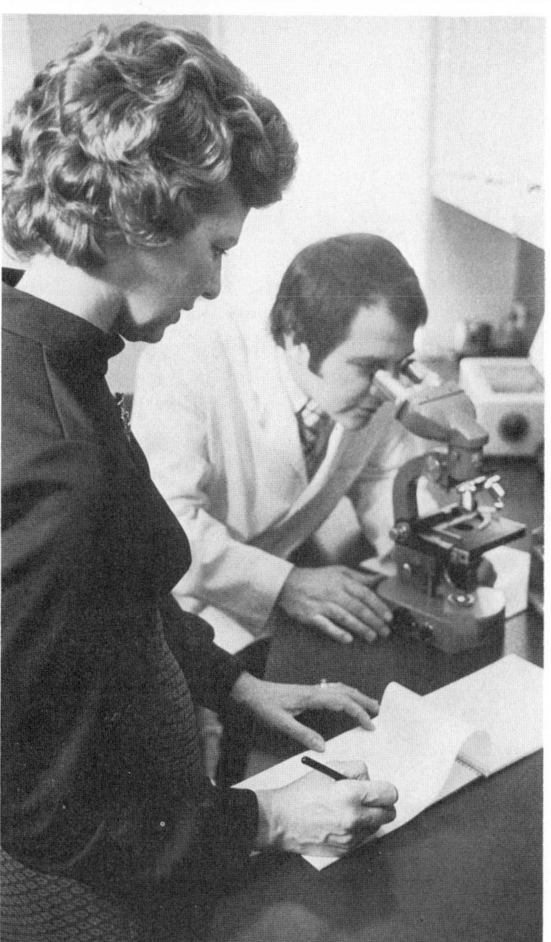

The person with talent in art, music, or drama, for example, finds keen competition when he tries to sell that talent to a commercial enterprise. In fact, more people seek jobs in those areas than there are jobs to be filled. Shorthand can be the key that opens the door for you to those hard-to-enter fields.

The English major who wants to work in business often finds it difficult to obtain that first job. But when he adds shorthand to his list of qualifications, the picture immediately brightens.

Each year thousands of women who have liberal arts degrees enroll in business schools to obtain secretarial skills. They know that with such skills, their chances of obtaining that ideal job are much better.

What is *your* major? Regardless of what it is, you have the best possible opportunity of marketing it when you can add shorthand to your qualifications on your data sheet.

Shorthand and liberal arts are a natural combination.

LESSON 13

Principles

106 Brief Forms

yesterday		were, year		enclose	
work		soon		order	
glad		very		thank	

107 Brief-Form Derivatives and Phrases

thanks		thank you		thank you for	
ordered		worker		gladly	

◈ Notice that *thanks* is written with a disjoined left *s* in the dot position; that the *d* representing the past tense of *order* is joined with a jog; that the dot in *thank* is omitted in phrases.

108 U, OO The hook that represents the sound of *oo,* as in *to*, also represents the vowel sounds in *does* and *foot.*

U

Spell: d-oo-s, does

does		none		us	
cover		number		just	
drug		enough		precious	

◈ Notice that the *oo* in *none, number, enough* is turned on its side; that *oo-s* join without an angle in *us, just, precious.*

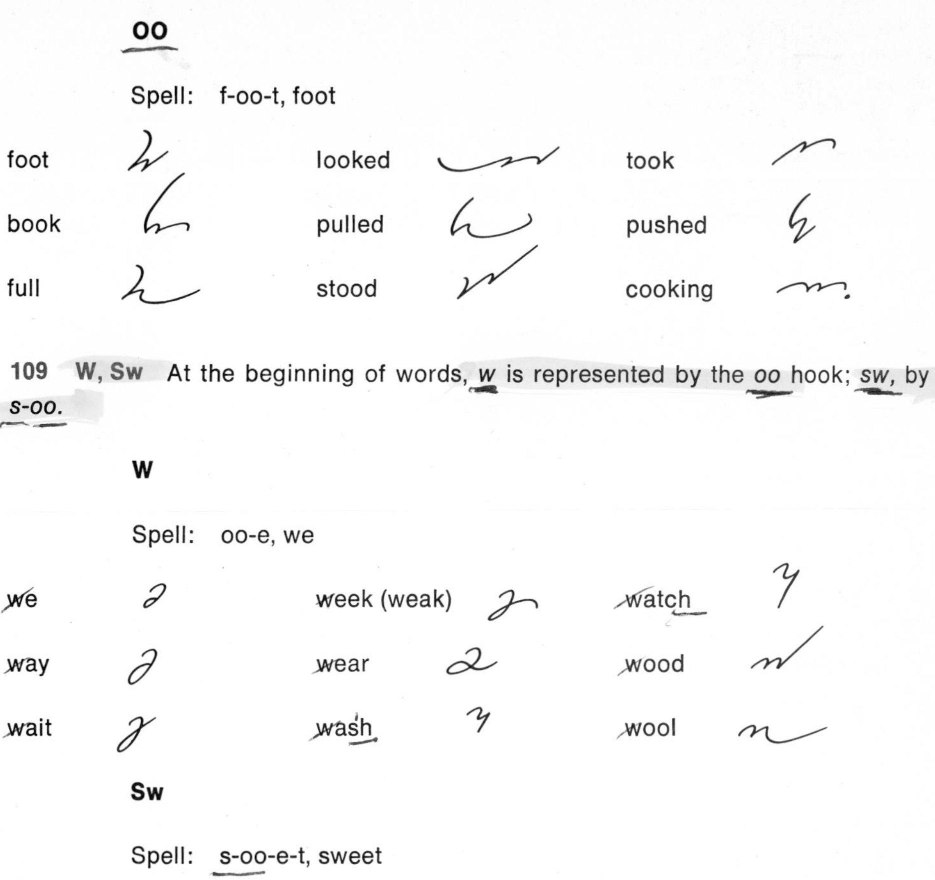

oo

Spell: f-oo-t, foot

foot	looked	took
book	pulled	pushed
full	stood	cooking

109 W, Sw At the beginning of words, *w* is represented by the *oo* hook; *sw,* by *s-oo.*

W

Spell: oo-e, we

we	week (weak)	watch
way	wear	wood
wait	wash	wool

Sw

Spell: s-oo-e-t, sweet

sweet	swim	sweater

Building Transcription Skills

110 BUSINESS VOCABULARY BUILDER

As a stenographer or secretary you will constantly be dealing with words. Consequently, the larger the vocabulary at your command, the easier will be your task of taking dictation and transcribing.

To help you build your vocabulary at the same time that you are learning shorthand, a Business Vocabulary Builder is provided in Lesson 13 and in many of the lessons that follow. The Business Vocabulary Builder consists of brief definitions of business words and expressions, selected from the Reading and Writing Practice of the lesson, that may be unfamiliar to you.

Be sure to read each Business Vocabulary Builder before you begin your work on the Reading and Writing Practice that follows it.

111

Business Vocabulary Builder

wearing apparel Clothing.

canceled Called off.

urgent Calling for immediate action; pressing.

testify Make a statement under oath.

Reading and Writing Practice

112 Brief-Form Letter

50 [124]

113

[77]

[90]

114

15

3

115

15

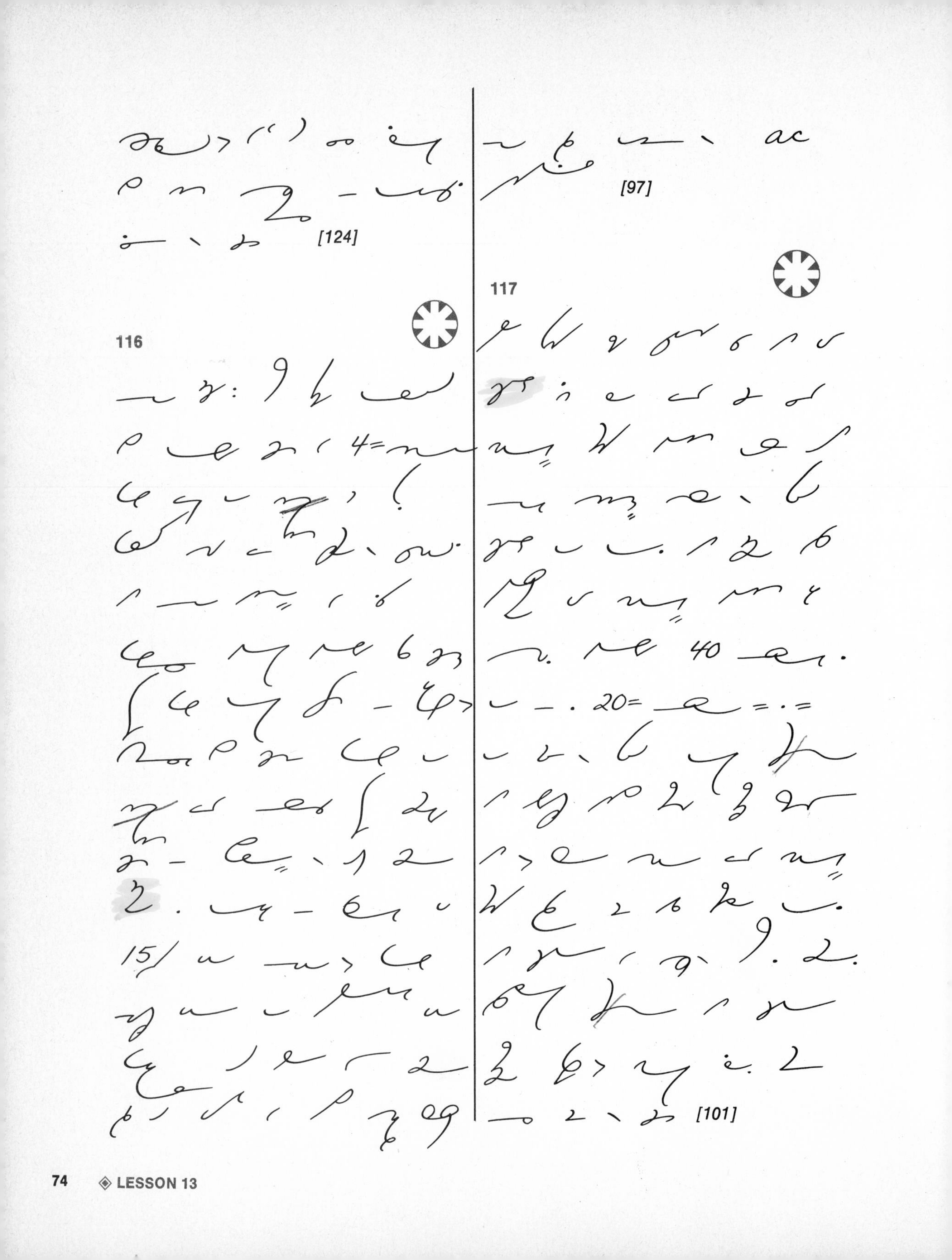

[124]

[97]

116

117

[101]

Principles

118 **Wh** *Wh,* as in *white,* is pronounced *hw*—the *h* is pronounced first. Therefore, in shorthand, we write the *h* first.

Spell: h-oo-ī-t, white

white | while | wheat

119 **W in the Body of a Word** When the sound of *w* occurs in the body of a word, as in *quick*, it is represented by a short dash underneath the vowel following the *w* sound. The dash is inserted after the rest of the shorthand outline has been written.

Spell: k-oo-e-k, quick

quick | equipped | always
quite | twice | roadway
quit | liquid | Broadway

120 **Ted** The combination *ted,* as in *heated,* is represented by joining *t* and *d* into one long stroke.

Ted

Compare: heat heed heated

Spell: h-e-ted, heated

acted | tested | dated
visited | located | steady
rested | listed | today

121 Ded, Dit, Det The long stroke that represents *ted* also represents *ded, dit, det.*

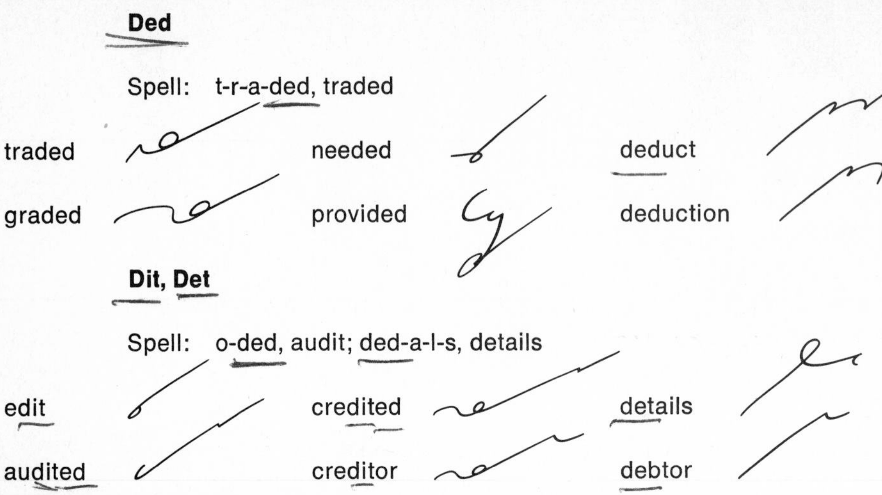

Ded

Spell: t-r-a-ded, traded

traded · needed · deduct

graded · provided · deduction

Dit, Det

Spell: o-ded, audit; ded-a-l-s, details

edit · credited · details

audited · creditor · debtor

◈ Notice that the *d* representing the past tense in *audit* and *credit* is joined with a jog.

Building Transcription Skills

122 Business Vocabulary Builder

drafted Outlined in rough form.

auditors Those who examine accounts for accuracy.

in vain Without success or result.

Reading and Writing Practice

123 Brief-Form Review Letter

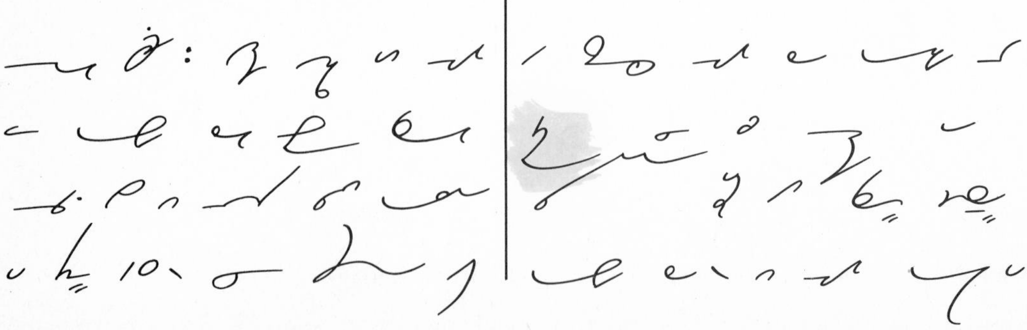

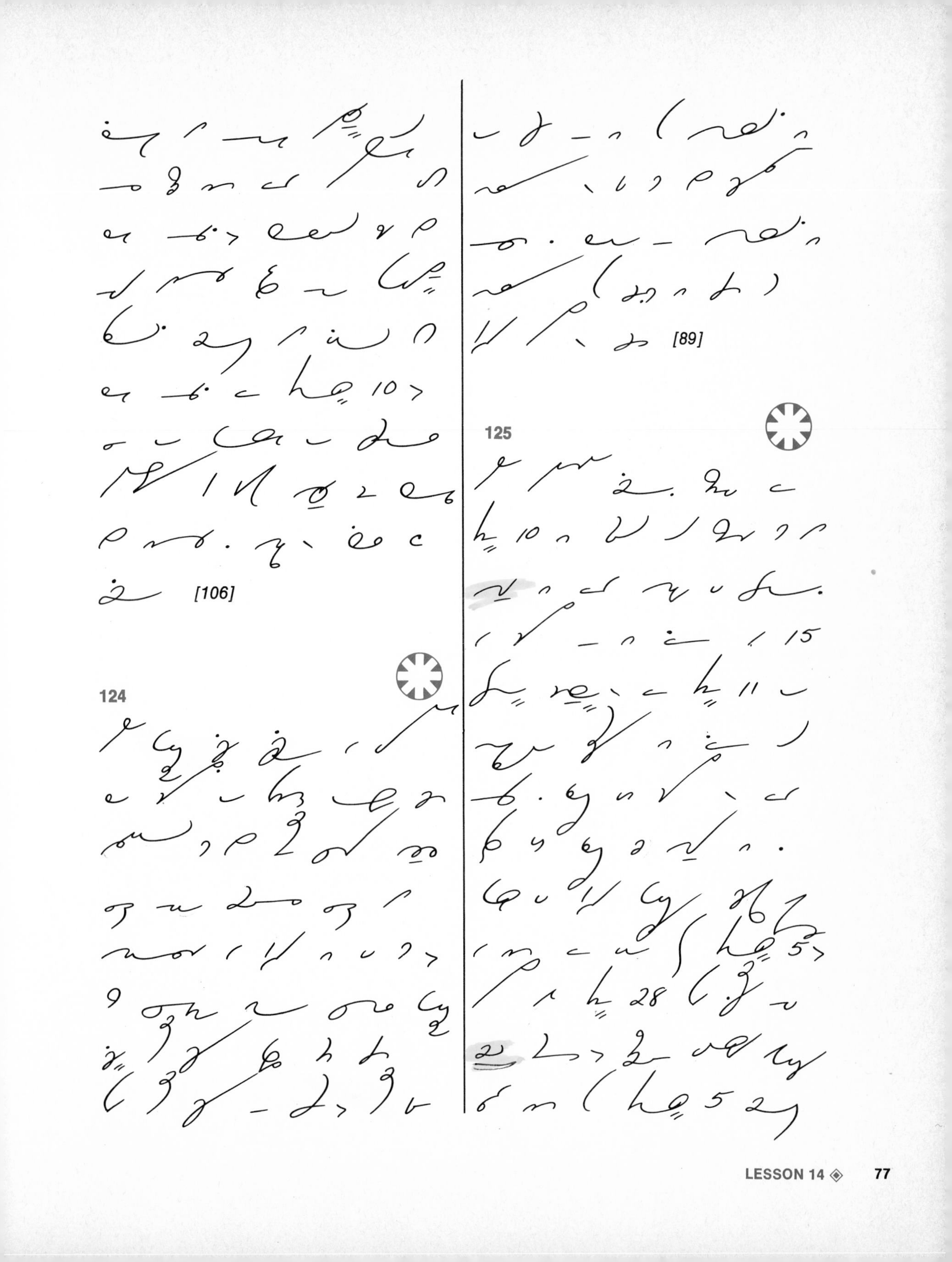

[106]

124

[89]

125

[125]

126

[127]

127

[81]

128

[107]

SHORTHAND READING CHECK LIST

When you read shorthand, do you—

■ **1** Read aloud so that you know that you are concentrating on each outline that you read?

■ **2** Spell each outline that you cannot immediately read?

■ **3** Reread each Reading and Writing Practice a second time?

■ **4** Occasionally reread the suggestions for reading shorthand given on pages 10 and 11?

LESSON 15

Principles

129 Brief Forms

what	value	one (won)
about	why	thing, think
great	business	than

◈ Note: *Than* is a combination of the over *ith* and *n* joined without an angle.

130 Brief-Form Derivatives

once	things, thinks	businessman
greater	thinking	businesses
greatly	values	businesslike

◈ Notice that a disjoined left *s* is used to express *things, thinks;* that the plural of *business* is formed by adding another left *s.*

131 Word Ending -ble The word ending *-ble* is represented by *b.*

Spell: p-o-s-bul, possible

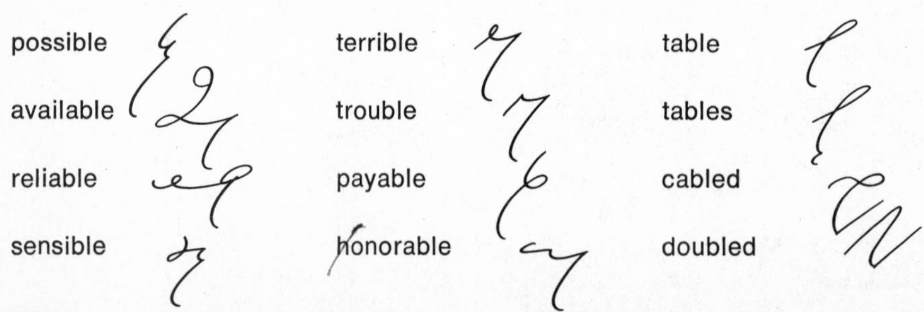

possible	terrible	table
available	trouble	tables
reliable	payable	cabled
sensible	honorable	doubled

132 **Word Beginning Re-** The word beginning *re-* is represented by *r*.

Spell: re-s-e-v, receive

receive	replace	reference
resist	revise	receipt
research	repeat	reopen
reply	repaired	rearrange

Building Transcription Skills

133 **Business Vocabulary Builder**

jeopardy Peril; danger.

precisely Exactly.

authorization Permission.

amicable Friendly.

Reading and Writing Practice

134 **Brief-Form Letter**

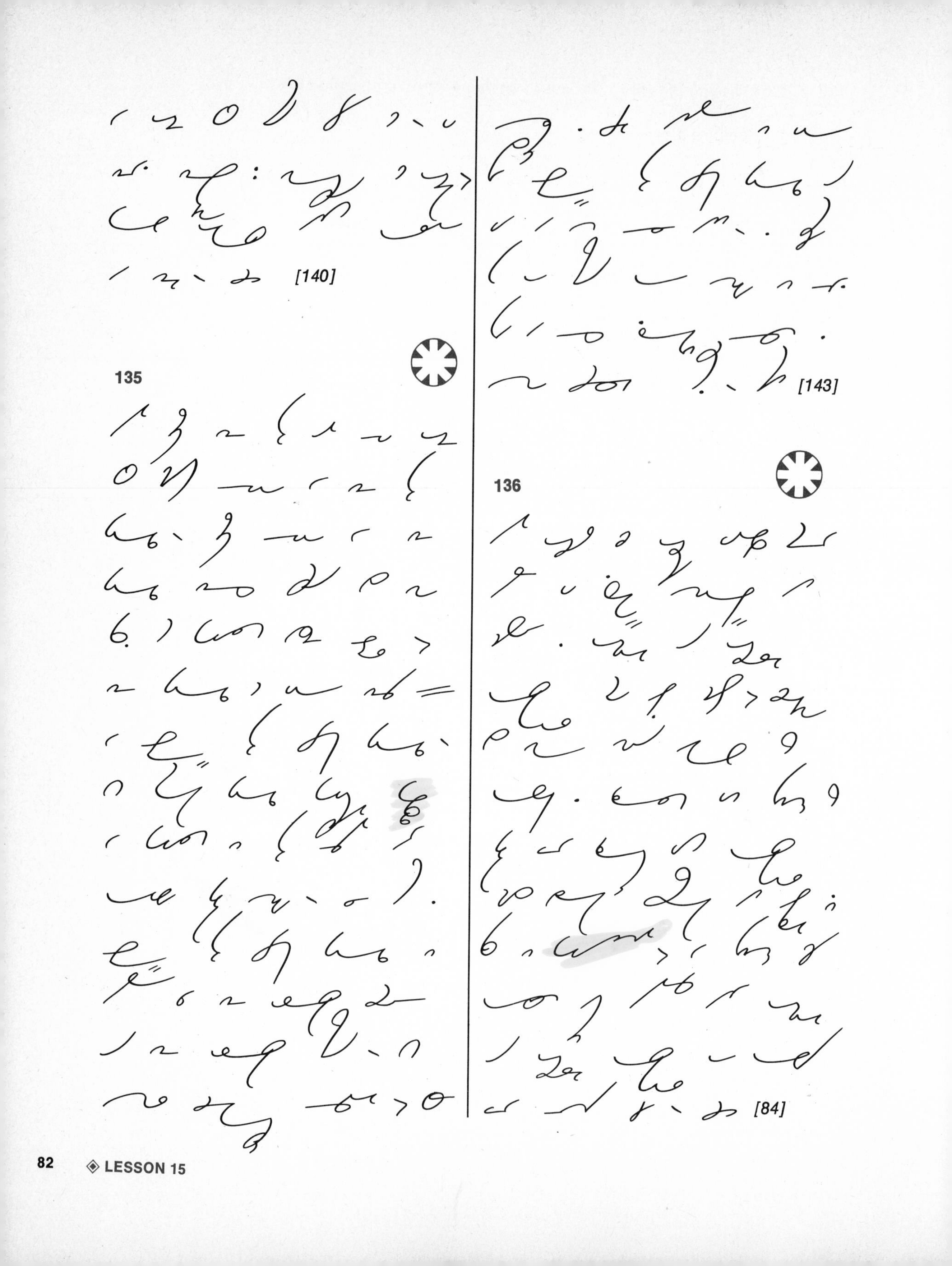

[140]

135

[143]

136

[84]

137

[125]

138

[117]

Principles

139 **Oi** The sound of *oi,* as in *toy,* is represented by .

Spell: t-oi, toy

toy	annoy	appoint
boy	oil	voice
joy	spoil	choice
join	boil	noises

140 **Men, Mem** The combinations *men, mem* are represented by joining *m* and *n* into one long forward stroke.

Men, Mem

Compare: knee me many

Men

Spell: men-t, meant

men	mending	businessmen
meant	mentally	women
mention	salesmen	amend

Mem

Spell: mem-r-e, memory

memory	member	remember
memorize	members	memorable

141 Min, Mon, Mun, etc. The long stroke that represents *men, mem* also represents the similar sounds of *min, mon, mun,* etc.

Spell: men-e-t, minute; men-r, manner

minute month manner

minimum monthly managed

eliminate money manager

142 Word Beginning Be- The word beginning *be-* is represented by *b.*

Spell: be-k-a-m, became

became because below

begin believe beyond

began belief betray

Building Transcription Skills

143 Business Vocabulary Builder

pointers Hints, tips.

hampered Interfered with.

business machines Typewriters, adding machines, calculators, etc.

Reading and Writing Practice

144 Brief-Form Review Letter

450

[129]

116-1117

[94]

145

146

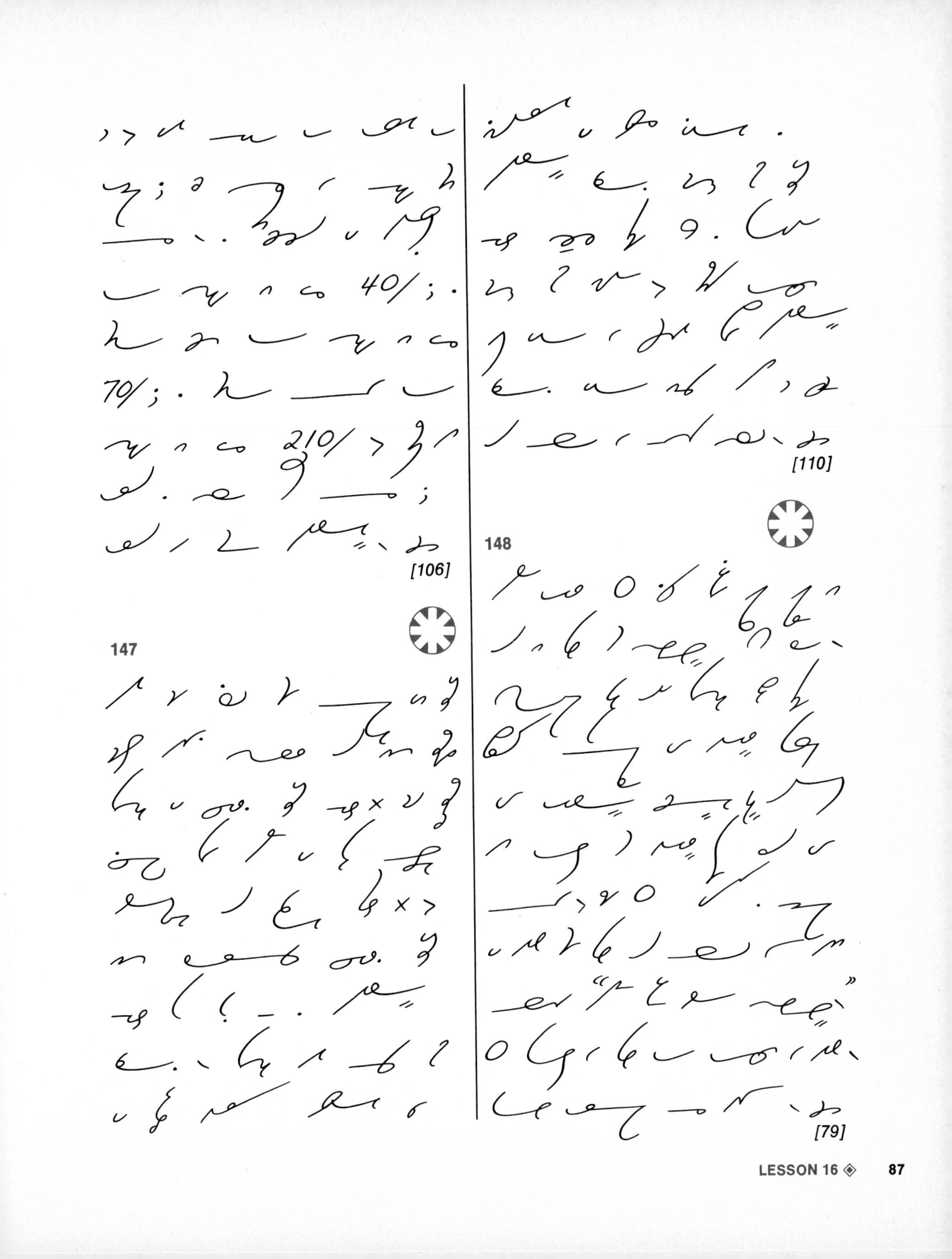

40%; 70%; 210%

[106]

[110]

148

[79]

147

LESSON 17

Principles

149 Brief Forms When you have learned the following six brief forms, you will have learned more than half the brief forms of Gregg Shorthand.

morning — important, importance — where
gentlemen — those — manufacture

150 Word Beginnings Per-, Pur- The word beginnings *per-, pur-* are represented by *pr.*

Per-

Spell: pur-s-n, person

person — persisted — persuade
permit — perfect — personnel

Pur-

Spell: pur-chay-a-s, purchase

purchase — purple — purse

151 Word Beginnings De-, Di- The word beginnings *de-, di-* are represented by *d.*

De-

Spell: de-l-a, delay

delay — deposit — derive
deserve — delivery — desired

Di-

Spell: de-r-e-k-t, direct

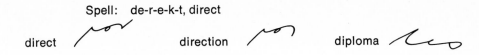

direct direction diploma

Building Transcription Skills

152 SIMILAR-WORDS DRILL

The English language contains many groups of words that sound or look alike, but each member of the group is spelled differently and has its own meaning.

Example: **sent** (dispatched); **scent** (a smell); **cent** (a coin).

In addition, there are many groups of words that sound or look *almost* alike.

Example: **defer** (to put off); **differ** (to disagree).

The stenographer or secretary who is not alert may, while transcribing, select the wrong member of the group, with the result that her transcript makes no sense.

In this lesson and in a number of others that follow you will find a Similar-Words Drill that will call to your attention common groups of similar words on which the unwary stenographer can stumble.

Study these groups carefully so that when you transcribe, you will be able to select the correct member of the group and thus avoid the embarrassment of having your letters returned for correction.

SIMILAR-WORDS DRILL ■ personal, personnel

personal Individual; private; pertaining to the person or body.

Harry is a *personal* friend of mine.
You should watch your *personal* appearance with care.

personnel The people who work for a firm; the staff.

You can depend on our *personnel* to give you good service.
Mr. Smith is the *personnel* director of our firm.

153 **Business Vocabulary Builder**

minimum The least.

decisive Settling all doubt; definite.

established *(adjective)* Recognized and accepted without question.

Reading and Writing Practice

154 **Brief-Form Letter**

[113]

155

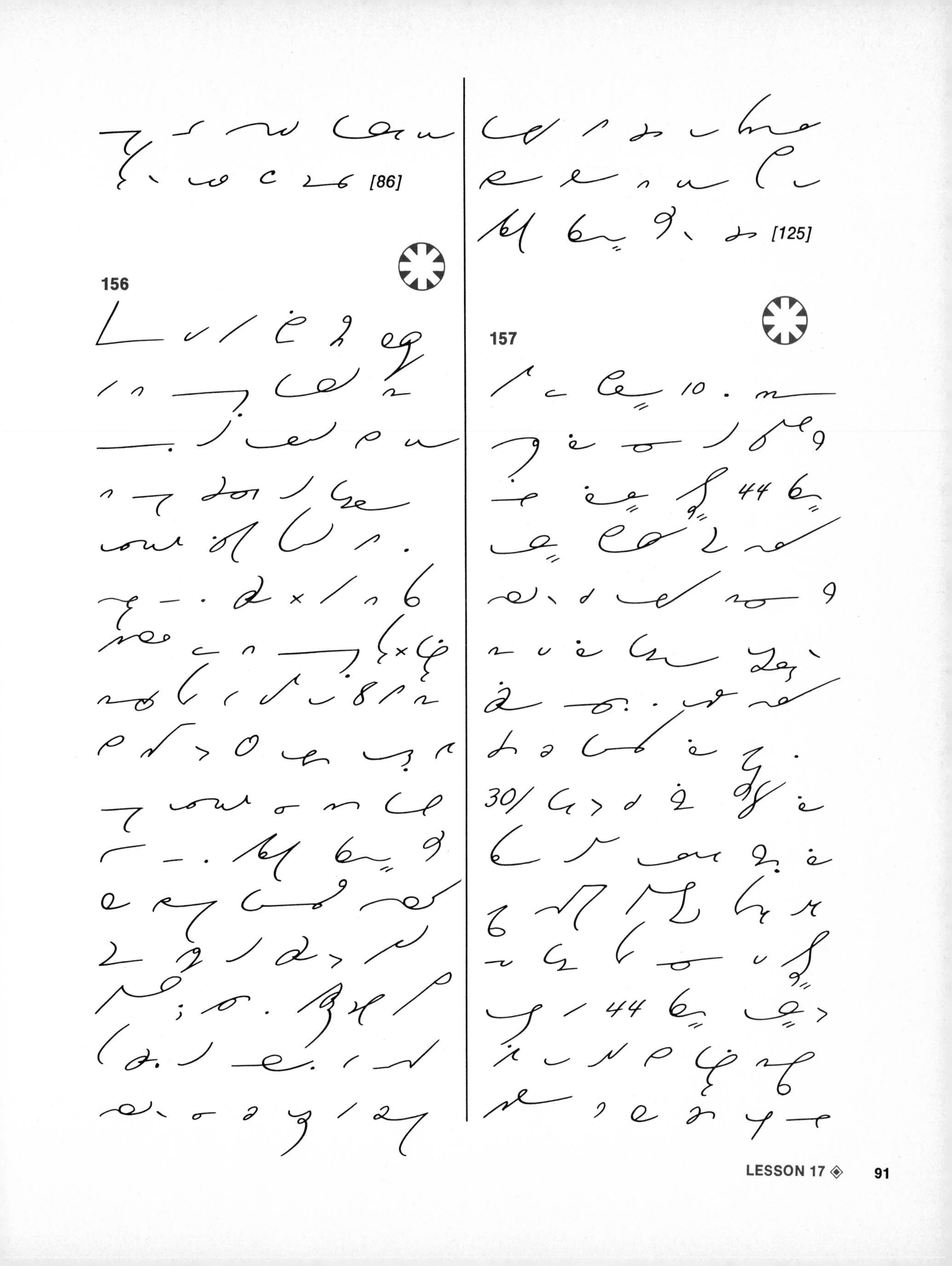

[86]

156

[125]

157

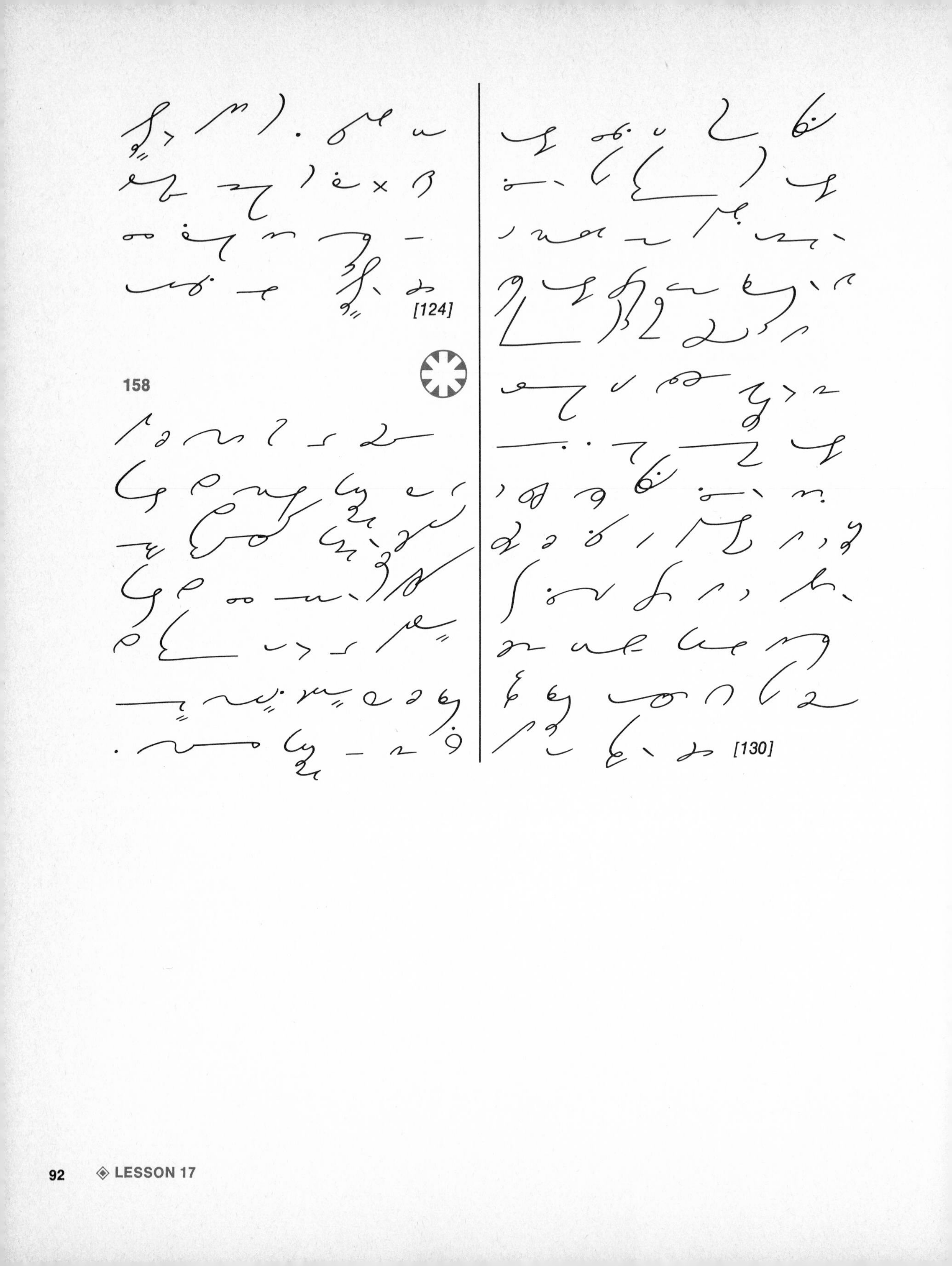

[124]

158

[130]

LESSON 18

RECALL

Lesson 18 is another "breather" for you; it contains no new shorthand devices for you to learn. Lesson 18 will give you an opportunity to consolidate what you have studied in Lessons 1-17.

Principles of Joining

159 At the beginning of a word and after *k* and *gay* or a downstroke, the combination *oo-s* is written without an angle.

husky gust just

but

loose does rust

160 The word beginning *re* is represented by *r* before a downstroke or a vowel.

research reference reopen

but

relate retake retreat

161 The word beginnings *de-, di-* are represented by *d* except before k *or gay.*

depressed deliver direction

but

declare decay degrade

162 As you have perhaps already noticed from your study of Lessons 1 through 17, the past tense of a verb is formed by adding the stroke for the sound that is heard in the past tense. In some words, the past tense has the sound of *t,* as in *baked;* in others, it has the sound of *d,* as in *saved.* In some words, the past tense is incorporated in a blend, as in *planned, feared, mailed.*

baked saved feared

missed planned mailed

163 **Recall Chart** The following chart reviews all the brief forms of Chapter 3 as well as all the shorthand devices you studied in Chapters 1, 2, and 3.

The chart contains 96 words and phrases. Can you read it in 8 minutes or less?

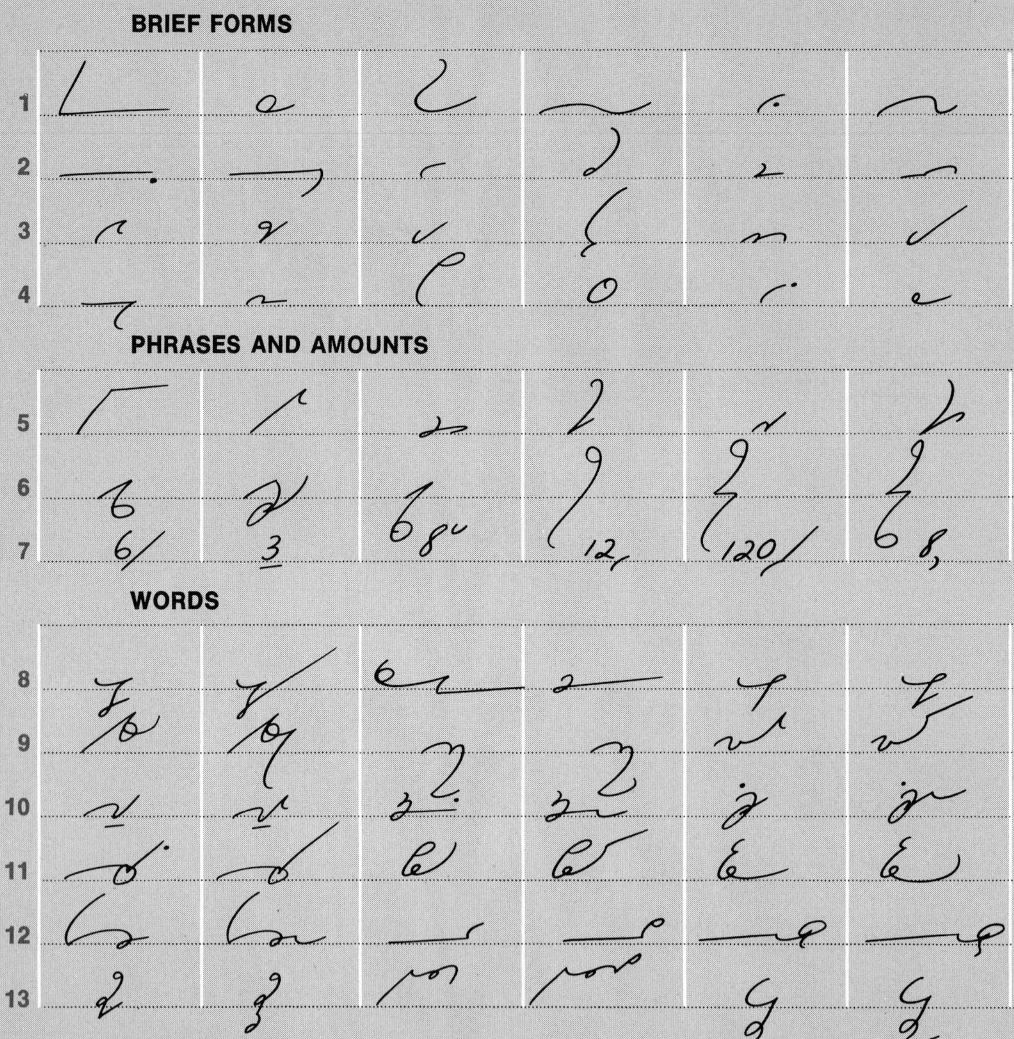

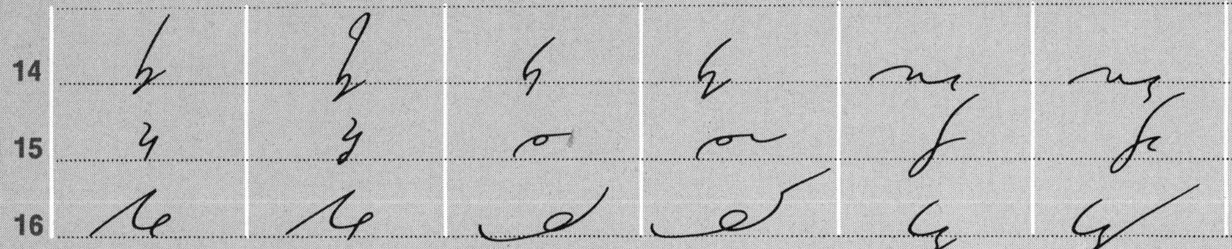

Building Transcription Skills

164

Business Vocabulary Builder	
	grates *(verb)* Causes a harsh sound.
	slur *(verb)* To pass over carelessly.
	diplomatic Tactful.

Reading and Writing Practice

Reading Scoreboard One of the factors in measuring shorthand growth is the rate at which you can read shorthand. Here is an opportunity for you to measure your reading speed on the *first reading* of the material in Lesson 18. The following table will help you determine how rapidly you can read shorthand.

Lesson 18 contains 429 words	
If you read Lesson 18 in	your reading rate is
17 minutes	**25 words a minute**
19 minutes	**22 words a minute**
21 minutes	**20 words a minute**
25 minutes	**17 words a minute**
29 minutes	**15 words a minute**
33 minutes	**13 words a minute**

If you can read Lesson 18 through the first time in less than 17 minutes, you are doing well indeed. If you take considerably longer than 33 minutes, here are some questions you should ask yourself:

1 *Am I spelling each outline I cannot read immediately?*

2 *Am I spending too much time deciphering an outline that I cannot read even after spelling it?*

3 *Should I perhaps reread the directions for reading shorthand on page 11?*

After you have determined your reading rate, make a record of it in some convenient place. You can then watch your reading rate grow as you time yourself on the Reading Scoreboards in later lessons.

165 Voice

If a

Why not

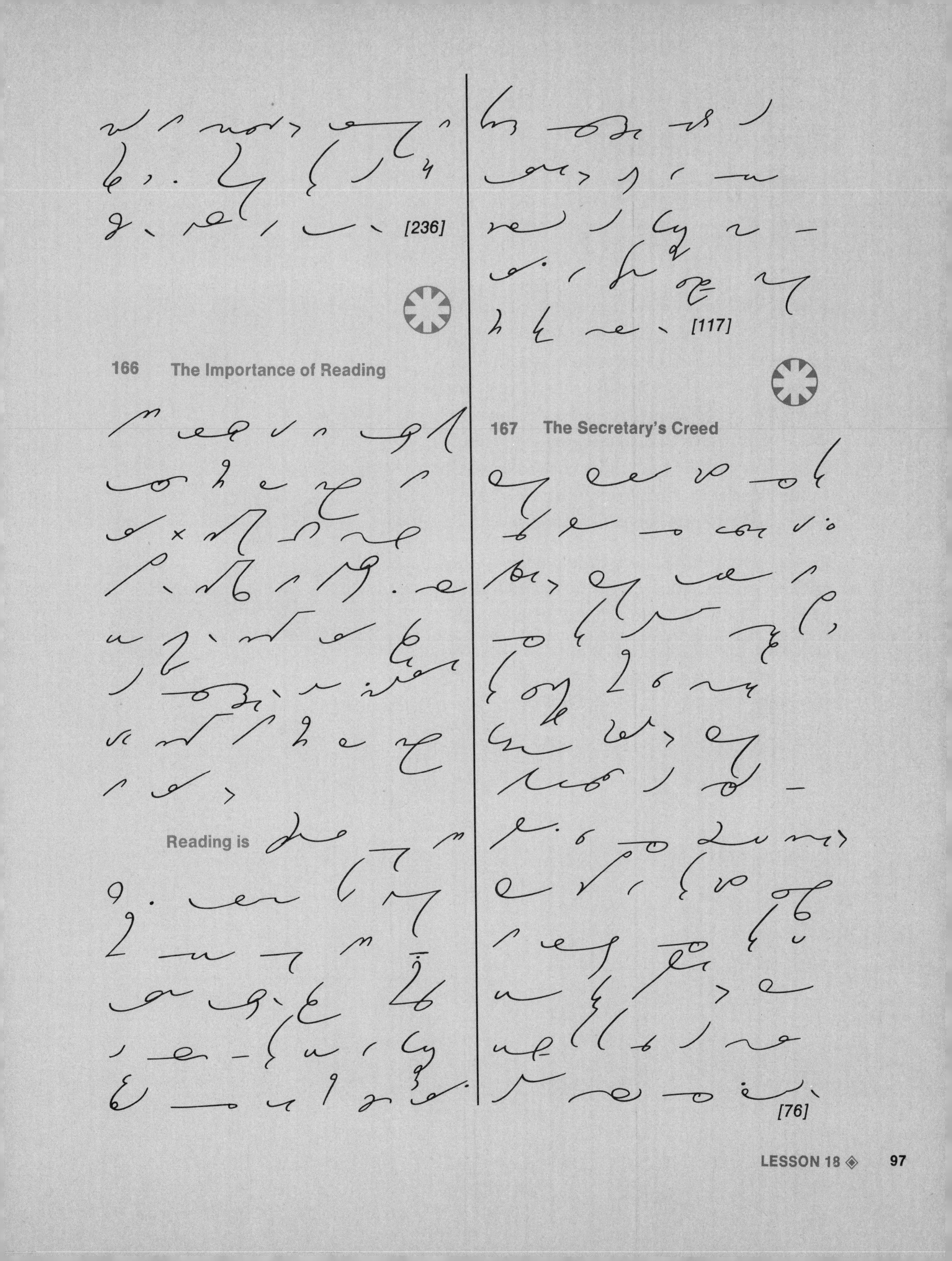

[236]

[117]

166 The Importance of Reading

Reading is

167 The Secretary's Creed

[76]

Chapter 4 The Growing Importance of the Secretary

Few professions offer women more opportunities to make a vital contribution to our society than does the secretarial profession. As business expands and the need arises for more and better executives, the demand for more and better secretaries rises accordingly. It is a well-known fact that executives cannot perform their functions effectively without the help of capable secretaries.

Today's secretary is more than a person who answers the telephone and brings coffee to her boss! Besides taking dictation and transcribing communications for her employer,

Photo Courtesy United Air Lines

she keeps track of his appointments, organizes his daily calendar, writes letters and reports, engages in research, follows up on pending business matters, arranges and reports conferences and meetings, and performs various public relations functions for customers and other important members of the organization.

The secretary is, in short, the executive's indispensable specialist in what is perhaps his most important job — communications. He depends on her to put his thoughts into type; to speak to subordinates, executives, top management, and to the public at large; to listen to the suggestions, ideas, and complaints of others; and to read business documents that cross his desk.

The secretary manages an efficient records system, including letter files, so that information can be obtained at a moment's notice. The modern secretary is indeed a communications specialist.

Meeting these challenges calls for a special type of person — a professional — who can take her place as an important member of the management team. She works closely with those who direct the activities of a business or government enterprise. She is in on many of the innumerable top-level decisions that are made every day in every American business.

The secretary plays a vital role indeed in American business, government, and industry. To prepare for this role, she must be exceptionally well trained. And shorthand is one of the most important skill subjects that she must master.

Principles

168 Brief Forms Here is another group of nine brief forms for common words.

present	advertise	immediate
part	company	must
after	wish	opportunity

◈ Notice that there is no angle between the *k* and the *p* in the brief form *company*.

169 U The sound of *u,* as in *few,* is represented by .

Spell: f-u, few.

few	unit	cute
refuse	united	acutely
reviewed	unique	usual

170 Word Ending -ment The word ending *-ment* is represented by *m.*

Spell: a-r-a-n-j-ment, arrangement

arrangement	advertisement	replacements
settlement	garments	shipments
payment	assignment	elementary

◈ Notice that in *assignment* the *m* for *-ment* is joined to the *n* with a jog.

Building Transcription Skills

171 SPELLING

When you look at the letter on page 102, you get a very favorable first impression. The letter is tastefully positioned; the right-hand margin is even; the date, inside address, and closing are all in their proper places. When you scan the letter casually, you will find that it makes good sense and apparently represents what the dictator said.

But that favorable first impression will vanish when you read the letter carefully. In fact, you will quickly realize that it will never be signed and that the director will have some harsh words for the stenographer who transcribed the letter. Why? It contains several misspelled words. No businessman will knowingly sign a letter that contains a misspelled word!

If you are to succeed as a stenographer or secretary, your letters must not only be accurate transcripts of what your employer dictated but they must also be free of spelling errors. A stenographer or secretary who regularly submits letters for her employer's signature that contain spelling errors will not be his stenographer or secretary long!

To make sure that you will be able to spell correctly when you have completed your shorthand course, you will from this point on give special attention to spelling in each Reading and Writing Practice.

As you read the Reading and Writing Practice, you will occasionally find shorthand outlines printed in color. These outlines represent words that stenographers and secretaries often misspell. When you encounter an outline printed in color, finish the sentence in which it occurs; then glance at the margin, where you will find the word in type, properly spelled and syllabicated.

Spell the word aloud if possible, pausing slightly after each word division. (The word divisions indicated are those given in *Webster's Seventh New Collegiate Dictionary.)*

172 Business Vocabulary Builder

handling costs Expenses such as postage, envelopes, clerical time, etc.

proof *(in printing)* A trial sheet of printed material on which corrections are made.

Reading and Writing Practice

173 Brief-Form Letter

Superior Heating Products Inc.

688 HARRISBURG AVENUE • PITTSBURGH • PENNSYLVANIA • 15227

Billings
Boise
Charlotte
Columbus
Denver
Dubuque
Elgin
Flint
Ft. Wayne
Ft. Worth
Huntington
Lexington
Madison
Memphis
Nashville
Norfolk
Portland
St. Louis
St. Paul
Santa Fe
Savannah
Seattle
Texarkana
Tucson
Tulsa
Wichita

September 22, 19--

Mr. James H. Graham
533 Second Avenue
Pittsburgh, Pennsylvania 15219

Dear Mr. Graham:

It is a comfortible feeling to know that the heating system in your home does not have to depend on the elements. Snow and ice cannot leave you shiverring when you heat with gas. It travels under ground.

The dependability of gas is only one of its many virtues. A gas heat system costs less to instal and less to operate. It needs lots less serviceing, and it lasts longer. It has no odor and makes no filmy deposits that cause extra work.

No wonder more than 400,000 users of other feuls changed to gas last year.

Why not let us show you how easy it is to instal gas heat in your home.

Yours truely,

Charles J. Parker
Sales Manager

CJP:re

Can you find all the errors in this letter?

re·view·ing

han·dling

im·me·di·ate·ly

ad·vice

[134]

174

en·clos·ing

ap·prov·al

[93]

175

Fu·el

per·son·nel

de·ci·sion

chal·leng·ing

[108]

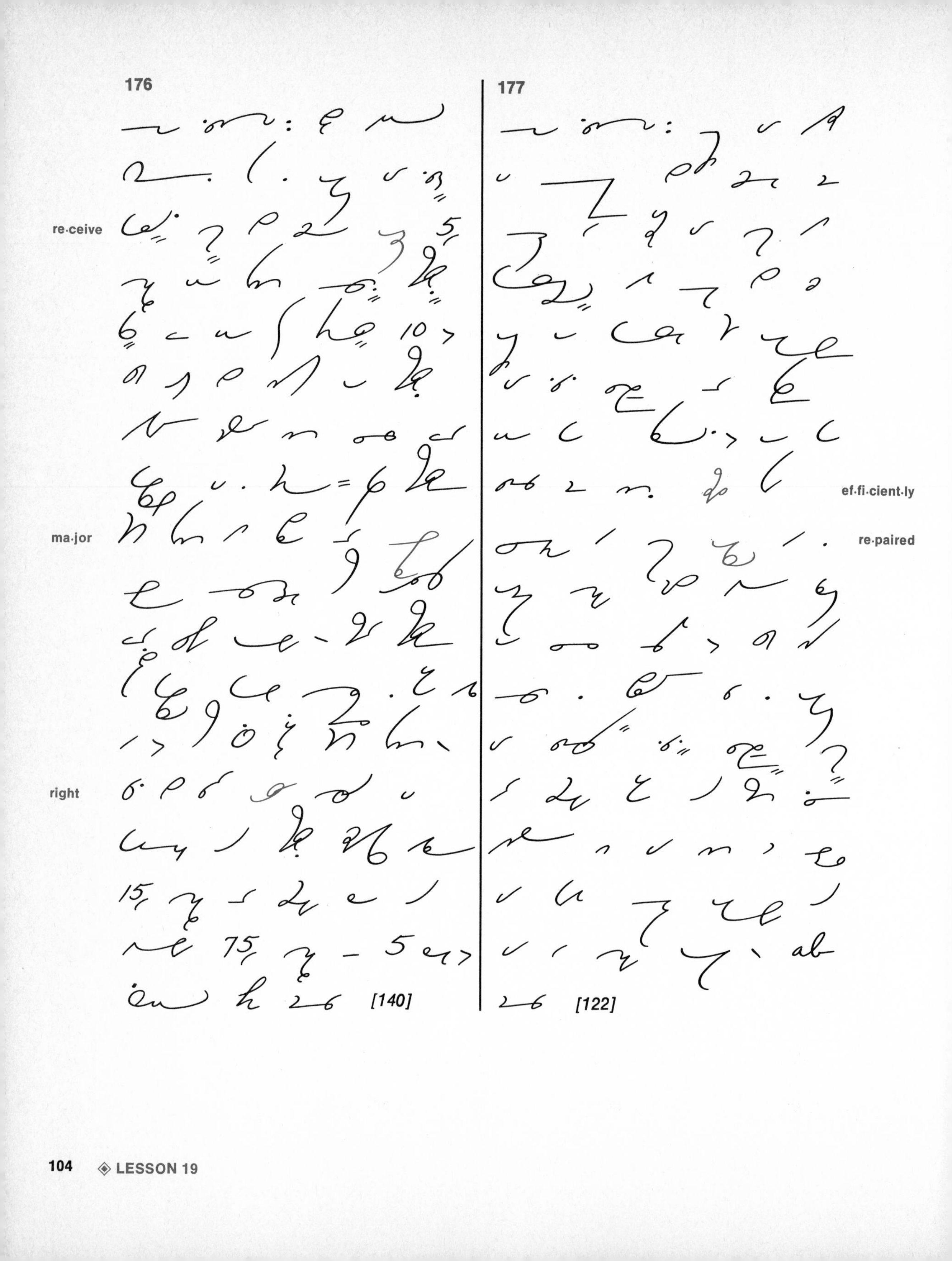

176

re·ceive

ma·jor

right

[140]

177

ef·fi·cient·ly

re·paired

[122]

Principles

178 **Ow** The sound of *ow,* as in *now,* is written [shorthand outline].

Spell: n-ow, now

now	sound	account
allow	found	loud
doubt	pound	house
proud	amount	ounce

179 **Word Ending -ther** The word ending *-ther* is represented by *ith.*

Spell: n-e-ith, neither

neither	brother	either
other	mother	rather
another	together	leather
gather	whether	bothered

180 **Word Beginnings Con-, Com-** The word beginnings *con-, com-* are represented by *k.*

Con-

Spell: con-s-e-r-n, concern

concern	considerable	confirm
consist	controlled	confusing

conference contract concrete

Com-

Spell: com-p-o-s, compose

compose combine compare

complete computer combined

comply complaint accomplish

181 Con-, Com- Followed by a Vowel When *con-, com-,* are followed by a vowel, these word beginnings are represented by *kn* or *km.*

connect connote committee

connection commerce accommodate

Building Transcription Skills

182 Business Vocabulary Builder

unique The only one of its kind. (It is incorrect, therefore, to say *more unique* or *most unique.*)

component A part.

commenced Started.

Reading and Writing Practice

183 Brief-Form Review Letter

unique

fu·el

com·pet·i·tive

lose

[118]

184

re·cent·ly

ac·com·pa·ny·ing

1902

grand·fa·ther's

50

al·ways

wheth·er

50

[172]

proud

185

com·mit·tee

no·ti·fied

[73]

186

leath·er

rep·u·ta·ble

[118]

187

con·fer·ence

week·end

[65]

LESSON 21

Principles

188 Brief Forms

several, big, correspond, correspondence, such, advantage, how, out, suggest, use, ever, every

189 Den By rounding off the angle between *d-n,* we obtain the fluent blend that represents *den.*

Den

Spell: s-oo-den, sudden; den-r, dinner

sudden, confident, dentist, wooden, evident, danger, deny, president, dinner

190 Ten The stroke that represents *den* also represents *t-n.*

Spell: ten-d-r, tender

tender, potential, stand, attend, competent, remittances, attention, consistent, assistance, sentence, bulletin, tonight

191 -tain The stroke that represents *d-n, t-n* also represents *-tain.*

Spell: o-b-tain, obtain

obtain	attain	certainly
maintain	detain	container
contain	certain	obtainable

Building Transcription Skills

192 Business Vocabulary Builder

mail-order house An organization that sells its products through the mails.

correspondents Those who write letters.

jeopardize Place in danger.

Reading and Writing Practice

193 Brief-Form Letter

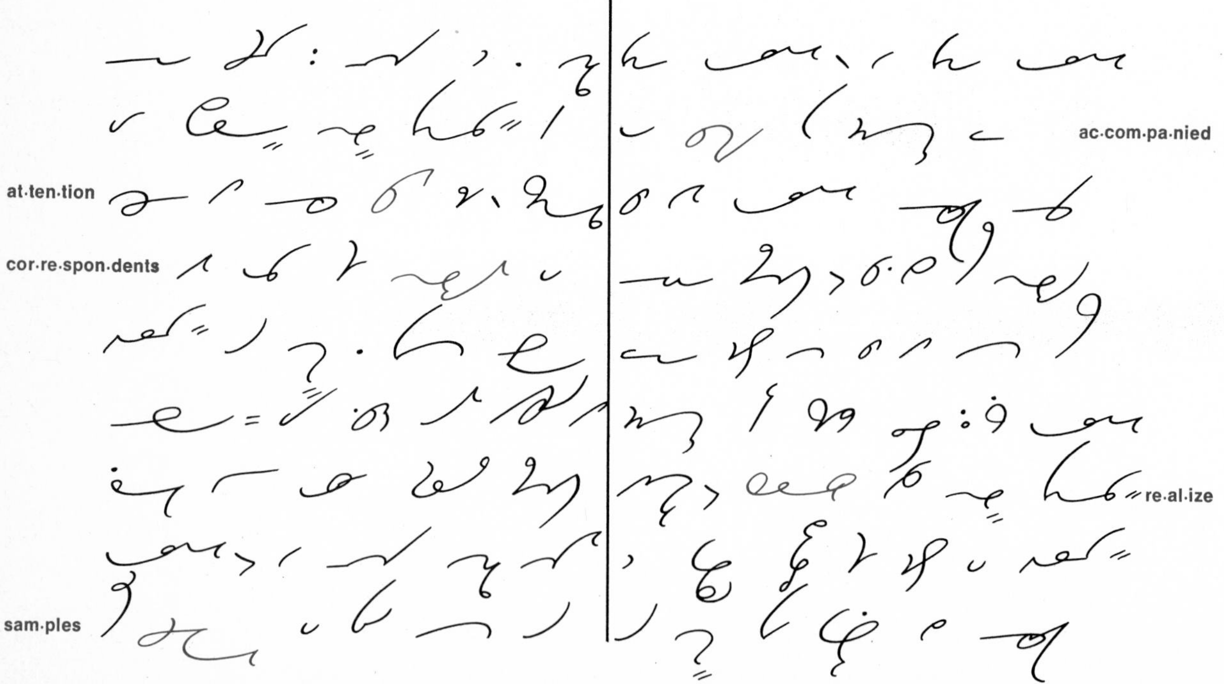

[153]

[128]

194

195

plea·sure

al·ways

hon·or

con·fi·dence

con·struct

re·ceiv·ing

[108]

196

re·mit·tance

agen·cy

jeop·ar·dize

[103]

197

bar·gain

con·nects

phy·si·cian

be·lieve

[144]

LESSON 22

Principles

198 Dem By rounding off the angle between *d-m,* we obtain the fluent *dem* blend.

Dem

Compare: den dem

Spell: dem-a-end, demand; m-e-dem, medium

demand random domestic

demonstration seldom damage

condemn freedom medium

199 Tem The stroke that represents *d-m* also represents *t-m.*

Spell: tem-p-r, temper

temper item estimate

temporary attempt contemplate

system tomorrow customers

200 Business Abbreviations Here are additional salutations and closings used in business letters.

Dear Mr. My dear Mr. Cordially yours

Dear Mrs. Yours sincerely Very cordially yours

Dear Miss

201 Useful Phrases The following useful phrases are formed with the *ten-tem* blends:

to know — to me — to make

202 Days of the Week

Sunday — Wednesday — Friday

Monday — Thursday — Saturday

Tuesday

203 Months of the Year You are already familiar with the shorthand outlines for several of the months, as they are written in full.

January — May — September

February — June — October

March — July — November

April — August — December

Building Transcription Skills

204 Business Vocabulary Builder

sturdy Strong.

opaque Not transparent; cannot be seen through.

contemplate Consider thoughtfully.

Reading and Writing Practice

205 Brief-Form Review Letter

cus·tom·ers

stur·dy
opaque

[148]

150

ar·range·ments

[133]

206

po·ten·tial

207

bus·i·est

60,

ef·fi·cient·ly

com·put·er

[140]

208

ur·gent

cus·tom·er's

30

55/

agree·ment

sim·i·lar

5/

[149]

209

re·ceived

18

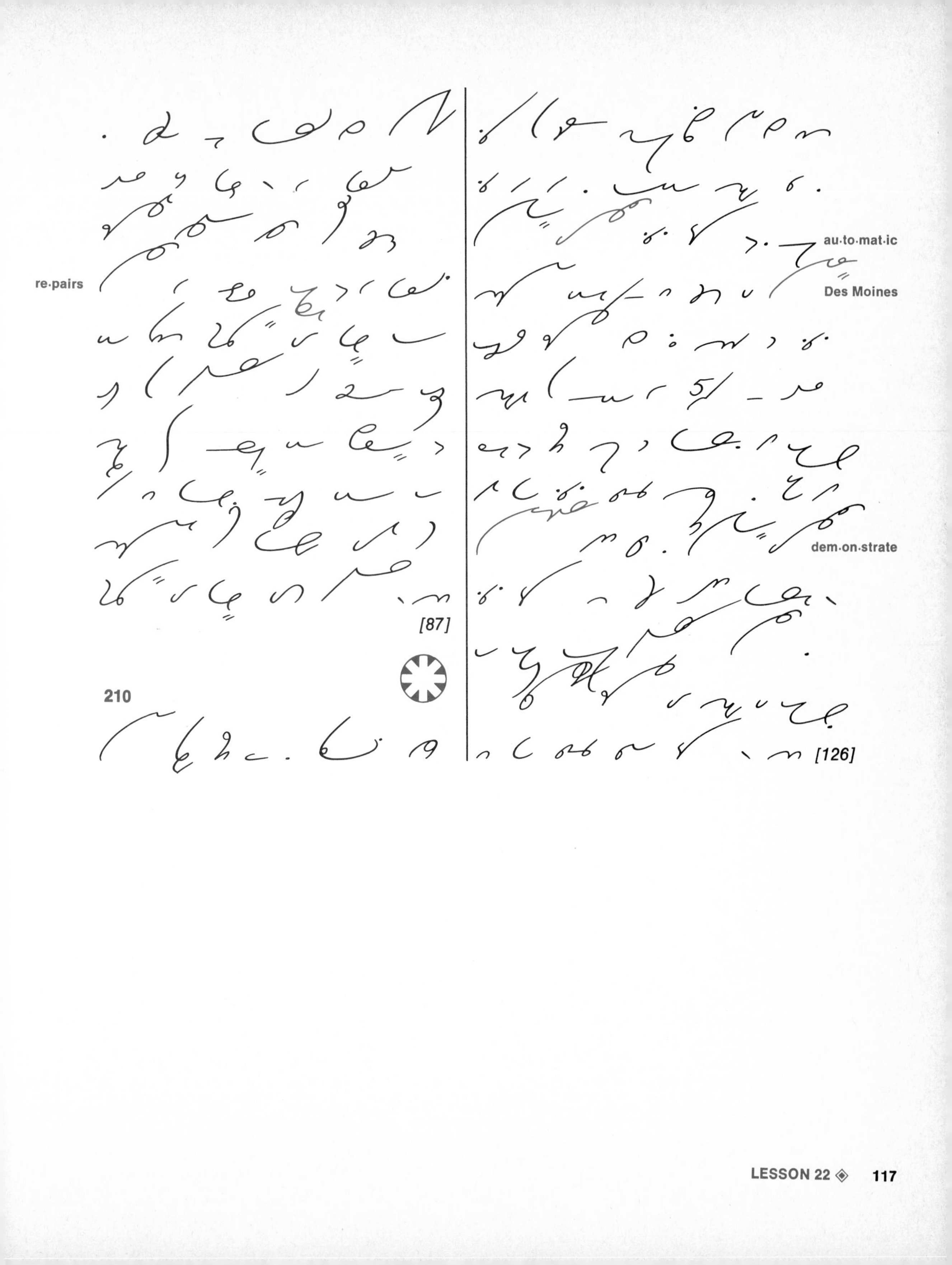

re·pairs

[87]

210

au·to·mat·ic

Des Moines

dem·on·strate

[126]

Principles

211 Brief Forms After this group, you have only five more groups to learn.

general | gone | question
acknowledge | during | yet
time | *over | worth

*The outline for *over* is written above the following character. It is also used as a prefix form, as in:

overcame | oversee | overdo

212 Def, Dif By rounding off the angle between *d-f,* we obtain the fluent *def, dif* blend.

Def, Dif

Spell: def-ī, defy

defy | defeat | different
defied | define | differences
defect | defined | diffident

213 Div, Dev The stroke that represents *def, dif* also represents *div* and *dev.*

Spell: div-ī-d, divide

divide | dividend | devised
division | devote | developed

214 U Represented by OO The *oo* hook is often used to represent the sound of *u,* as in *new.*

Spell: n-oo, new

new	issue	induce
due	duty	suit
avenue	continue	volume

Building Transcription Skills

215 SIMILAR-WORDS DRILL ■ to, too, two

to (*preposition*) In the direction of. (*To* is also the sign of the infinitive.)

I gave the book *to* him.
He plans *to* go *to* the theater.

too Also; more than enough.

He, *too,* is a member of the team.
She receives *too* many personal telephone calls in the office.

two One plus one.

It took me *two* weeks to finish the job.

◈ Note: The word to watch in this group is *too;* it is so easy to type *to* instead of *too!*

216 Business Vocabulary Builder

complicated (*adjective*) Difficult.

tentative Not definite; temporary.

confidentially Secretly.

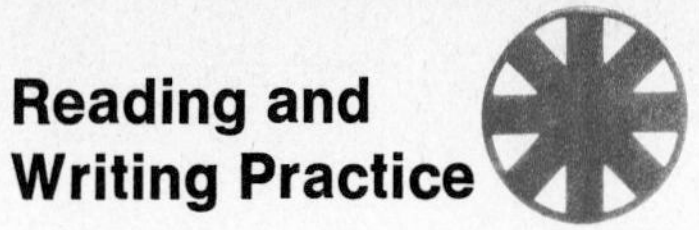

Reading and Writing Practice

217 Brief-Form Letter

ac·knowl·edg·ment

daily

at·tempt

[116]

of·fered

sur·gery

an·swer

[128]

218

de·vel·op·ment

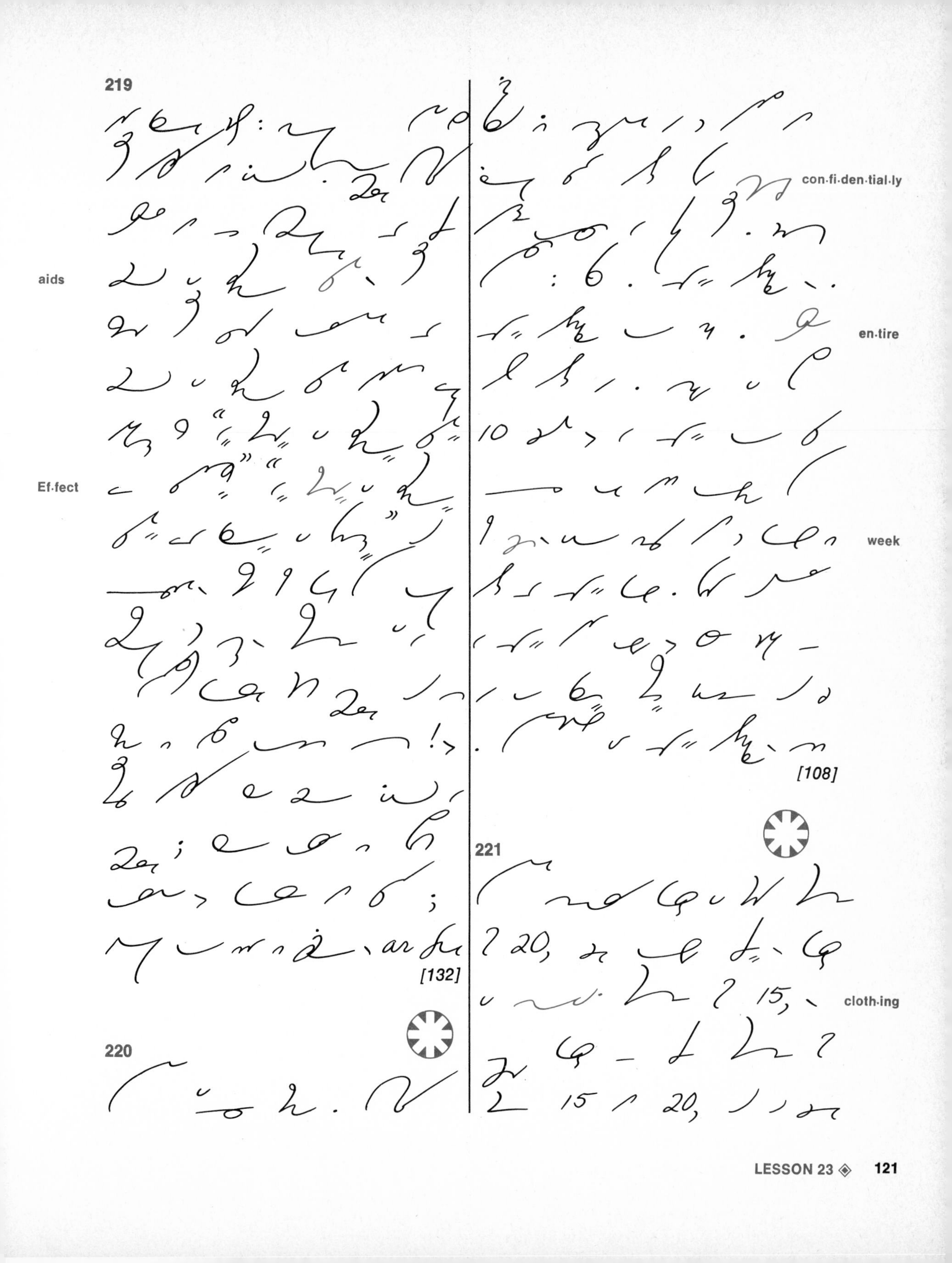

219

aids

Ef·fect

[132]

220

con·fi·den·tial·ly

en·tire

10

week

[108]

221

20,

15,

cloth·ing

15

20,

rise

re·duc·ing

rais·ing

[117]

222

ac·knowl·edg·ing

afraid

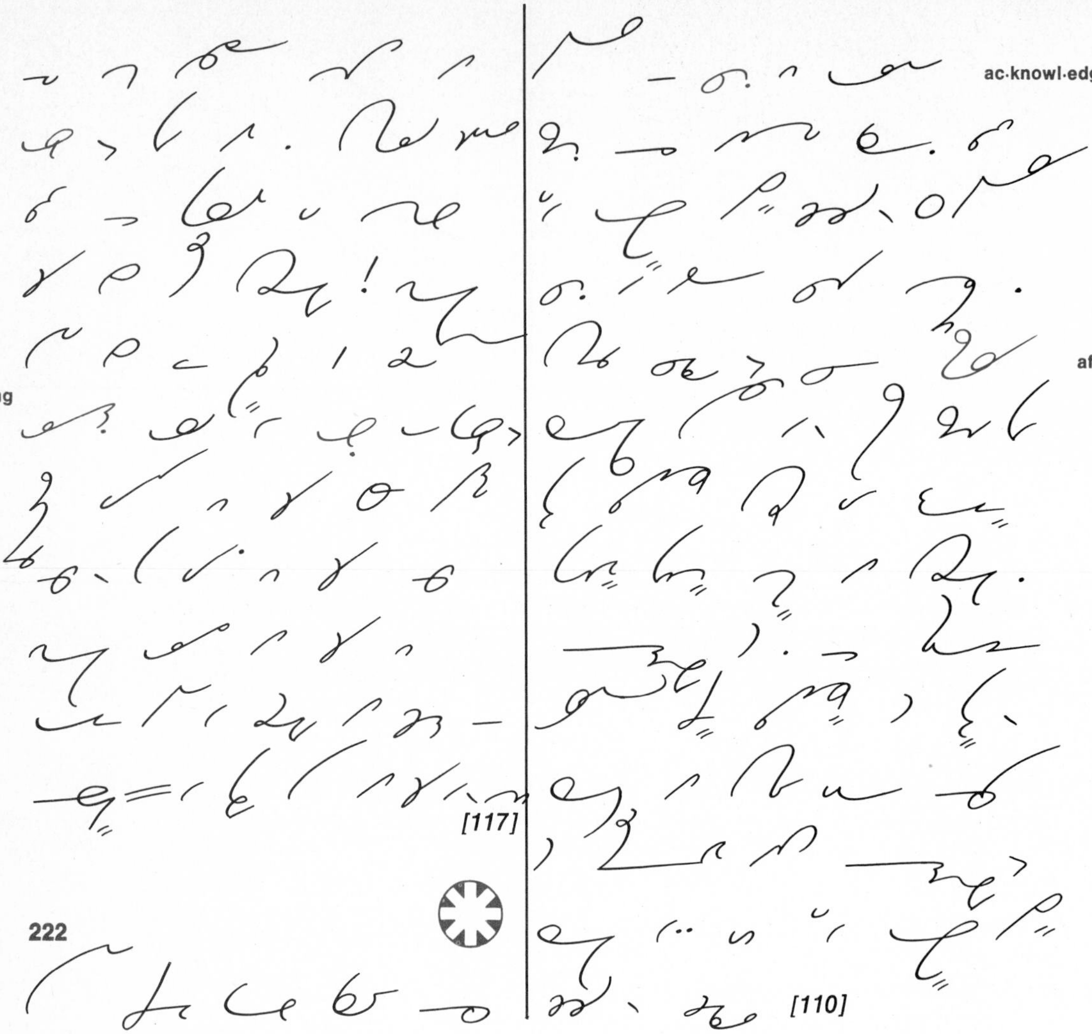

[110]

PROPORTION CHECK LIST

The writer who can read his shorthand notes fluently is the one who is careful of his proportions. In your shorthand writing, do you:

■ **1** Make the large *a* circle huge; the small *e* circle tiny?

■ **2** Make the straight strokes very straight and the curves very deep?

■ **3** Make the *o* and *oo* hooks deep and narrow?

■ **4** Make short strokes, such as *t* and *n*, very short and long strokes, such as *ted* and *men*, very long?

LESSON 24

RECALL

In Lesson 24 you will have no new shorthand devices to learn; you will have a little time to "digest" the devices that you have studied in previous lessons. In Lesson 24 you will find a new feature—Accuracy Practice—that will help you improve your shorthand writing style.

Accuracy Practice

The speed and accuracy with which you will be able to transcribe your shorthand notes will depend on how well you write them. If you follow the suggestions given in this lesson when you work with each Accuracy Practice, you will soon find that you can read your own notes with greater ease and facility.

So that you may have a clear picture of the proper shapes of the shorthand strokes that you are studying, enlarged models of the alphabetic characters and of the typical joinings are given, together with a short explanation of the things that you should keep in mind as you practice.

To get the most out of each Accuracy Practice, follow this simple procedure:

a *Read the explanations carefully.*

b *Study the model to see the application of each explanation.*

c *Write the first outline in the Practice Drill.*

d *Compare what you have written with the enlarged model.*

e *Write three or four more copies of the outline, trying to improve your outline with each writing.*

f *Repeat this procedure with the remaining outlines in the Practice Drill.*

223 **R** **L** **K** **G**

To write these strokes accurately:

a *Start and finish each one on the same level of writing.*

b *Make the* **beginning** *of the curve in* **r** *and* **l** *deep. Make the* **end** *of the curve in* **k** *and* **g** *deep.*

c *Make the* **l** *and* **g** *considerably longer than* **r** *and* **k**.

practice drill

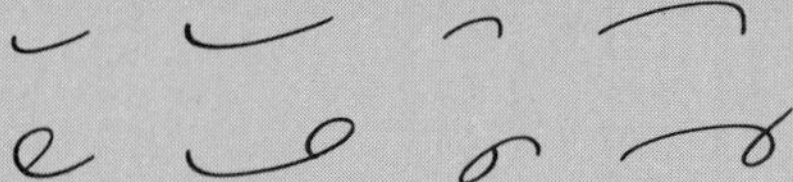

Are-our-hour, will-well, can, good.
Air, lay, ache, gate.

224 Kr **Rk** **Gl**

To write these combinations accurately:

a *Make the curves rather flat.*

b *Make the combinations* **kr** *and* **rk** *somewhat shorter than the combined length of* **r** *and* **k** *when written separately.*

c *Make the combination* **gl** *somewhat shorter than the combined length of* **g** *and* **l** *when written separately.*

practice drill

Cream, crate, maker, mark, dark.
Gleam, glean, glare, eagle.

225 Recall Chart This chart contains all the brief forms in Chapter 4 and one or more illustrations of all the shorthand devices you have studied in Chapters 1 through 4.

The chart contains 90 words. Can you read the entire chart in 7 minutes or less?

WORDS

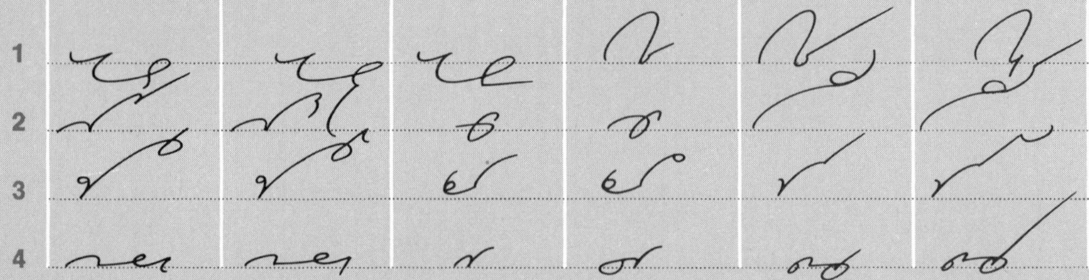

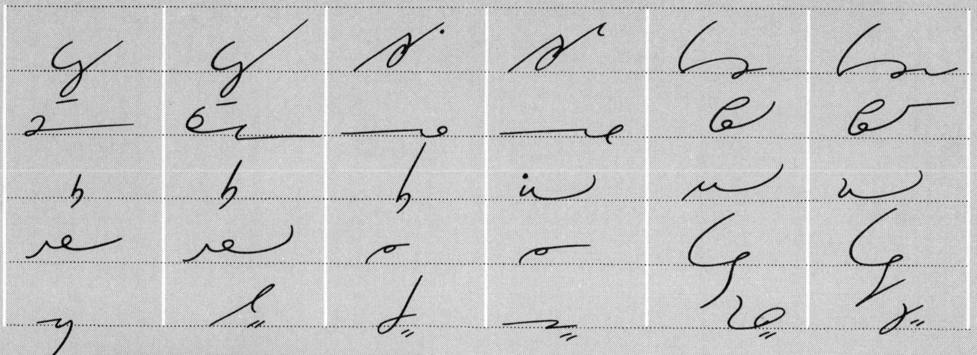

5

6

7

8

9

BRIEF FORMS AND PHRASES

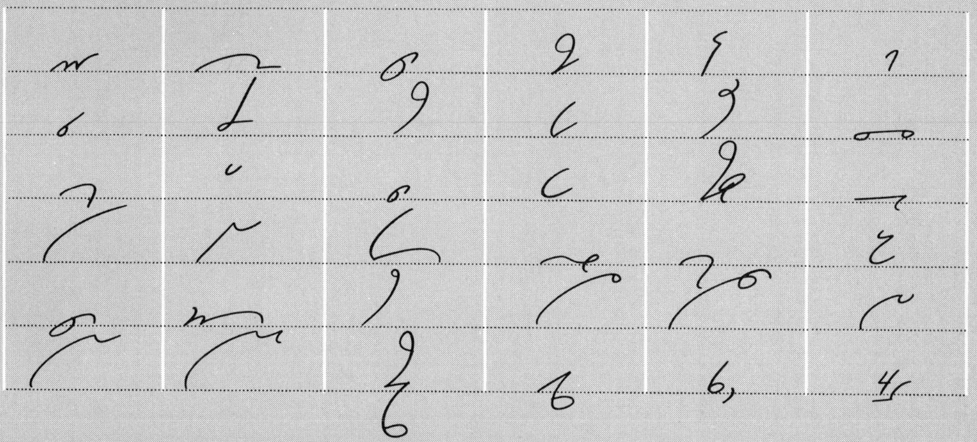

10

11

12

13

14

15

Building Transcription Skills

226 Business Vocabulary Builder

legitimate Reasonable.

common knowledge Something known to everybody.

resolve Make a firm decision about.

Reading and Writing Practice

227 Greeting People

greet

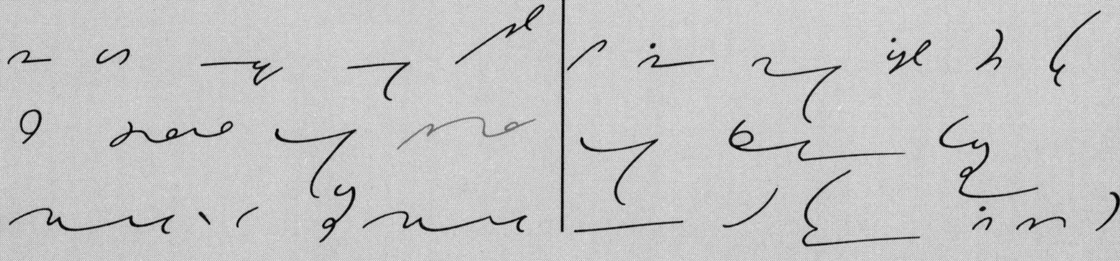

com·pa·nies

Visitors are

le·git·i·mate

at·tend

de·vise

oc·ca·sion·al·ly

cal·en·dar

You will find

ad·vis·able

pleas·ant

tre·men·dous

[273]

228 Strictly Confidential

con·fi·dence

knowl·edge

ur·gent

wor·thy

[213]

In your

unique

be·ware

229 Health

mus·cles

①

②

③

④

[53]

Chapter 5 The Road to Promotion

The term *stenographer* is rarely heard in the business office today. Today, the title *secretary* is preferred to identify those who perform stenographic duties for an executive. The term *secretary* seems to have more prestige.

Even though the term *secretary* now identifies all those who act as "girl Fridays," the level of job is usually distinguished by grade —Secretary 1, Secretary 2, Secretary 5, and so on—the higher the number, the higher the grade. Of course, the grade is determined by the importance of the executive for whom the secretary works.

In attempting to distinguish between levels of secretarial jobs, it is difficult to dispense with the term *secretary* because everyone has a pretty clear idea of what is done by the person who holds the title. Thus, the term *secretary* may identify the top executive assistant in a large corporation, or it may identify the newest beginner.

Nowadays the term *stenographer* is used mainly in government job classifications. It is also used by some firms to designate a person who works for several executives, for another secretary, or in a pool (a group of stenographers who are on call to take dictation from any executive). The next step up from the job of stenographer is to *private*

secretary, that is, one who works for only one executive. The secretary who earns the right to work for a high-ranking executive in a business organization is often given the title *executive secretary.* In this case, the word *executive* does not refer to the person for whom the secretary works but implies that the secretary is an executive in her own right, with the privilege of making important decisions and often supervising other secretaries and office employees. A more current term for this high-level position is *administrative assistant*—and it is a job worth working for. Administrative assistants are actually executives, and they command salaries and prestige equal to those of some supervisors and department managers.

Where to from the position of administrative assistant? This depends on your special talents and aspirations. You may become a supervisor of office personnel, an assistant department manager, a department manager, a personnel specialist, and so on. It is not as unusual as you might think for a secretary to advance into the top ranks of management.

But keep this in mind: Most secretaries progress as their bosses progress. If the boss moves up the ladder of management, his secretary moves with him. Her future, then, is very much tied in with her boss's future. The good secretary can shorten the boss's route to advancement by taking from his shoulders every assignment she can successfully handle and by keeping him efficiently organized. When the secretary helps her boss, she helps herself.

LESSON 25

Principles

230 Brief Forms

request	success	progress
state	difficult	satisfy, satisfactory
next	envelope	under

The outline for *under* is written above the following shorthand character. It is also used as a prefix, as in:

undergo	understudy	underground
underneath	underpaid	understand
underwrite	undermine	understood

231 Cities and States In your work as a stenographer or secretary, you will frequently have occasion to write geographical expressions. Here are a few important cities and states.

Cities

New York	Boston	Los Angeles
Chicago	Philadelphia	St. Louis

States

Michigan	Massachusetts	Missouri
Illinois	Pennsylvania	California

232 Useful Business Phrases The following phrases are used in business letters so frequently that special forms have been provided for them. Study these phrases as you would study brief forms.

I hope	as soon as	let us
we hope	as soon as possible	to us
your order	of course	to do

Building Transcription Skills

233 Business Vocabulary Builder

marked *(adjective)* Clearly defined.

successor One who comes after.

valises Small pieces of hand luggage.

Reading and Writing Practice

234 Brief-Form Letter

ef·fect

of·fi·cers

sim·ply

lose

suc·ces·sor

[147]

235

Chi·ca·go

shipped

re·ceive

oc·ca·sion

[120]

236

cus·tom·ers

due

en·ve·lope

[120]

237

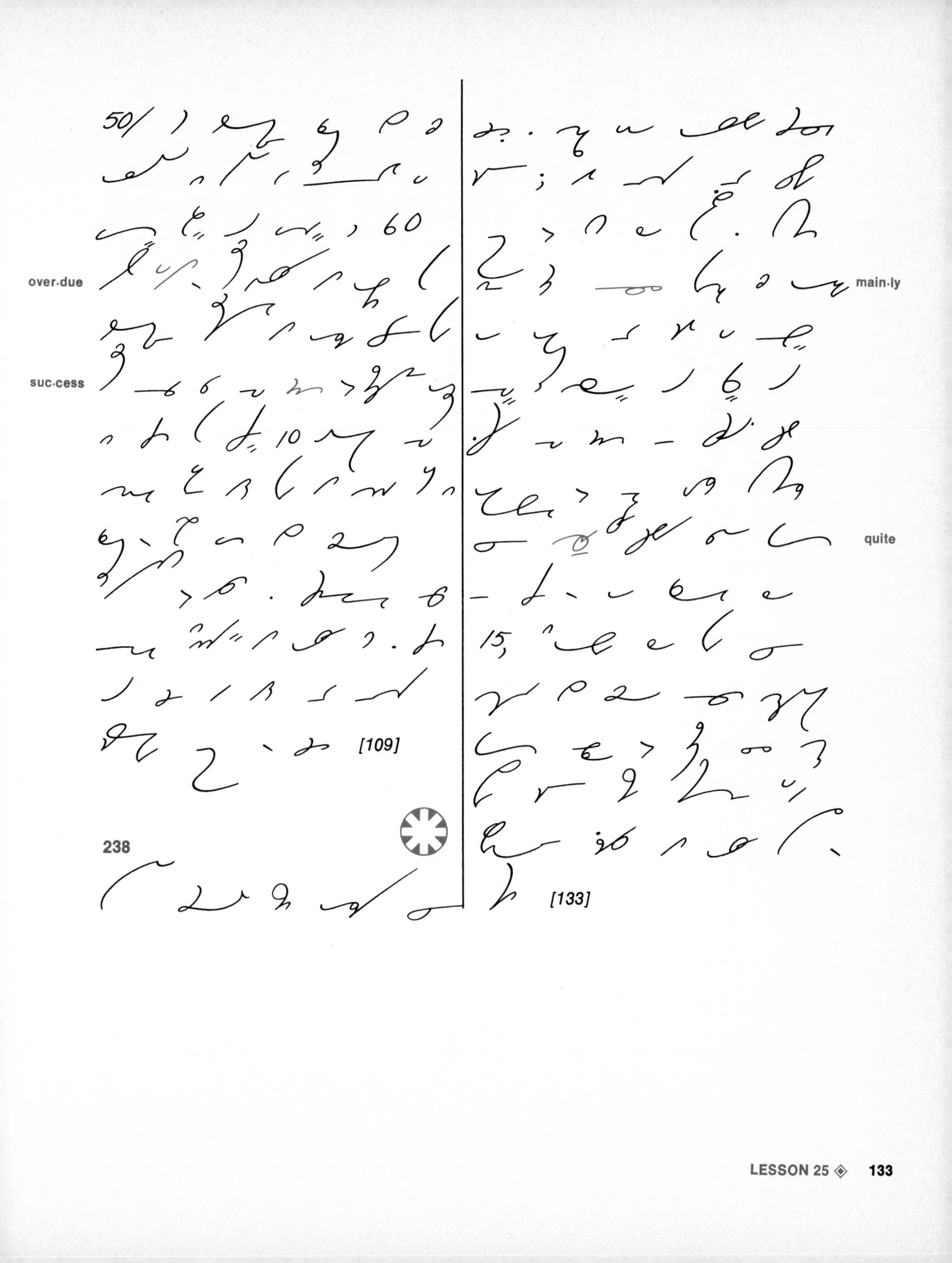

over·due

suc·cess

main·ly

quite

[109]

238

[133]

LESSON 26

Principles

239 Long I and a Following Vowel Any vowel following long *i* is represented by a small circle within a large circle.

Compare: signs science

Spell: t-r-īah-l, trial

trial prior reliance

dial client compliance

drier quiet appliance

240 Ia, Ea The sounds of *ia,* as in *piano,* and *ea,* as in *create,* are represented by a large circle with a dot placed within it.

Spell: a-r-eah, area

area appropriate radiate

piano initiate create

appreciate brilliant created

241 Word Beginnings In-, Un-, En- The word beginnings *in-, un-, en-* are represented by *n* before a consonant.

In-

Spell: in-k-r-e-s, increase

increase instead insist

insure invest instance

Un-

Spell: un-t-e-l, until

until unfair unfilled

unless unpaid uncertain

En-

Spell: en-j-oi, enjoy

enjoy enlarge endanger

encourage enrolled engage

242 In-, Un-, En- Followed by a Vowel When *in-, un-, en-* are followed by a vowel, they are written in full.

innovation unable enact

Building Transcription Skills

243 Business Vocabulary Builder

endeavored Tried.

invoices Bills.

apprehensive Fearful; uneasy.

Reading and Writing Practice

244 Brief-Form Review Letter

cli·ents re·quest·ing en·deav·ored

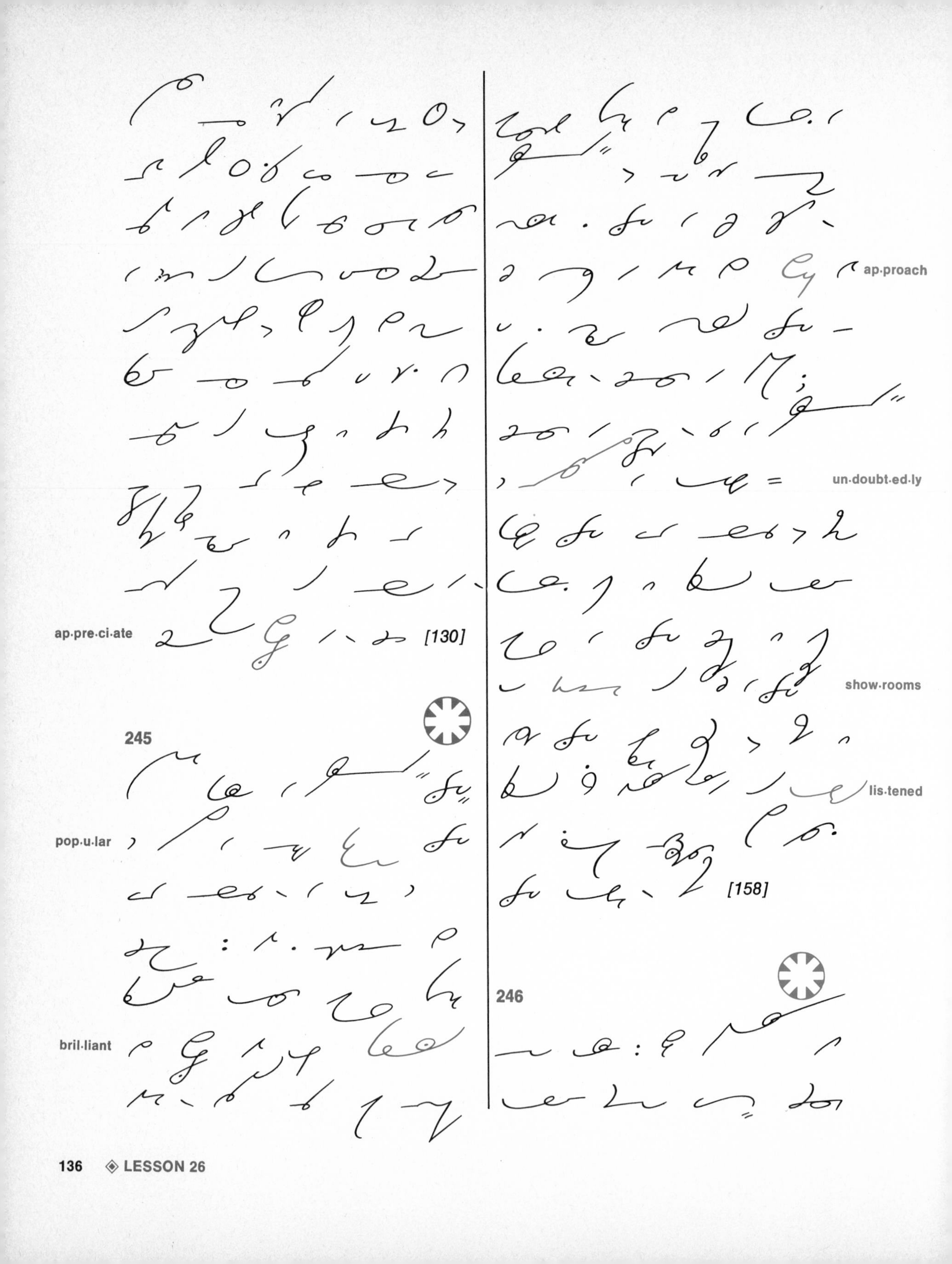

ap·pre·ci·ate

[130]

245

pop·u·lar

bril·liant

ap·proach

un·doubt·ed·ly

show·rooms

lis·tened

[158]

246

en·cour·ag·ing

ar·ea

un·veiled

brought

[134]

247

re·ceipt

con·vic·tion

brib·ery

[85]

248

to·day's

en·gi·neer·ing

ini·tia·tive

40=

sal·a·ries

[86]

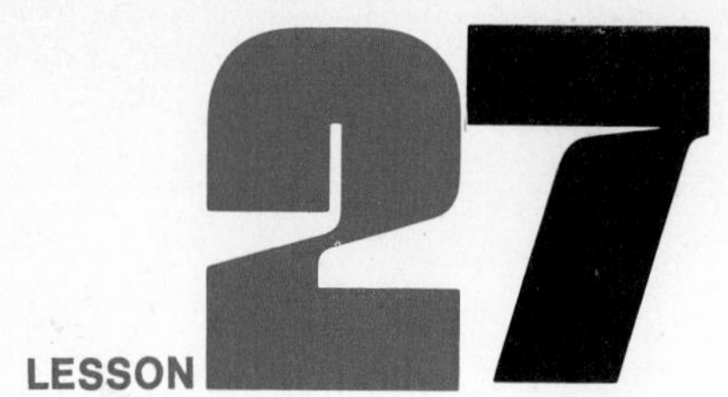

LESSON 27

Principles

249 Brief Forms After you have learned the following nine brief forms, you have only three more groups to go!

speak — upon — particular
idea — street — probable
subject — newspaper — regular

250 Ng The sound of *ng* is written .

Compare: seen sing

Spell: s-e-ing, sing

sing — bring — spring
sang — wrong — length
song — long — strength
ring — strong — single

251 Ngk The sound of *ngk* (usually spelled *nk*) is written .

Compare: seem sink

Spell: r-a-ink, rank

rank — blank — drink
frank — bank — shrink

tank | banquet | uncle
ink | link | anxious

252 Omission of Vowel Preceding -tion When *t, d, n,* or *m* is followed by *-ition* or *-ation,* the circle is omitted.

addition | commission | quotation
permission | reputation | estimation
condition | combination | station
admission | accommodation | stationed

Building Transcription Skills

253 Business Vocabulary Builder

role Part.

fluently Effortlessly; flowing easily.

quotations Bids or prices offered.

Reading and Writing Practice

254 Brief-Form Letter

As·so·ci·a·tion

anx·ious

at·ten·dance

Role

ac·cept

[138]

255

fi·nan·cial

hu·mor

per·mis·sion

[114]

256

pop·u·lar

ear

lis·ten

con·fi·dent

[154]

257

edi·tion

Prin·ci·ples

10

Res·tau·rant

12

16

[85]

258

pried

mu·ti·lat·ed

piece

pos·ses·sions

[121]

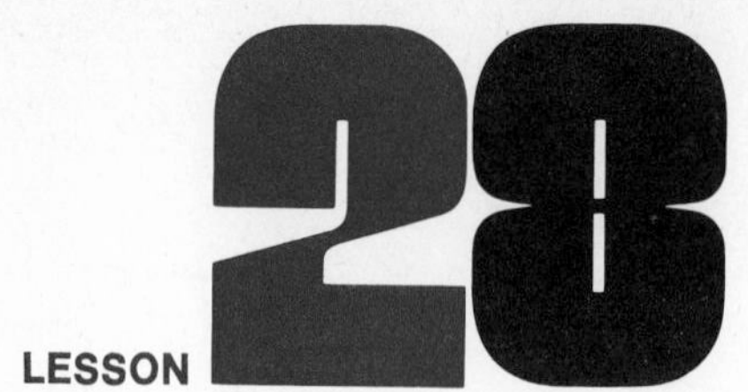

LESSON 28

Principles

259 **Ah, Aw** A dot is used for *a* in words that begin *ah* and *aw*.

Spell: a-h-e-d, ahead; a-oo-a, away

ahead, awaken, awoke, away, await, award, awake, awaited, aware

260 **Y** Before *o* and *oo, y* is represented by the small *e* circle, as *y* is pronounced *e*. *Ye* is represented by a small loop; *ya*, by a large loop.

Spell: e-oo-ith, youth; wī-ē-l-o, yellow; wī-ē-ärd, yard

youth, yellow, yard, yawn, yield, yarn

261 **X** The letter *x* is represented by an *s* written with a slight backward slant.

Compare: miss, mix, fees, fix

Spell: t-a-ex, tax; t-a-exes, taxes

tax, indexes, box, taxes, relax, boxes, index, relaxes, perplex

262 **Omission of Short U** In the body of a word, short *u*, as in *fun*, is omitted before *n*, *m*, or a straight downstroke.

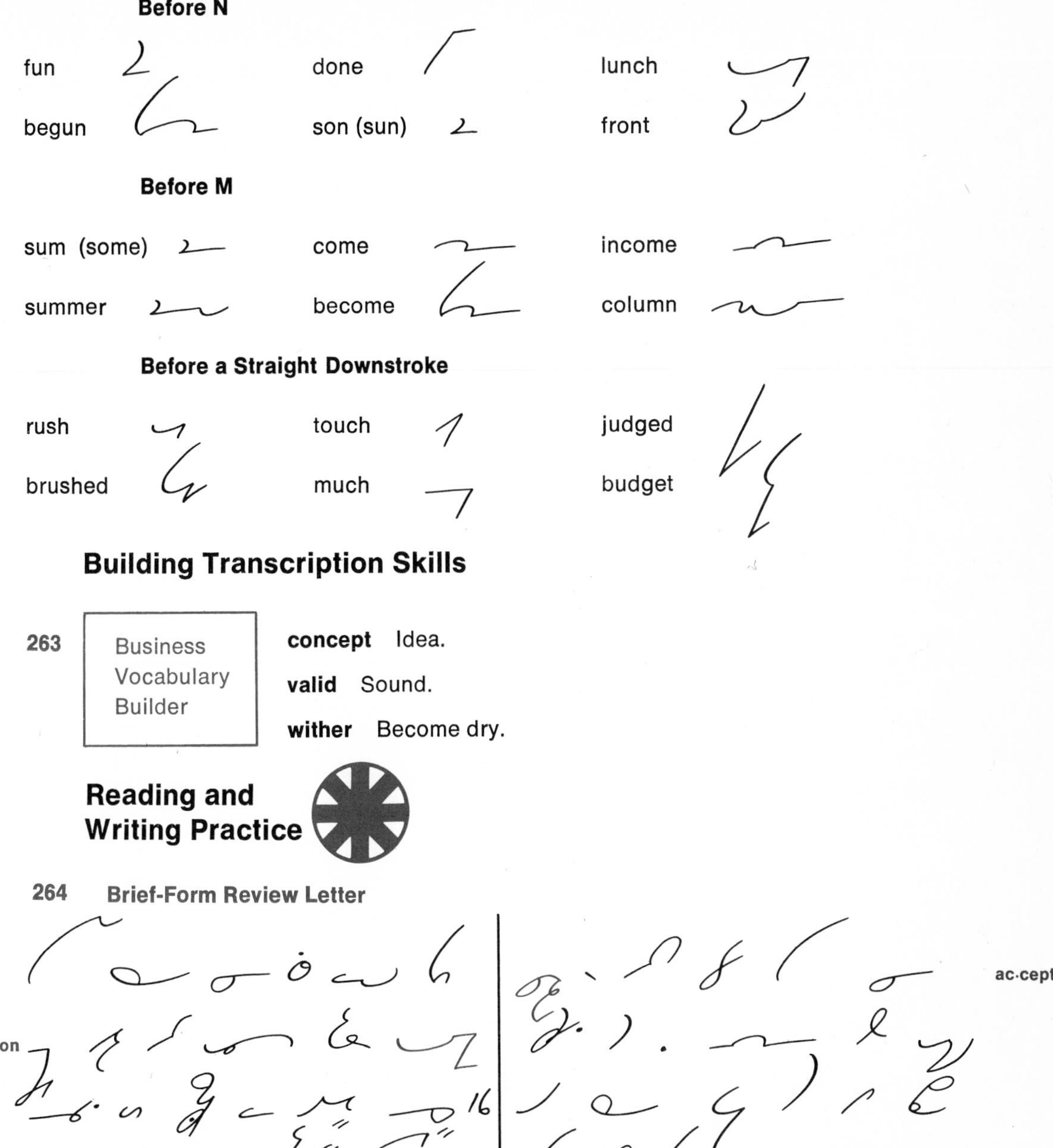

Before N

fun, done, lunch

begun, son (sun), front

Before M

sum (some), come, income

summer, become, column

Before a Straight Downstroke

rush, touch, judged

brushed, much, budget

Building Transcription Skills

263 Business Vocabulary Builder

concept Idea.

valid Sound.

wither Become dry.

Reading and Writing Practice

264 **Brief-Form Review Letter**

lun·cheon

ac·cept

plead

ban·quet

rec·om·mend

[153]

265

com·mut·ers

judg·ment

be·lieve

res·i·dents

wel·come

[147]

266

proud

[84]

[98]

safe·ty

re·li·able

267

sys·tem

268

weath·er

en·gi·neer

rec·om·mend

[119]

269

bud·get

en·ve·lope

ten·ta·tive

year's

judg·ment

ab

[114]

LESSON 29

Principles

270 Brief Forms

organize, ordinary, public
responsible, opinion, publish, publication
circular, regard, purpose

271 Word Beginning Ex-

The word beginning *ex-* is represented by *e-s.*

Spell: ex-t-r-a, extra

extra, explanation, excuse
examine, expression, exist
example, expenses, expect
extend, except, expired

272 Md

By rounding off the angle between m-d, we obtain the fluent *md* blend.

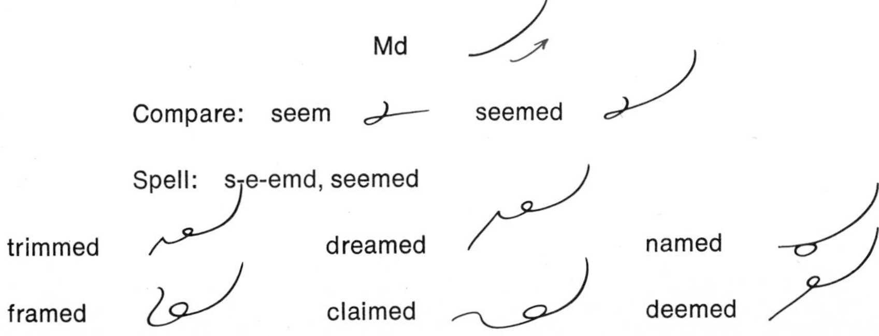

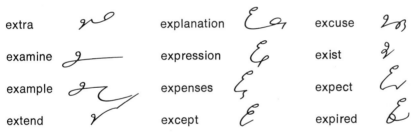

Md

Compare: seem seemed

Spell: s-e-emd, seemed

trimmed, dreamed, named
framed, claimed, deemed

273 **Mt** The stroke that represents *md* also represents *mt.*

Spell: p-r-o-emt, prompt

prompt exempt empty

274 **Word Ending -ful** The word ending *-ful* is represented by *f.*

Spell: k-a-r-ful, careful

careful useful hopeful

doubtful grateful hopefully

delightful powerful helpful

thoughtful beautiful helpfulness

◈ Notice that the *p* and the *f* in *hopeful* and *helpful* join without an angle.

Building Transcription Skills

275 **SIMILAR-WORDS DRILL** ■ **write, right**

write To put words on paper.

I will *write* you about our problems.

right *(noun)* Something to which one has a just claim; *(adjective)* correct; *(adverb)* directly.

You have a *right* to expect good service from us.
I do not have the *right* time.
John is going *right* home after the meeting.

276 Business Vocabulary Builder

confirmed Assured the validity of.

acoustics The quality of sound.

curtail To cut short.

excessive Too much.

Reading and Writing Practice

277 **Brief-Form Letter**

prompt·ly

over·whelmed

write

al·ways

com·plet·ing

right

ad·di·tion

[161]

278

at·ten·dance

edi·tion

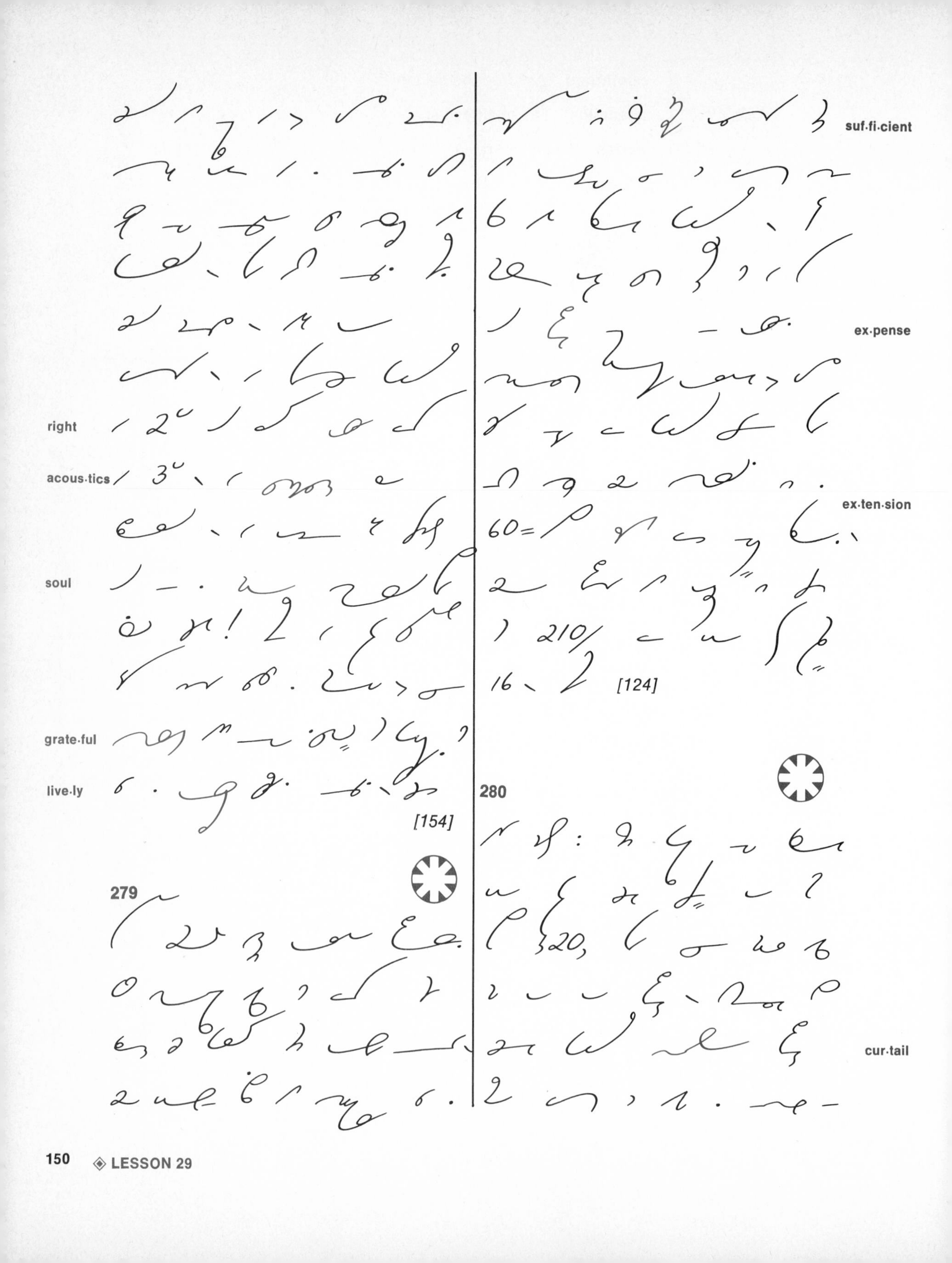

suf·fi·cient

ex·pense

right

acous·tics

ex·ten·sion

soul

[124]

grate·ful

live·ly

280

[154]

279

cur·tail

itin·er·aries

ac·com·mo·da·tions

ex·ces·sive

[158]

281

ex·ten·sion

ru·in·ing

kitch·en

enough

[133]

RECALL

There are no new shorthand strokes or principles in Lesson 30. In this lesson you will find an Accuracy Practice devoted to the curved strokes of *Gregg Shorthand,* a Recall Chart, and a Reading and Writing Practice.

Accuracy Practice

To get the most benefit from the Accuracy Practice, be sure to follow the procedures suggested on page 123.

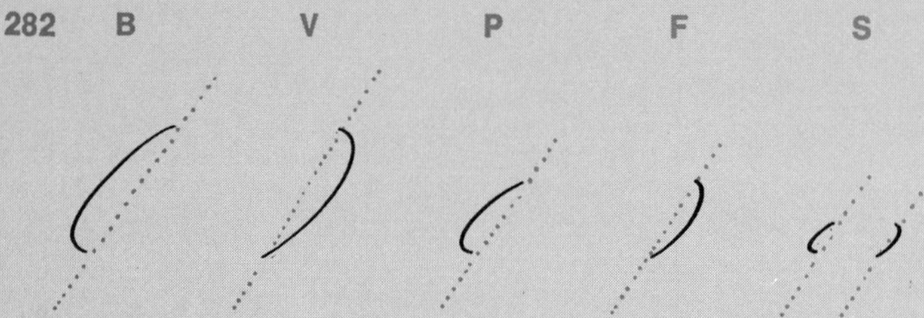

To write these strokes accurately:

a *Give them approximately the slant indicated by the dotted lines.*

b *Make the curve deep at the* **beginning** *of* v, f, *comma* s; *make the curve deep at the* **end** *of* b, p, *left* s.

practice drill

Puts, spare, business, bears, stairs, sphere, leaves, briefs.

283 Pr Pl Br Bl

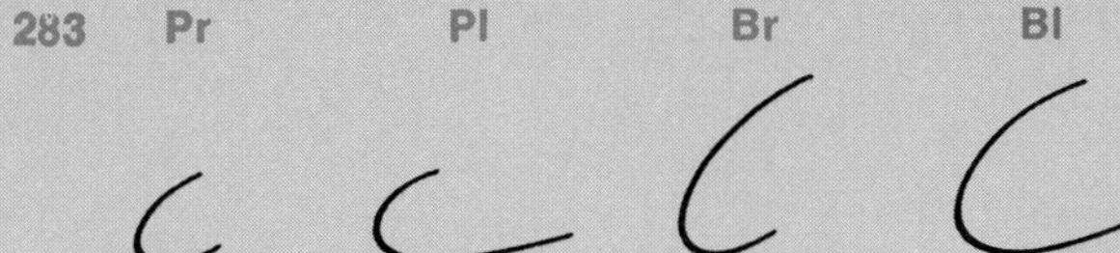

To write these combinations accurately:

a *Write each without a pause between the first and second letter of each combination.*

b *Watch your proportions carefully.*

practice drill

Press, pray, prim, plan, plate, place.
Brim, brief, bread, blame, blast.

284 Fr Fl

To write these combinations accurately:

Write them with one sweep of the pen, with no stop between the f *and* r *or* l.

practice drill

Free, freeze, frame, flee, flame, flap.

285 Recall Chart This chart contains all the brief forms in Chapter 5 and one or more illustrations of the word-building principles you studied in Chapters 1 through 5.

As you read through the words in this chart, be sure to spell each word that you cannot read immediately.

Can you read the 90 words in the chart in 6 minutes or less?

BRIEF FORMS

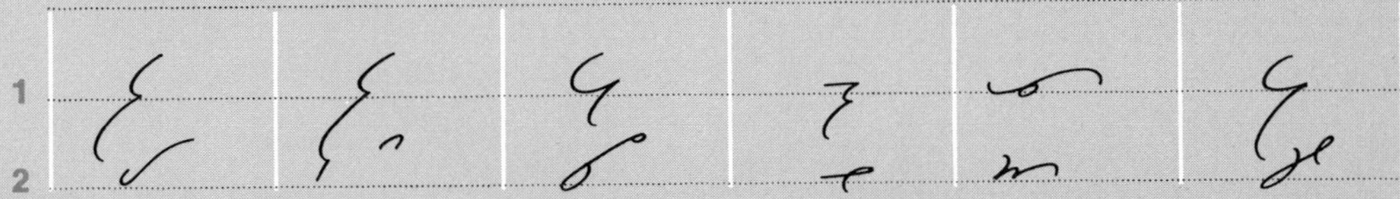

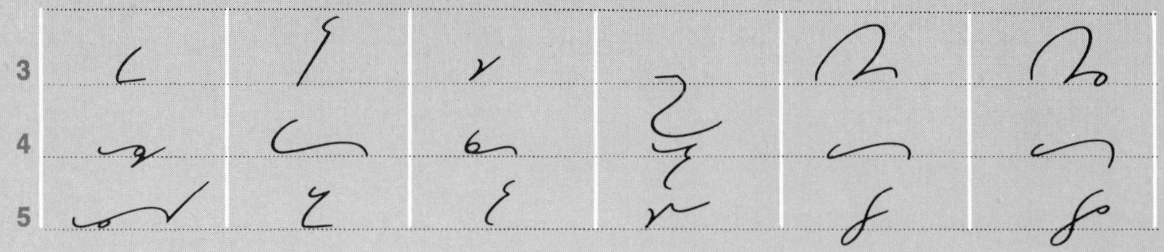

3

4

5

WORDS

6

7

8

9

10

11

12

13

14

15

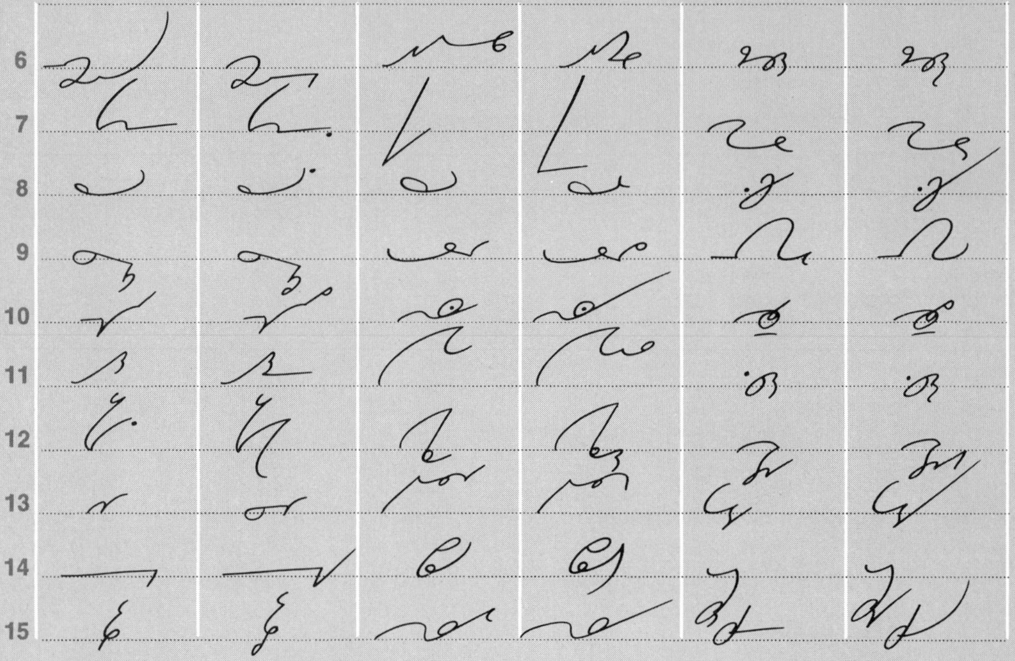

Building Transcription Skills

286 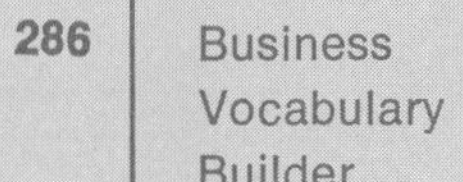

brevity Briefness.

convert Change over.

clarify Make clear.

Reading and Writing Practice

Reading Scoreboard The previous Reading Scoreboard appeared in Lesson 18. If you have been studying each Reading and Writing Practice faithfully, you have no doubt increased your reading speed. Measure that increase on your first reading of the material in Lesson 30. The following table will help you:

Lesson 30 contains 461 words	
If you read Lesson 30 in	your reading rate is
15 minutes	**30 words a minute**
16 minutes	**28 words a minute**
18 minutes	**26 words a minute**
19 minutes	**24 words a minute**
21 minutes	**22 words a minute**
23 minutes	**20 words a minute**
26 minutes	**18 words a minute**

If you can read Lesson 30 in 15 minutes or less, you are doing well. If you take considerably longer than 26 minutes, perhaps you should review your homework procedures. For example, are you:

1 *Practicing in a quiet place at home?*

2 *Practicing without the radio or television set on?*

3 *Spelling aloud any words that you cannot read immediately?*

287 Effective Writing

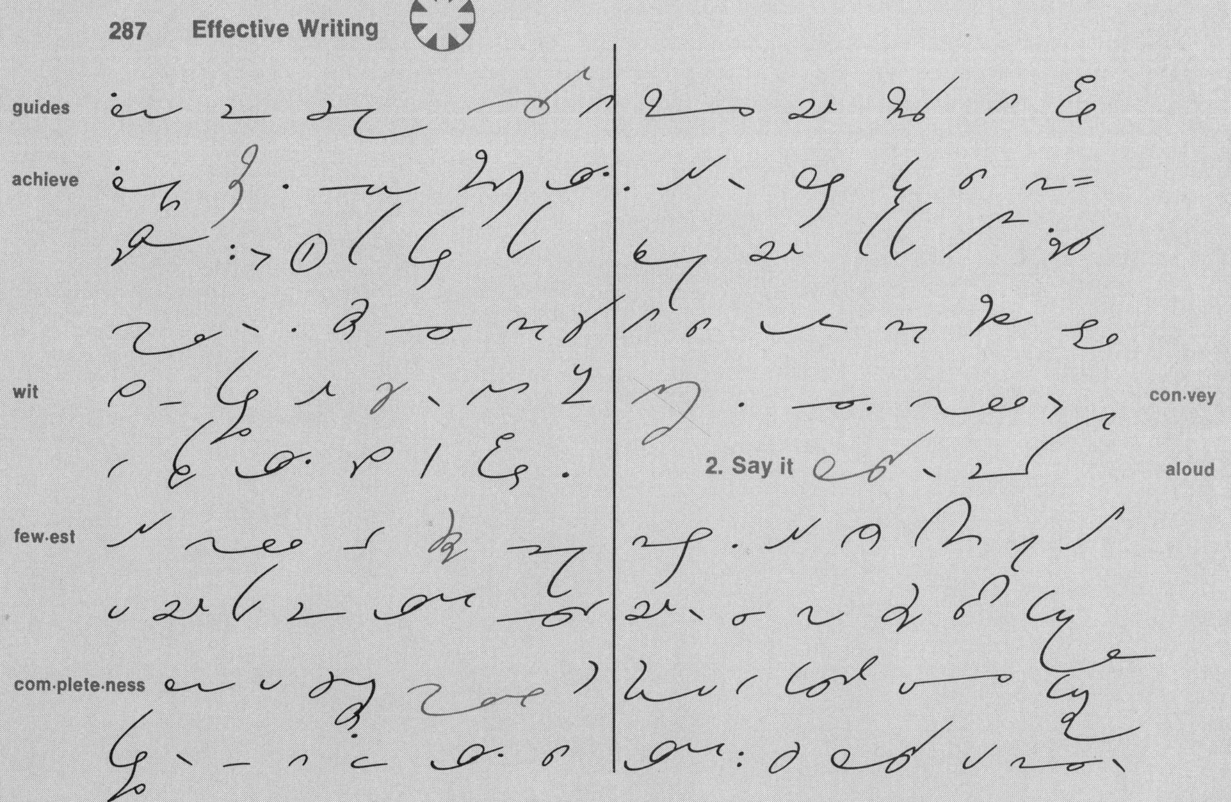

draft

aware

ac·cept

The thing

rough

over·all

omit·ted

5. Search for

oc·ca·sion·al·ly

con·clu·sion

de·ci·sive

ma·jor

[461]

UP-AND-DOWN CHECK LIST

Do you always write the following strokes upward?

■ **1**	and	their-there	
■ **2**	it-at	would	

Do you always write the following strokes downward?

■ **1**	is-his	for	have
■ **2**	shall	which	

Chapter 6 The Specialized Secretary

This is an age of specialization, a trite expression. Still, it's true. You know that many professional people specialize. A doctor may be a heart specialist, a lung specialist, a radiologist, or a neurologist. Lawyers specialize in criminal law, corporation law, tax law, or international law. Accountants specialize, too—in tax matters, internal auditing, or public accounting. Engineers have always specialized — electrical, mechanical, civil, chemical, and aeronautical, to mention a few areas.

This age of specialization has also affected secretarial work. Today some secretaries specialize in medicine, law, education, or various other scientific and technical fields. Specialization has become so widespread that there are several national organizations of specialized secretaries.

Why specialize? There are wonderful opportunities for the secretary who goes beyond the general secretarial curriculum to take special courses in vocabulary, procedures, and dictation in a special field. A popular college curriculum is the medical secretarial area. Many private secretarial schools and colleges offer a complete curriculum in medical secretarial training. Courses include laboratory techniques, prin-

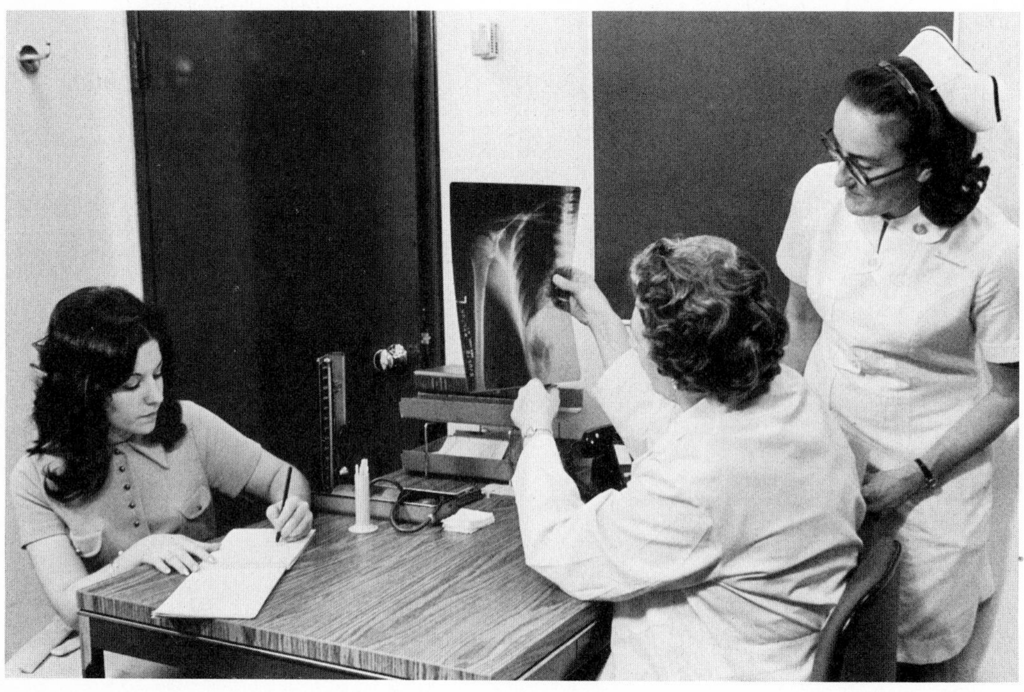

ciples of anatomy and physiology, medical vocabulary, and medical dictation and transcription. A growing number of colleges are offering similar programs for legal secretaries.

Perhaps the fastest growing field of secretarial specialization is the scientific and technical field. This includes a wide variety of careers with engineering firms, textile manufacturers, chemical manufacturing enterprises, and various business and government operations that deal in aeronautical engineering, rocket engineering, and electronics.

Obviously, specialization for secretaries has the same appeal as specialization for those in other areas. Specialists do a better job because they bring more training to their work. For the same reason they earn more.

Should you specialize after you have completed your general training? The decision is yours, but the advantages are many—and there is growing prestige in the "specialist" designation.

LESSON 

Principles

288 Brief Forms Only one more group to learn after this one!

merchant	between	situation
merchandise	experience	quantity
recognize	never	short

289 Word Ending -ure The word ending *-ure* is represented by *r.*

Spell: f-a-l-r, failure

failure	lecture	nature
figure	procedure	naturally

290 Word Ending -ual The word ending *-ual* is represented by *l.*

Spell: a-n-l, annual

annual	equal	actual
annually	gradual	eventual

Building Transcription Skills

291 PUNCTUATION PRACTICE

Another "must" for the successful stenographer or secretary is the ability to punctuate correctly. Most businessmen rely on their stenographers or secretaries to supply the proper punctuation when they transcribe. Because the inclusion or omission of a punctuation mark may completely alter the meaning of a sentence, it is important that you know when to use each punctuation mark.

To sharpen your punctuation skill, you will hereafter give special attention to punctuation in each Reading and Writing Practice.

In the lessons ahead you will review nine of the most common uses of the comma. Each time one of these uses of the comma occurs in the Reading and Writing Practice, it will be encircled in the shorthand, thus calling it forcefully to your attention.

PRACTICE SUGGESTIONS

If you follow these simple suggestions in your homework practice hereafter, your ability to punctuate should improve noticeably.

1 Read carefully the explanation of each comma usage (for example, the explanation of the parenthetical comma given below) to be sure that you understand it. You will encounter many illustrations of each comma usage in the Reading and Writing Practice exercises, so that eventually you will acquire the knack of applying it correctly.

2 Continue to read and copy each Reading and Writing Practice as you have done before. However, add these two important steps:

a *Each time you see an encircled comma in the Reading and Writing Practice, note the reason for its use, which is indicated directly above the encircled comma.*

b *As you copy the Reading and Writing Practice in your shorthand notebook, insert the commas in your shorthand notes, encircling them as in the textbook.*

PUNCTUATION PRACTICE ■ , parenthetical

A word or a phrase or a clause that is used parenthetically (that is, one not neccessary to the grammatical completeness of the sentence) should be set off by commas.

If the parenthetical expression occurs at the end of the sentence, only one comma is used.

There is, of course, no charge for this service.

Never hesitate to let us know, Mr. Strong, when our organization can help you.

We actually print your picture on the card, Mr. Short.

Each time a parenthetical expression occurs in the Reading and Writing Practice, it will be indicated thus in the shorthand: par (,)

292 Business Vocabulary Builder

miniature A small model of a large object.

departure Leaving.

booked to capacity Filled up; sold out.

Reading and Writing Practice

293 Brief-Form Letter

Mer·chan·dis·ing

an·nu·al·ly

par

par

sit·u·a·tion

con·ven·tions

rec·og·nize

car·tridge

par

com·plete·ly

par

Christ·mas

[184]

294

par

filled

prompt·ly

116-1117 aj [136]

295

man·u·al

par

cope

equal·ly

sched·uled

par

as·sis·tance

[166]

296

Cen·tu·ry

par

par

per·son·al·ly

par

ac·com·mo·date

praise

par

[157]

297

ex·cept

par

fail·ure

par

de·vel·op

aj

[97]

LESSON 

Principles

298 Word Ending -ily The word ending *-ily* is represented by a narrow loop.

Compare: steady steadily

Spell: r-e-d-ily, readily

readily	hastily	heartily
temporarily	necessarily	heavily
easily	speedily	family

299 Word Beginning Al- The word beginning *al-* is represented by the shorthand letter *o*.

Spell: all-t-r, alter

alter	alters	almost
altered	although	also
alteration	altogether	already

300 Word Beginning Mis- The word beginning *mis-* is represented by *m-s*.

Spell: mis-t-a-k, mistake

mistake	mistaken	misery
misplace	miscarry	mystery
misprint	mislaid	misunderstood

301 Word Beginning Dis- The word beginning *dis-* is represented by *d-s.*

Spell: dis-k-oo-s, discuss

discuss   distance   discontinue

discussion   discover   discount

dismiss   discourage   dismay

302 Word Beginning Des- The word beginning *des-* is also represented by *d-s.*

Spell: dis-k-r-ī-b, describe

describe   description   despite

desperate   destiny   destroy

Building Transcription Skills

303 PUNCTUATION PRACTICE ■, apposition

An expression in apposition (that is, a word or a phrase or a clause that identifies or explains other terms) should be set off by commas. When the expression in apposition occurs at the end of a sentence, only one comma is necessary.

Her employer, Mr. John H. Smith, is out of town.

I have an appointment for Friday, April 15, at noon.

His book, Accounting Principles and Practice, *is out of stock.*

I gave the report to Mr. Green, our personnel manager.

Each time an expression in apposition appears in the Reading and Writing Practice, it will be indicated thus in the shorthand: ap (,)

304 Business Vocabulary Builder

indispensable Absolutely necessary.

dispel To clear away.

dismayed Filled with dread; discouraged.

Reading and Writing Practice

305 Brief-Form Review Letter

dis·ap·point·ed

re·ceived

15

tem·po·rar·i·ly

par

non·pay·ment

par

ap

owe

560

[137]

306

in·dis·pens·able

mys·tery

dis·pel

ap

con·cepts

par

func·tions

com·plete·ly

ap

prompt·ly

par

[174]

307

dis·turb·ing

ap

15

ap

dis·mayed

par

as·sis·tant

ap

cam·paign

ar·ea

par

[156]

308

of·fered

ap

par

de·scrip·tive

ap

pol·i·cies

pos·sess

ap

[115]

309

re·ferred

ap

al·ready

par

over·due

60

par

150

ap

par

[98]

310 Thought for the Day

week·end

cap·ti·vat·ing

[77]

Principles

311 Brief Forms This is the last group of brief forms you will learn.

character	world	object
railroad	govern	throughout

312 Word Beginnings For-, Fore- The word beginnings *for-, fore-* are represented by *f.* The *f* is joined with an angle to *r* or *l* to indicate that it represents a word beginning. The *f* is disjoined if the following character is a vowel.

Spell: for-gay-e-t, forget

forget	informed	forerunner
forgive	force	forlorn
form	forth	forever
foreman	effort	forewarn

313 Word Beginning Fur- The word beginning *fur-* is also represented by *f.*

Spell: fur-n-ish, furnish

furnish	furniture	furthermore
furnace	further	furlough

314 Ago in Phrases In expressions of time, *ago* is expressed by *gay.*

days ago	years ago	long ago
weeks ago	minutes ago	months ago

Building Transcription Skills

315 PUNCTUATION PRACTICE ■ , series

When the last member of a series of three or more items is preceded by *and* or *or*, place a comma before the conjunction as well as between the other items.

For his birthday he received a shirt, a tie, and a pair of cuff links.

I saw him on July 18, on July 19, and again on July 30.

I need a girl to take dictation, to answer the telephone, and to greet callers.

Each time a series occurs in the Reading and Writing Practice, it will be indicated thus in the shorthand: ser (,)

316 Business Vocabulary Builder

air pollution Impure air.

commuters People who travel back and forth regularly.

exhibit Show.

Reading and Writing Practice

317 Brief-Form Letter

its

pol·lu·tion

nu·cle·ar

fumes

ar·ea

sim·i·lar

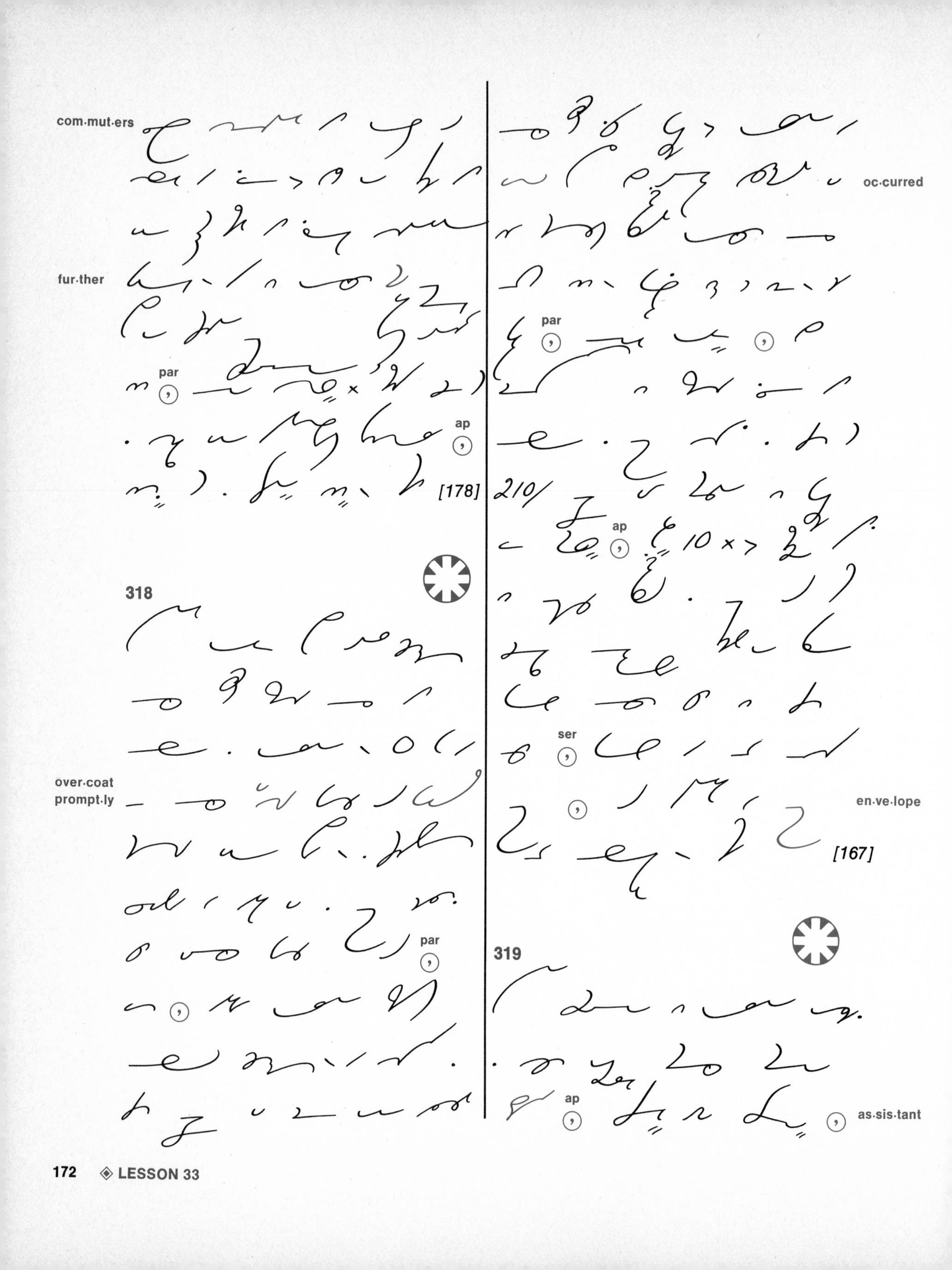

com·mut·ers

oc·curred

fur·ther

par

par

ap

[178]

210

ap

318

ser

over·coat
prompt·ly

en·ve·lope

[167]

par

319

ap

as·sis·tant

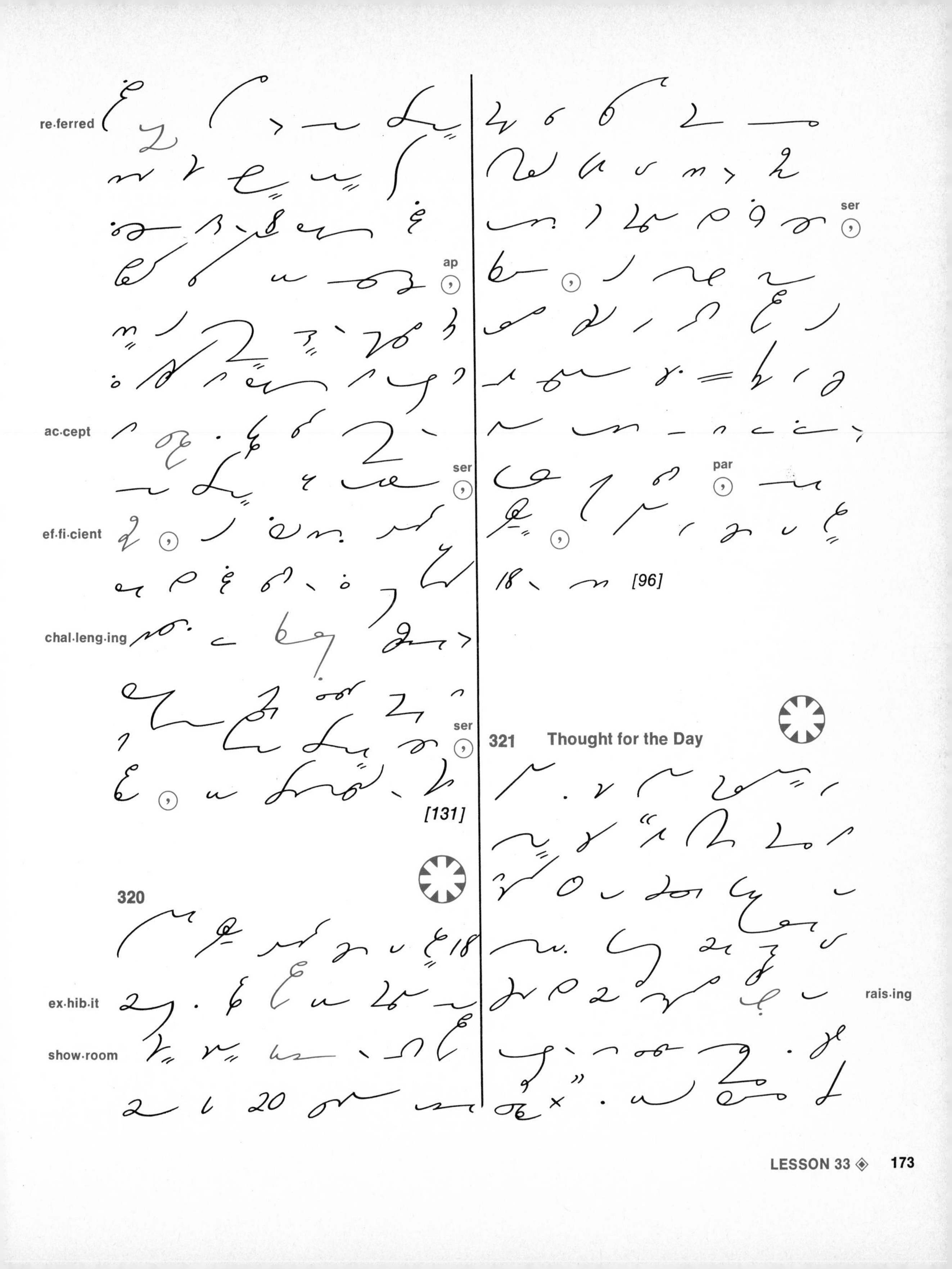

re·ferred

ap

ac·cept

ser

ef·fi·cient

chal·leng·ing

ser

[131]

320

ex·hib·it

show·room

ser

par

18 [96]

321 Thought for the Day

rais·ing

dry·ly

piece

[117]

pea

SHORTHAND NOTEBOOK CHECK LIST

Your shorthand notebook is another important tool of your trade. Do you:

■ **1** Use a notebook with a spiral binding so that the pages always lie flat as you write?

■ **2** Write on the front cover your name and the first and last dates on which you use the notebook?

■ **3** Place a rubber band around the used portion of your notebook so that it opens automatically to the first blank page?

■ **4** Date the first page of each day's dictation at the bottom of the page for quick and convenient reference—just as a stenographer in an office would do?

■ **5** Check before class to see that there are sufficient pages remaining in your notebook for the day's dictation and, if not, supply yourself with a second notebook so that you will not run out of paper in the middle of dictation?

Principles

322 Want in Phrases In phrases, *want* is represented by the *nt* blend.

I want	I wanted	if you want
you want	he wants	do you want

323 Ort The *r* is omitted in the combination *ort.*

Spell: re-p-o-t, report

report	quart	sort
export	quarterly	portable

324 R Omitted in -ern, -erm The *r* is omitted in the combinations *tern, term, thern, therm, dern, derm.*

Spell: t-e-n, turn

turn	term	southern
return	termed	thermometer
eastern	determine	modern

325 Word Endings -cal, -cle The word endings *-cal, -cle* are represented by a disjoined *k.*

Spell: l-o-j-ical, logical

logical	technical	article
chemical	practical	physically
medical	critical	musically

Building Transcription Skills

326 Business Vocabulary Builder

misfortunes Troubles.

harassed Annoyed continually; worried.

competent Capable; well qualified.

Reading and Writing Practice

327 Brief-Form Review Letter

los·ing

so·lu·tion

cur·tail

ar·ti·cle

ser

suf·fered

ha·rassed

par

de·vel·op·ments

par

be·gin·ning

[170]

328

ap

15

Chem·i·cal

145

Bou·le·vard

bright

ser

140

mod·ern

quar·ters

par

[102]

329

ser

com·mer·cial

par

fur·ther

[140]

330

com·plete·ly

331

par

par

ser

con·vinc·ing

par

par

par

ar·ea

plan·ning

en·hance

[134]

ap

15

[130]

Principles

332 Word Beginnings Inter-, Intr-, Enter-, Entr- The word beginnings *inter-, intr-, enter-, entr-* are represented by a disjoined *n.* This disjoined word beginning, as well as other disjoined word beginnings that you will study in later lessons, is placed above the line of writing, close to the remainder of the word.

Inter-

Spell: inter-s-t, interest

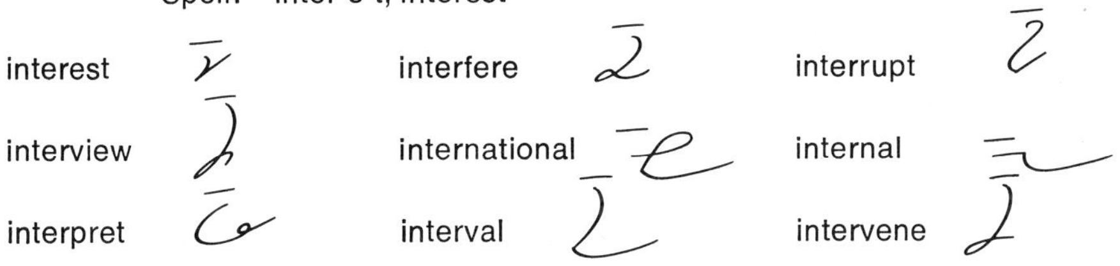

interest	interfere	interrupt
interview	international	internal
interpret	interval	intervene

Intr-

Spell: intro-d-oo-s, introduce

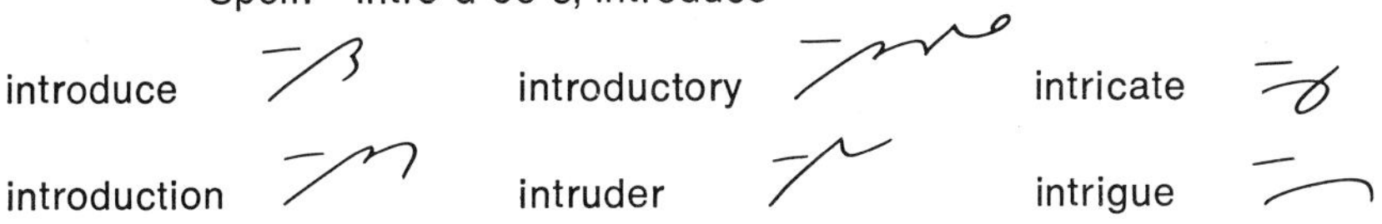

introduce	introductory	intricate
introduction	intruder	intrigue

Enter-

Spell: enter-ing, entering

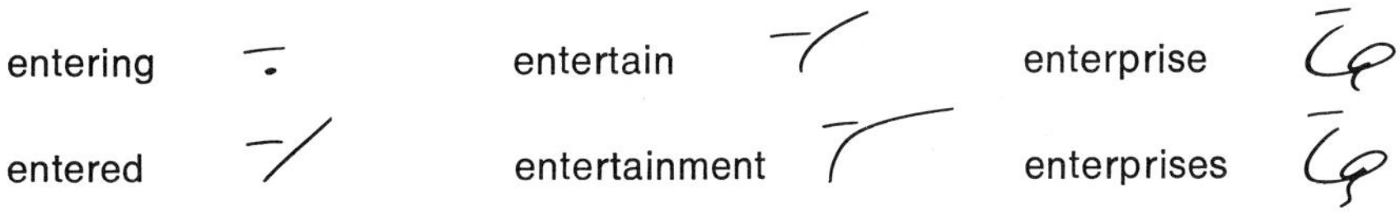

entering	entertain	enterprise
entered	entertainment	enterprises

Entr-

Spell: enter-n-s, entrance

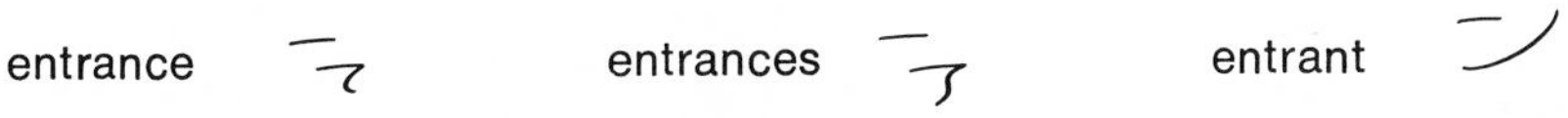

entrance	entrances	entrant

333 **Word Ending -ings** The word ending *-ings* is represented by a disjoined left *s*.

Spell: s-a-v-ings, savings

savings	proceedings	trimmings
openings	furnishings	hearings
drawings	earnings	evenings

334 **Omission of Words in Phrases** It is often possible to omit one or more unimportant words in a shorthand phrase. In the phrase *one of the,* for example, the word *of* is omitted; we write *one the.* When transcribing, the stenographer would insert *of,* as the phrase would make no sense without that word.

one of the	some of the	many of the
one of them	up to date	in the future
some of our	in the world	during the past

Building Transcription Skills

335 **SIMILAR-WORDS DRILL ■ hear, here**

hear To gain knowledge of by listening; to be informed.

I will *hear* his side of the story later.

here In this place.

Our staff is *here* to serve your needs.

336 Business Vocabulary Builder

turnover The number of employees hired by a company to replace those who have left.

recruiters Those who supply a company with new employees.

realize To obtain or achieve, as a gain or profit.

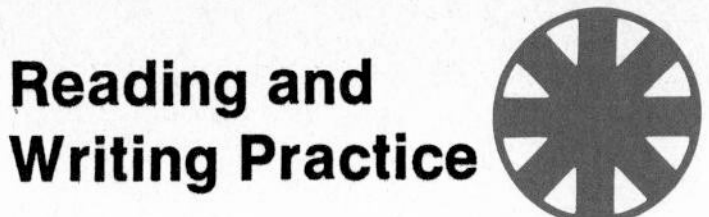

Reading and Writing Practice

337 Phrase Letter

turn·over

re·al·ize

lose

ap

re·cruit·ers

rec·om·mend

par

ser

[150]

338

ser

haven't

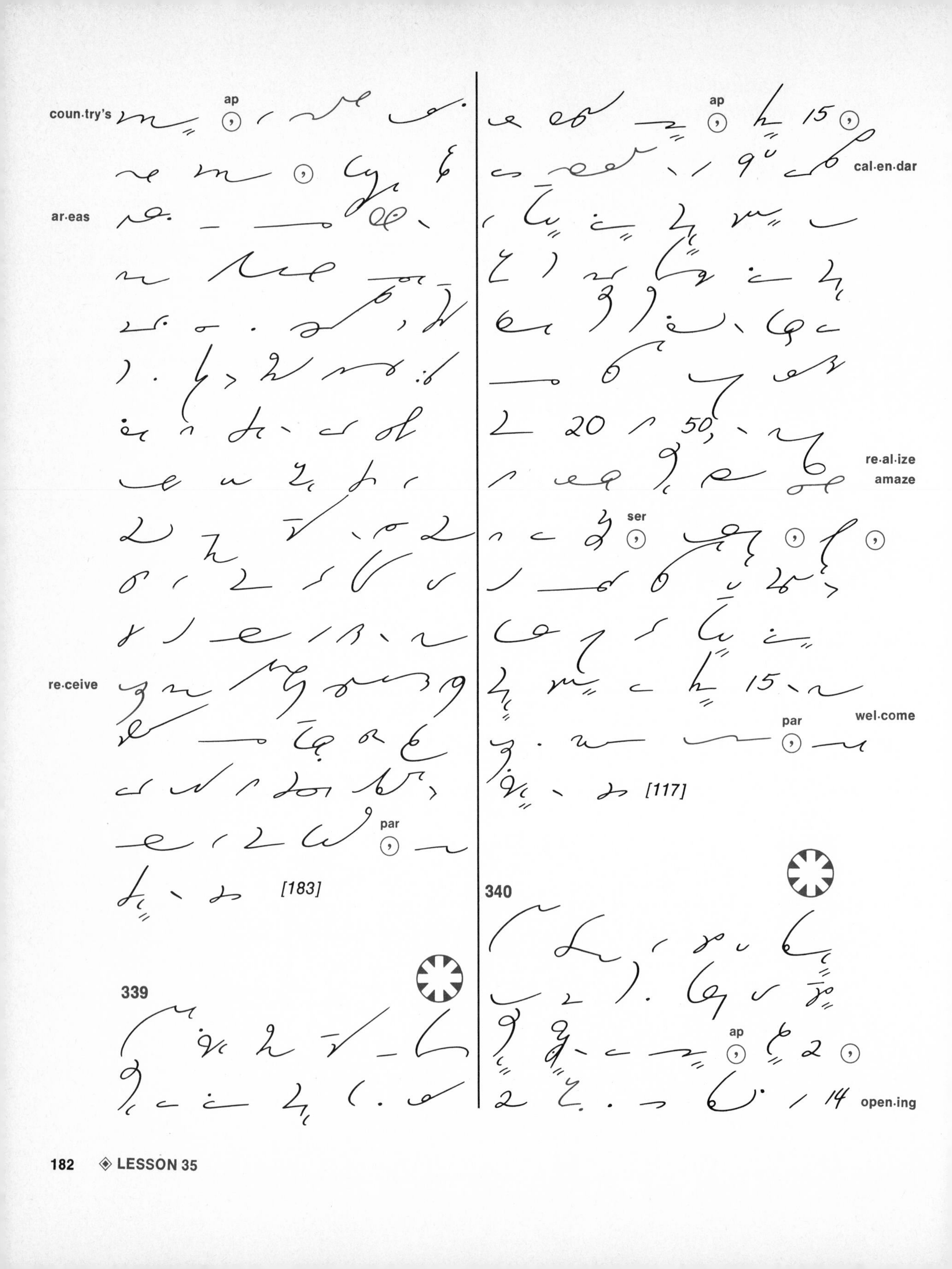

coun·try's ap

ar·eas

re·ceive

par

[183]

339

cal·en·dar ap 15

re·al·ize

amaze

ser

20 50

15

wel·come par

[117]

340

ap

14 open·ing

per·mit·ted

be·gin·ning

sou·ve·nir

[125]

341

en·ter·pris·ing

par

par

ap

ap

ser

ser

Rus·sian

Bell

[118]

PERSONAL-USE CHECK LIST

Do you put your shorthand knowledge to work for you by:

- **1** Writing all your assignments in shorthand?
- **2** Making drafts of term papers and reports in shorthand?
- **3** Corresponding with friends in shorthand?
- **4** Keeping your diary in shorthand?
- **5** Making notes to yourself on things to do, people to see, and appointments to keep in shorthand?

LESSON 36

RECALL

Lesson 36 is another breather. In Lesson 36 you will find the last principle of joining, a chart that contains a review of the shorthand devices you studied in Lessons 1 through 35, and a Reading and Writing Practice.

Principles of Joining

342 The word endings *-ure* and *-ual* are represented by *r* and *l* except when those endings are preceded by a downstroke.

nature	procedure	creature
equal	gradual	annual

but

pressure	treasure	insure
casual	usual	visual

Accuracy Practice

343 O On Sho Non

To write these combinations accurately:

a *Keep the* **o** *hook narrow, being sure that the* **beginning** *and* **end** *are on the same level of writing as indicated by the dotted line.*

b *Keep the* **o** *in* **on** *and* **sho** *parallel with the consonant, as indicated by the dotted line.*

c *Make the* **beginning** *of the* **o** *in* **non** *retrace the* **end** *of the first* **n**.

d *Avoid a point at the* **curved** *part indicated by the arrows.*

practice drill

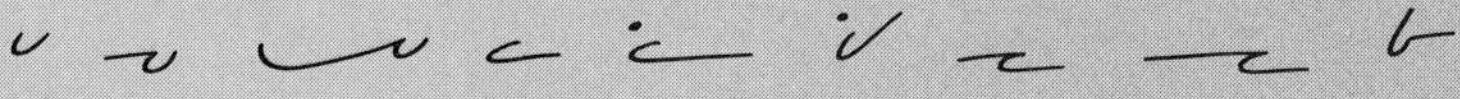

Of, know, law, own, home, hot, known, moan, shown

344 OO  **Noo**  **Noom**

To write these combinations accurately:

a *Keep the* **oo** *hook narrow and deep.*

b *Keep the* **beginning** *and* **end** *of the hook on the same level of writing.*

c *In* **noo** *and* **noom**, *keep the hook parallel with the straight line that precedes it.*

d *In* **noom**, *retrace the* **beginning** *of the* **m** *on the* **bottom** *of the* **oo** *hook.*

e *Avoid a point at the places indicated by arrows.*

practice drill

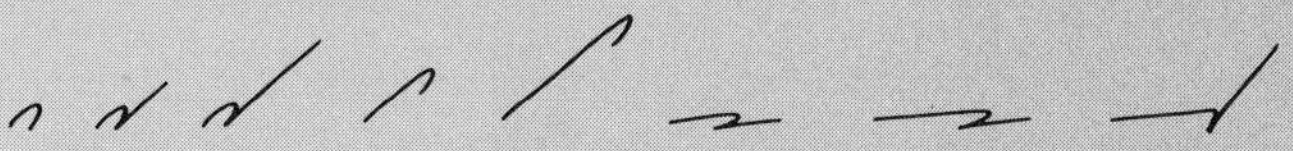

You-your, Yours truly, you would, to (too-two), do, noon, moon, mood.

345 Hard  **Hailed**

To write these combinations accurately:

a *Give the* **end** *of the* **r** *and the* **end** *of the* **l** *a lift upward.*

b *Do not lift the* **end** *too soon, or the strokes may resemble the* **nd, md** *combinations.*

practice drill

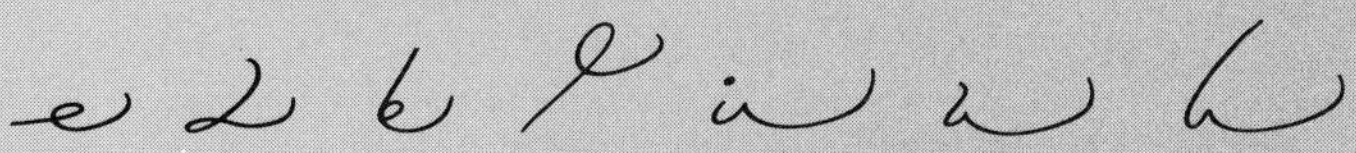

Neared, feared, cheered, dared, hold, sold, bold.

346 Recall Chart This chart contains a review of the shorthand devices you studied in previous lessons. It contains 90 brief forms, words, and phrases. Can you read the entire chart in 5 minutes?

BRIEF FORMS

1

2

3

PHRASES

4

5

WORDS

6

7

8

9

10

11

12

13

14

15

Building Transcription Skills

347 Business Vocabulary Builder

versatile Capable of doing many things.

irate Angry.

aspect Phase; view.

voluminous Very big; having great bulk.

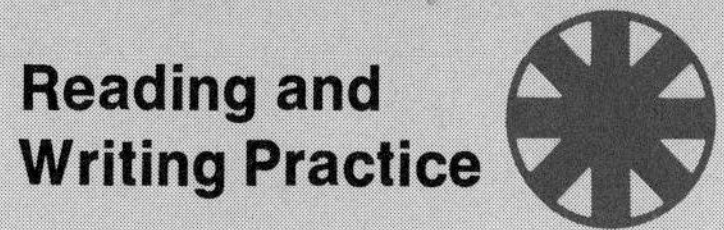

Reading and Writing Practice

348 You and Your Boss

than

wor·ry

busi·ness·man

chat·ting

ser

Skillful.

par

ac·cu·rate·ly

par

ser

an·swer·ing

weight

ver·sa·tile

sit·u·a·tions

ser

los·ing

Calm.

irate

ser

de·ci·sive

ap

won't

[270]

349 The Complete Treatment

per·son·nel

ser

stir

par

un·for·tu·nate·ly

par

pol·i·cies

(250)

vo·lu·mi·nous

ser

an·a·lyzed

Finally,

ser

tapped

neigh·bor's

[222]

350 Humor

hu·mor

par

josh·ing

whole·some

in·no·cent

There are

par

ac·cept

cru·el

in·tol·er·a·ble

ser

re·frain

dou·bly

re·sent

In your

in·dulge

[227]

Chapter 7 What Is an "Adequate" Shorthand Skill?

Some people say that if you can write 80 words a minute, you can hold a secretarial job. Others maintain that you need a speed of 100 words a minute. Still others consider that to be a well-trained secretary, you must write 120 or 140 words a minute.

Actually, the term *words a minute* can be misleading. To understand what it means, we must know what kind of material was dictated and for what length of time. A secretary can take simple, short business letters at much faster speeds than she can long, technical ones. And the rate of 120 words a minute means little if the dictation was for only a minute and on simple material. You can say that you are a 100- or 120-word writer only if you can write for a sustained period of several minutes at that rate on average material that you have never seen before.

Why do we make such a point of *words a minute?* No executive sits with a stopwatch in his hand to time the dictation. He probably couldn't even guess the speed of his dictation. In fact, *words a minute* is only meaningful as a *measurement of progress* while you're in training. If you are writing 60 words a minute, you must have a goal if you are to be spurred on—a goal, say, of 80 words a minute. And the 80-word writer has

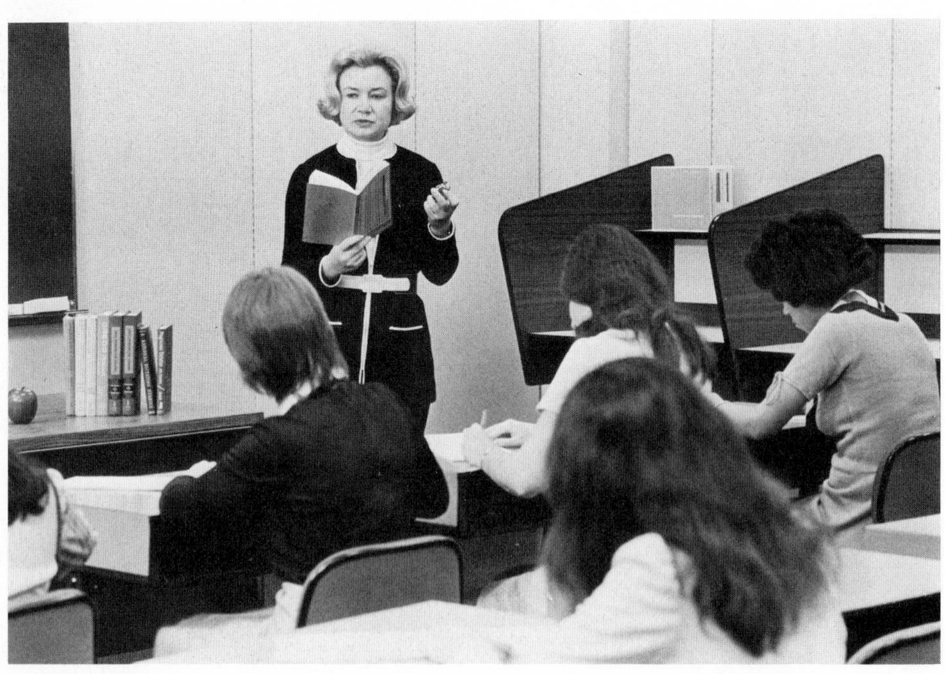

a goal of 100. In order to help you achieve greater speed, your shorthand instructor uses a stopwatch to time the dictation.

Does a speed of 80 words a minute mean that 80 actual words are dictated every 60 seconds? Not necessarily. What about short words like *a*, *of*, and *to* and long words like *incomprehensible* and *tintinnabulation* — should they count the same? No. In order to equalize the short and long words, the sounds uttered by the dictator are broken down into syllables and the dictation speed is actually measured in syllables. Studies have shown that for standard dictation a typical word contains 1.4 syllables. Thus 80 words a minute is 112 syllables a minute (80 x 1.4).

Now, after all this discussion, what is an adequate speed for a shorthand writer? You will hear from time to time that the average dictation speed in the business office is about 80 words a minute. And studies have shown this to be true. But mark the word *average*. If you are going to take the dictation of an executive whose rate averages 80 words a minute, you will need to be able to write about 100 words a minute, because a good part of the dictation will be at more than 80. If you work for an executive whose average speed is 100 words a minute, you will need a speed of about 120 words a minute.

It has been proved that only the secretary who can write for a substantial period at 120 words a minute can be reasonably sure that she can handle the dictation of every executive.

The point is this: Don't be satisfied with a minimum speed of 80 words a minute just because someone told you that's all you need. Continue to build your skill to the highest degree possible. Aim for a speed of 120 words a minute or more so that you can be sure of handling the dictation of any executive who might become your employer. You will never be sorry that you possess this reserve power for the inevitable emergencies.

LESSON 

Principles

351 Word Ending -ingly The word ending *-ingly* is represented by a disjoined *e* circle.

Spell: n-o-ingly, knowingly

knowingly	increasingly	appealingly
exceedingly	willingly	encouragingly
accordingly	surprisingly	decreasingly

352 Word Beginning Im- The word beginning *im-* is represented by *m.*

Spell: im-p-o-s, impose

impose	impossible	imply
impressed	improve	impolite
import	improper	improbable

353 Word Beginning Em- The word beginning *em-* is also represented by *m.*

Spell: em-p-l-oi, employ

employ	embarrass	emphasis
employer	embrace	empower
employment	emphatic	empire

354 Im-, Em-, Followed by a Vowel When *im-, em-* are followed by a vowel, they are written in full.

immodest	immoral	emotional

355 Omission of Minor Vowel When two vowel sounds come together, the minor vowel may be omitted.

courteous		genuine		period	
serious		theory		ideal	
previous		union		situated	

Building Transcription Skills

356 PUNCTUATION PRACTICE ■ , if clause

A frequent error made by the beginning transcriber is the failure to make a complete sentence. In most cases the incomplete sentence is a dependent or subordinate clause introduced by a word such as *if, when,* or *as.* The dependent or subordinate clause deceives the transcriber because it would be a complete sentence if it were not introduced by a word such as *if;* therefore, it requires another clause to complete the thought.

The dependent or subordinate clause often signals the coming of the main clause by means of a subordinate conjunction. The commonest subordinating conjunctions are *if, as* and *when.* Other subordinating conjunctions are *though, although, whether, unless, because, since, while, where, after, whenever, until,* and *before.* In this lesson you will consider clauses introduced by *if.*

A subordinate clause introduced by *if* and followed by a main clause is separated from the main clause by a comma.

If you complete the work before 5 o'clock, you may leave.

If you would like to have more information about our products, please fill out and return the enclosed card.

If you cannot complete the work by February 15, please call me at my home in Washington.

Each time a subordinate clause beginning with *if* occurs in the Reading and Writing Practice, it will be indicated thus in the shorthand: if (,)

357 Business Vocabulary Builder

impose Force oneself upon another.

Impartial Not favoring one more than the other.

impressive Commanding attention.

implement To carry out.

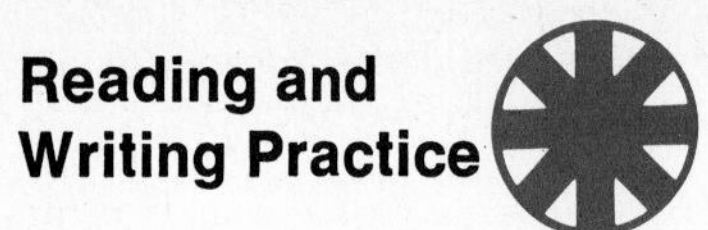

358 Brief-Form Review Letter

ap

em·ploy·ee

of·fer·ing

par

ser

fair

grate·ful

if

par

par

[137]

359

va·ca·tion

if

heart

ser

the·aters

par

if

pace

ser

if

sce·nery

ser

par

com·pli·ment

ap

cour·te·ous

gen·u·ine·ly

sim·i·lar

di·rec·to·ry

par

if

[196]

ser

writ·ing

if

[150]

360

ap

361

its

if

grad·u·a·tion

ide·al

ser

ap

prac·ti·cal

ap

ser

fair·ly

im·par·tial·ly

ser

if

adop·tion

busy

if

[120]

ap·pre·ci·ate

362

[118]

BRIEF-FORM CHECK LIST

Are you making good use of the brief-form chart that appears on the inside back cover of your textbook? Remember, the brief forms represent many of the commonest words in the language and the better you know them, the more rapid progress you will make in developing your shorthand speed.

Are you—

■ **1** Spending a few minutes reading from the chart each day?

■ **2** Timing yourself and trying to cut a few seconds off your reading time with each reading?

■ **3** Reading the brief forms in a different order each time—from left to right, from right to left, from top to bottom, from bottom top?

Principles

363 Word Ending -ship The word ending *-ship* is represented by a disjoined *ish.*

Spell: s-t-e-m-ship, steamship

steamship friendship township

relationship membership scholarships

364 Word Beginning Sub- The word beginning *sub-* is represented by *s.*

Spell: sub-m-e-t, submit

submit substantial sublease

subscribed subdivide suburbs

365 Joining of Hook and Circle Vowels When a hook and a circle vowel come together, they are written in the order in which they are pronounced.

poet poetry folio

poem radio portfolio

Building Transcription Skills

366 PUNCTUATION PRACTICE ■ , as clause

A subordinate clause introduced by *as* and followed by the main clause is separated from the main clause by a comma.

As you can well imagine, an effective credit letter is not an easy one to write.

As you may have read in the newspapers, Frank Smith was made president of the New York Publishing Company.

Each time a subordinate clause beginning with *as* occurs in the Reading and Writing Practice, it will be indicated thus in the shorthand: as ⦅,⦆

367 Business Vocabulary Builder

suburban Relating to a residential area outlying a city.

quarterly Four times a year.

sublet To rent (property one holds by lease) to another.

Reading and Writing Practice

368 Brief-Form Review Letter

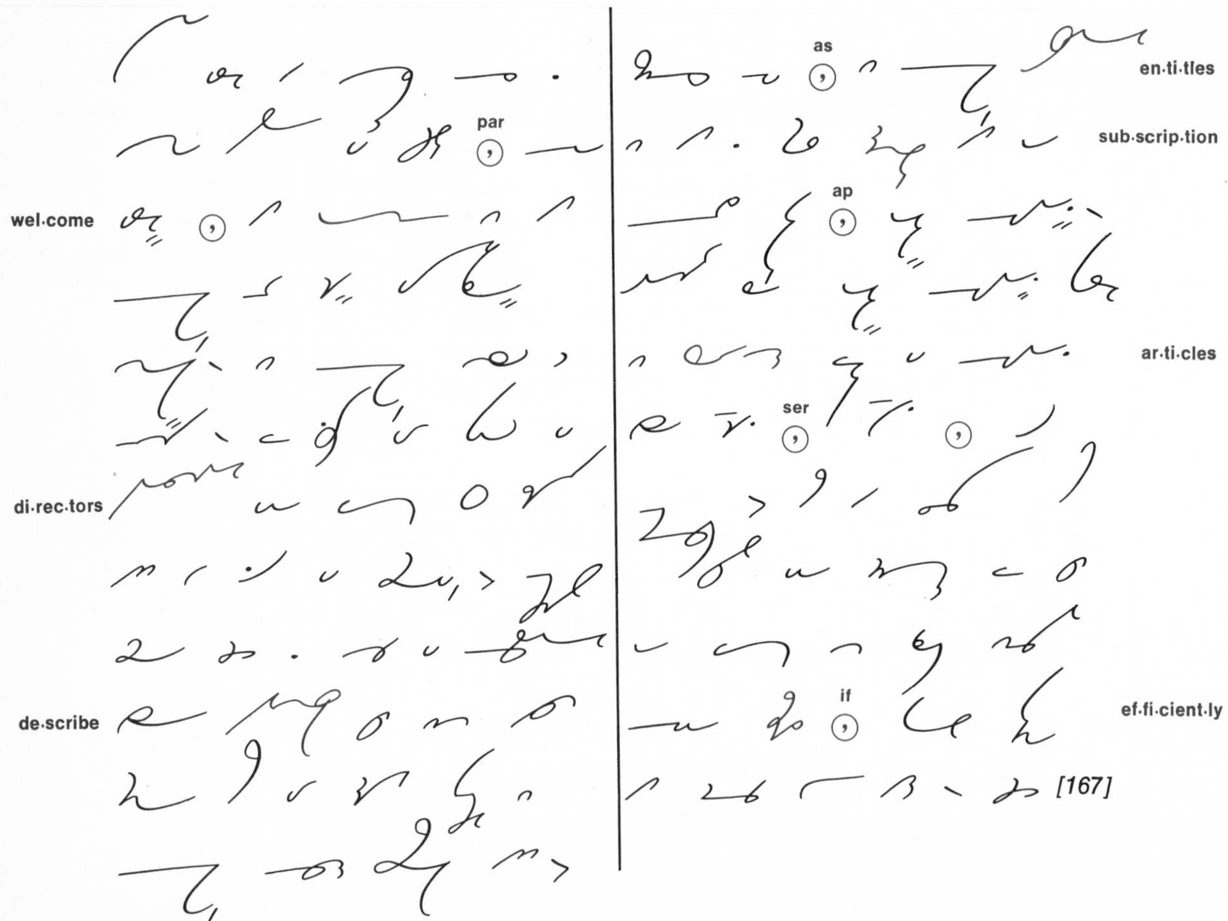

369

ap 15 con·vey com·mit·tee as grate·ful sub·mit·ting 30 par oc·cu·py [142]

370

as spon·sor·ship ap par sub·mit·ted sub·ur·ban par par if en·ve·lope [147]

371

en·ter·prise

as

sub·urbs

180

sub·lease

if

prompt·ly

[130]

372

ap

as

se·nior

an·nu·al

stud·ied

if

[115]

LESSON 39

Principles

373 Word Ending -rity The word ending *-rity* is represented by a disjoined *r.*

Spell: s-e-n-s-rity, sincerity

sincerity majority priority
security minority integrity
maturity popularity authorities

374 Word Ending -lity The word ending *-lity* is represented by a disjoined *l.*

Spell: a-b-lity, ability

ability vitality quality
facility locality responsibility
utility personality reliability

375 Word Ending -lty The word ending *-lty* is also represented by a disjoined *l.*

Spell: f-a-k-ulty, faculty

faculty penalty loyalty

376 Word Ending -self The word ending *-self* is represented by *s.*

Spell: h-e-r-self, herself

herself myself oneself
himself itself yourself

377 Word Ending -selves The word ending *-selves* is represented by *ses.*

Spell: your-selves, yourselves

yourselves themselves ourselves

Building Transcription Skills

378 PUNCTUATION PRACTICE ■ , when clause

A subordinate clause introduced by *when* and followed by the main clause is separated from the main clause by a comma.

When I was in Chicago last week, I visited your company.

When you delay paying your account after it is due, you endanger your credit standing.

Each time a subordinate clause beginning with *when* occurs in the Reading and Writing Practice, it will be indicated thus in the shorthand: when (,)

379 Business Vocabulary Builder

exacting (*adjective*) Demanding a definite standard.

mediocrity The state of being neither good nor bad; ordinary.

precedents Similar events that took place in the past.

Reading and Writing Practice

380 Brief-Form Review Letter

quan·ti·ties

fa·cil·i·ties

ser

sched·ules

ser

ex·pe·ri·enced

15

dif·fi·cul·ty

when

par

cus·tom·ers

[150]

381

suc·cess

ser

me·di·oc·ri·ty

if

ap

de·scribes

ser

par

fac·ul·ty

as

[163]

382

par

than

par

piece

when

qual·i·ty

in·fe·ri·or·i·ty

Stu·di·os

ex·cel·lence

par

[158]

383 The Qualities of Leadership

when

prec·e·dents

2. Popularity,

when

③

so·cia·bil·i·ty

af·fect

judg·ment

im·plic·it·ly

5. Desire

if

ev·ery·one

when

cheer·ful·ly

pos·sess

[287]

TRANSCRIPTION CHECK LIST

Are you getting the full benefit from the spelling and punctuation helps in the Reading and Writing Practice by—

■ **1** Encircling all punctuation in your notes as you copy each Reading and Writing Practice?

■ **2** Noting the reason for the use of each punctuation mark to be sure that you understand why it was used?

■ **3** Spelling aloud at least once the spelling words given in the margin of the shorthand?

Principles

384 Abbreviated Words—in Families Many long words may be abbreviated in shorthand by dropping the endings. This device is also used in longhand, as *Jan.* for *January.* The extent to which you use this device will depend on your familiarity with the words and with the subject matter of the dictation. When in doubt, write it out! The ending of a word is not dropped when a special shorthand word ending has been provided, such as *-lity,* in *ability.*

Notice how many of the words written with this abbreviating device fall naturally into families of similar endings.

-tribute

tribute, contribute, distribute

attribute, contributed, distributor

attributes, contribution, distribution

-quent

consequent, consequence, subsequent, eloquent, eloquence

consequently, subsequently, frequent

-quire

require, inquire, inquiries

requirement, inquired, acquire

-titute

substitute, institute, constitute

substitution, institution, constitution

-titude

aptitude | gratitude | latitude

-ology

psychology | sociology | apology

psychological | sociological | apologies

Building Transcription Skills

385 PUNCTUATION PRACTICE ■ , introductory

A comma is used to separate the subordinate clause from a following main clause. You have already studied the application of this rule to subordinate clauses introduced by *if, as,* and *when.* Here are examples of subordinate clauses introduced by other subordinating conjunctions.

Although the car cost more than he had planned to pay, he bought it.

Before you sign the contract, you should discuss it with your lawyer.

Unless I hear from you by March 18, I will have to refer your account to a collection agency.

While I am in Chicago on business, I will stop in to see my uncle.

A comma is also used after introductory words or phrases such as *furthermore, on the contrary,* and *for instance.*

Furthermore, the report was not prepared in the proper form.

On the contrary, you are the one who made the mistake.

Each time a subordinate (or introductory) word, phrase, or clause other than one beginning with *if, as,* or *when* occurs in the Reading and Writing Practice, it will be indicated thus in the shorthand: intro (,)

◈ Note: If the subordinate clause or other introductory expression follows the main clause, the comma is usually not necessary.

I am enclosing a stamped envelope for your convenience in sending me your check.

386 Business Vocabulary Builder

comprehend Understand.

subsequently Later.

constitute Make up.

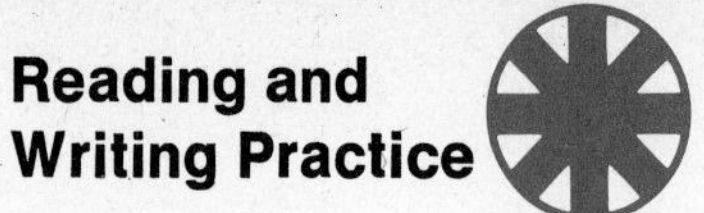

Reading and Writing Practice

387 Brief-Form Review Letter

opin·ion intro

intro

as·sis·tance

as

fre·quent

ac·knowl·edg·ing

if

[145]

388

in·qui·ries

look·out

ap

Ecol·o·gy

ser

if

plan·ning

intro

if

avail·able

ex·pense

intro

par

[154]

389

wheth·er

[167]

re·ferred

390

psy·cho·log·i·cal

ap

par

intro

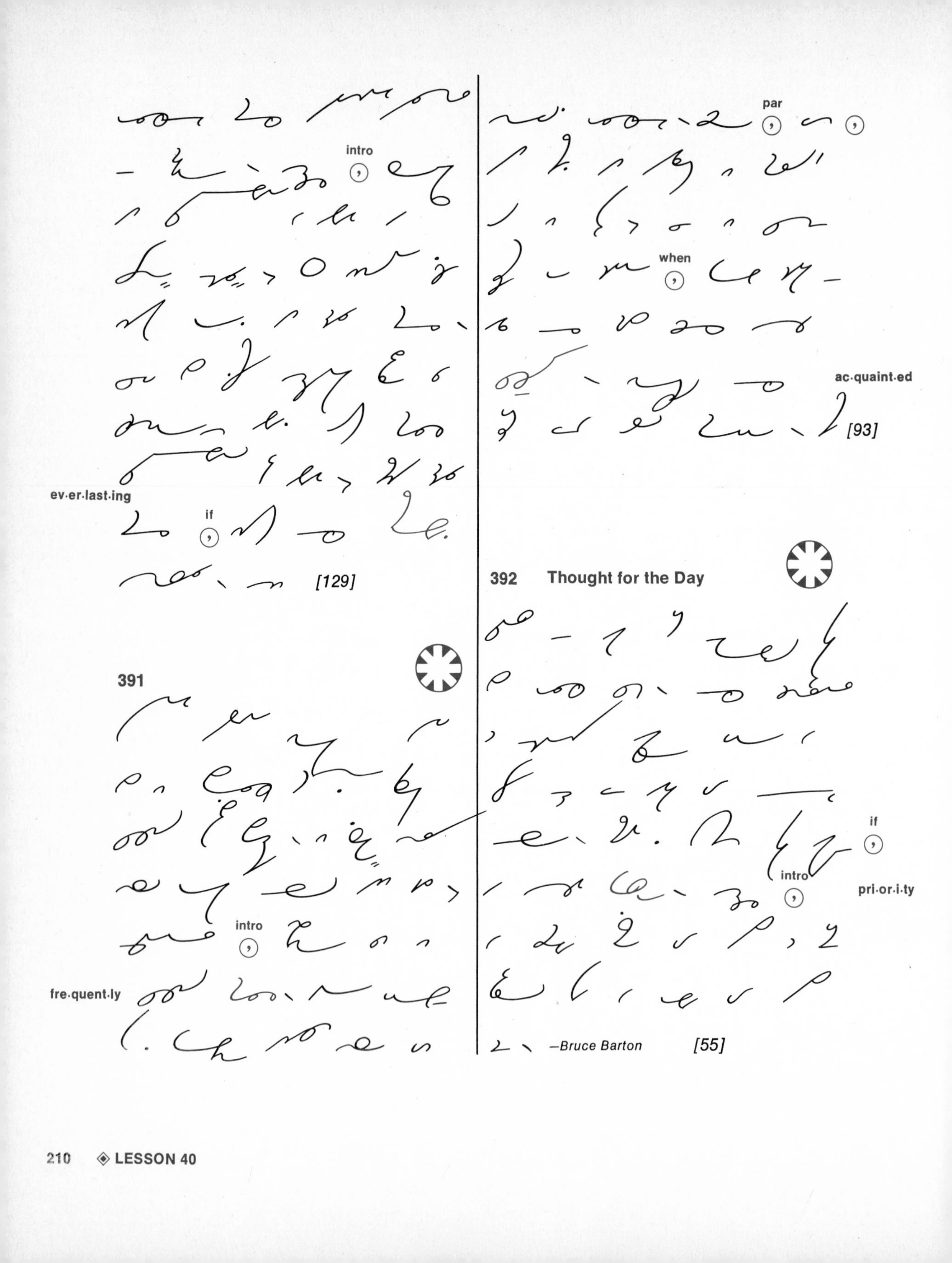

intro

ev·er·last·ing

if

[129]

391

intro

fre·quent·ly

par

when

ac·quaint·ed

[93]

392 Thought for the Day

if

intro

pri·or·i·ty

—Bruce Barton [55]

LESSON 41

Principles

393 Abbreviated Words—Not in Families The ending may be omitted from some long words even though they do not fall into a family.

memorandum	significant, significance	philosophy
convenient, convenience	reluctant, reluctance	privilege
equivalent	anniversary	privileged

394 Word Beginning Trans- The word beginning *trans-* is represented by a disjoined *t.*

Spell: trans-l-a-t, translate

translate	transport	transplant
transact	transcribe	transit
transfer	transcript	transistor

395 Word Ending -ification The word ending *-ification* is represented by a disjoined *f.*

Spell: n-o-t-ification, notification

notification	ratification	modification
classification	verification	specifications
justification	identification	qualifications

Building Transcription Skills

396 SIMILAR-WORDS DRILL ■ assistance, assistants

assistance Help.

If we can be of any *assistance* to you, please let us know.

assistants Helpers.

My *assistants* and I will need more time to complete the job.

397 Business Vocabulary Builder

periodically At regular intervals.

transmitted Handed from one person to another.

reluctance Unwillingness.

Reading and Writing Practice

398 Brief-Form Review Letter

as

priv·i·lege

par

con·ve·nient

hon·ored

intro

ser

intro

when

rou·tine

par

[153]

399

as

hand·i·capped

intro

in·con·ve·nienced

for·mal·ly

par

ex·pan·sion

as·sis·tants

[150]

400

ap

trans·mit·ted

re·luc·tance

im·me·di·ate·ly

dis·cussed

as·sis·tance

[172]

401

sub·mit·ted

ver·sus

than

con·nec·tion

re·ceive

[166]

LESSON 42

RECALL

There are no new shorthand devices for you to learn in Lesson 42. However, Lesson 42 does contain an Accuracy Practice, a review of the word beginnings and endings you have studied thus far, and a Reading and Writing Practice.

Accuracy Practice

402 My **Lie** **Fight**

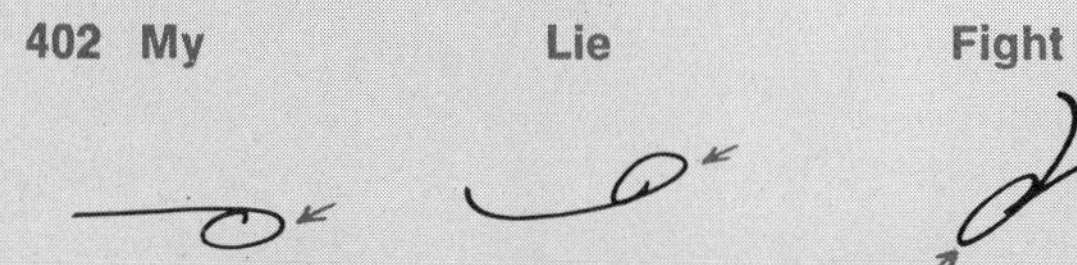

To write these combinations accurately:

a *Join the broken circle in the same way that you would join an* **a** *circle, but turn the* **end** *inside the circle.*

b *Before turning the* **end** *of the circle inside, be sure that the stroke touches the stroke to which the* **i** *is joined.*

c *Avoid making a point at the places indicated by arrows.*

practice drill

My, night, sight, line, mile.

403 Ow **Oi**

To write these combinations accurately:

a *Keep the hooks deep and narrow.*

b *Place the circles* **outside** *the hooks as indicated by the dotted lines.*

practice drill

How-out, now, doubt, scout; toy, soil, annoy.

404 Ith **Nt, Nd** **Mt, Md**

To write these combinations accurately:

a *Slant the strokes as indicated by the dotted lines.*

b *Start these strokes to the right and upward.*

practice drill

There are, and will, empty, health, lined, ashamed.

Compare:

Hint, heard; tamed, detailed.

405 Recall Chart There are 90 word beginnings and endings in the following chart. Can you read them in 5 minutes?

WORD BEGINNINGS AND ENDINGS

1

2

3

4

5

6

7

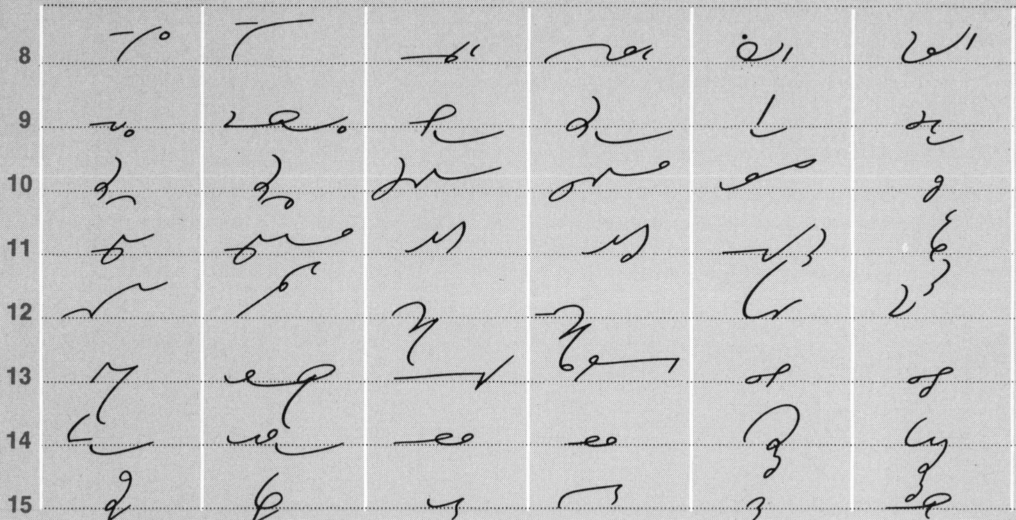

Building Transcription Skills

406 **Business Vocabulary Builder**

accelerator The gas pedal of a car.

extended (*adjective*) Long.

generate Produce.

Reading and Writing Practice

Reading Scoreboard Twelve lessons have gone by since you last measured your reading speed. You have, of course, continued to do each Reading and Writing Practice faithfully, and, consequently, your reading speed will reflect this faithfulness! The following table will help you measure your reading speed on the *first reading* of Lesson 42.

Lesson 42 contains 469 words	
If you read Lesson 42 in	your reading rate is
16 minutes	**30 words a minute**
17 minutes	**28 words a minute**
18 minutes	**26 words a minute**
20 minutes	**24 words a minute**
21 minutes	**22 words a minute**
24 minutes	**20 words a minute**

If you can read Lesson 42 through the first time in less than 12 minutes, you are doing well. If you take considerably longer than 22 minutes, perhaps you should:

1 *Pay closer attention in class while the shorthand devices are being presented to you.*
2 *Spend less time trying to decipher outlines that you cannot read.*
3 *Review, occasionally, all the brief forms you have studied by referring to the chart on the inside back cover of your text.*

407 Improve Your Mileage

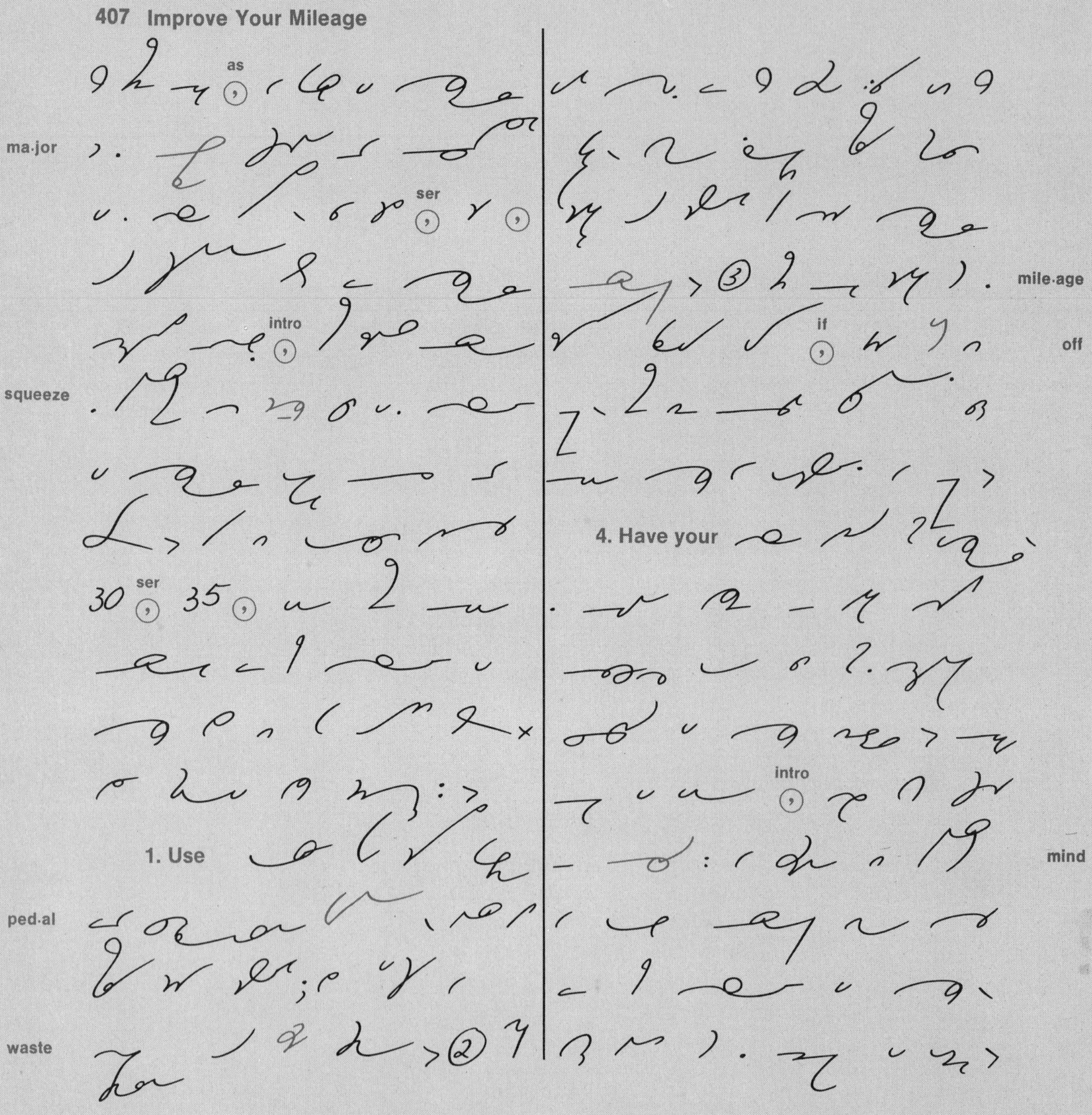

en·gine

intro

intro

re·sis·tance

intro

35

bi·cy·cle

If you

if

lei·sure·ly

if

[354]

408 The Secretary

if

em·ploy·er

oc·ca·sion·al

The person

weight

[115]

Chapter 8 Choosing a Job

As far as secretarial jobs are concerned, it is still a seller's market. This means that the secretary can *choose* the company or organization for which she would like to work—assuming, of course, that she has the proper skills to bring to the job.

Because your first job may be your most important one, you will be smart to choose it carefully. If you jump at the first opportunity, you may be forced to leave the job soon after because it wasn't what you wanted. And changing jobs is always disagreeable.

How can you find out which is the right job for you? First, determine where your interests are. If you like an academic atmosphere, you might find a position in a school office or a college dean's office exciting. If the advertising world fascinates you, there are plenty of jobs for secretaries in advertising agencies and in advertising departments of companies. Or you might prefer to work for a doctor, a personnel manager, or a hotel

Photo Courtesy United Air Lines

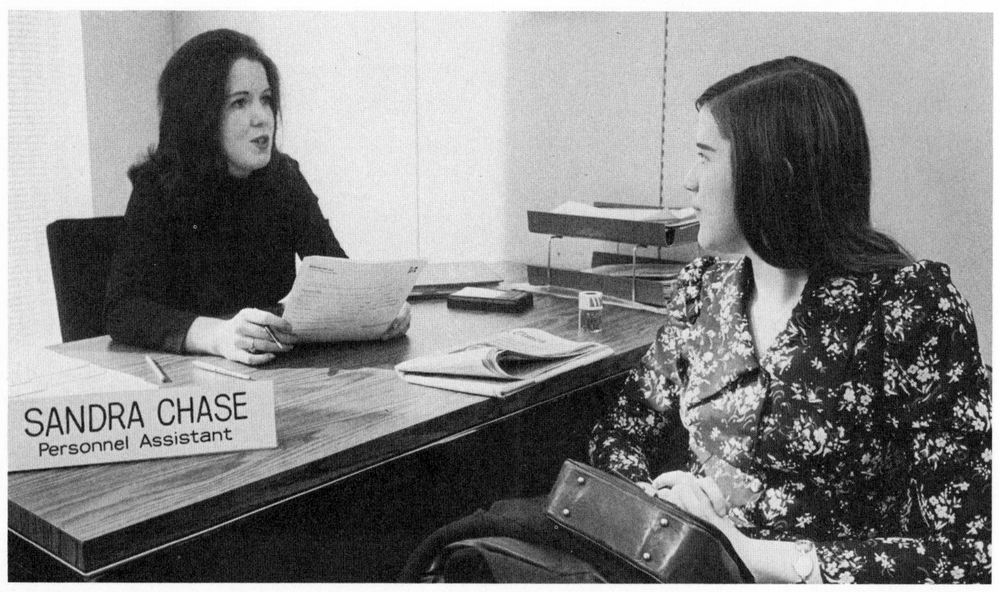

manager. Perhaps you would like a government job in Washington or on a military base, a position with a major airline, or a job in a newspaper office. Decide in what general surroundings you would probably be happiest, and aim in that direction.

Another factor you need to consider is the reputation of the company. Do people talk favorably about it, and do they think it has a bright future? What do the employees of the company think of it as a place to work? What fringe benefits are offered, such as insurance, vacation, hospitalization, recreation, etc.?

Location is important to some people. You may feel it is more important to live within walking distance of your job than to have the ideal job in another part of town. Or you may prefer working in a big city to working in a small town.

We haven't mentioned money, but of course it is enormously important. The reason we come to it last is that too many people rank it first.

Secretarial jobs in a given location do not vary greatly in beginning salaries. Find out from your placement counselor what beginning salaries are being paid in your area to people of your background, and don't be afraid to ask for a comparable wage. Don't raise the salary issue, however, unless it is clear that your interviewer does not intend to.

Basically, the three most important questions you should ask yourself before you accept a position are these:

1. Will I find the work interesting and challenging?
2. Will I enjoy the people I work with and for?
3. Will I be given reasonable opportunity for financial and professional advancement?

LESSON 43

Principles

409 Word Ending -ulate The word ending *-ulate* is represented by a disjoined *oo* hook.

Spell: s-t-e-p-ulate, stipulate

stipulate congratulate formulate
accumulate stimulate formulates
circulate calculate formulated

410 Word Ending -ulation The word ending *-ulation* is represented by *oo-shun.*

Spell: p-o-p-ulation, population

population tabulation congratulations
circulation stimulation calculations

411 Word Beginning Post- The word beginning *post-* is represented by a disjoined *p.*

Spell: post-j, postage

postage postpaid postpone
postmark postal postponed

412 Word Beginning Super- The word beginning *super-* is represented by a disjoined comma *s.*

Spell: super-v-ī-s, supervise

supervise superintendent superior

supervision superhuman superb

Building Transcription Skills

413 PUNCTUATION PRACTICE ■ , conjunction

A comma is used to separate two independent clauses that are joined by one of the following conjunctions: *and, but, or, for, nor.*

An independent clause (sometimes called a main or a principal clause) is one that has a subject and a predicate and that could stand alone as a complete sentence.

There are twelve men in the department, but only six of them have been with us for more than one year.

The first independent clause is:

There are twelve men in the department

and the second independent clause is:

only six of them have been with us for more than one year.

Both clauses could stand as separate sentences, with a period after each. Because the thoughts of the two clauses are closely related, however, the clauses were joined to form one sentence. Because the two independent clauses are connected by the coordinating conjunction *but,* a comma is used between them, before the conjunction.

Each time this use of the comma occurs in the Reading and Writing Practice, it will be indicated thus in the shorthand: conj (,)

414 Business Vocabulary Builder

circulating your report Passing the report from person to person.

simulation Imitation.

superlative Of the highest quality.

superficial Minor.

Reading and Writing Practice

415 Brief-Form Review Letter

ap (,) Ex·plo·sion 12

conj

ti·tles

ap

Cen·tu·ry

20

when

de·scrib·ing

[127]

416

af·fect

su·pe·ri·or

conj

ris·ing

conj

judg·ment

ser

su·per·vi·so·ry

if

con·sid·er·a·bly

par

[158]

su·perb

417

ap

15

ap

Sim·u·la·tion

as

anx·ious·ly

par

su·per·la·tive

conj

su·per·fi·cial

com·ple·tion

intro

50

5 [142]

418

if

post·al

se·ri·ous·ly

if

if

ser

weath·er

if

par

[148]

419

intro

right

intro

fu·el

if

con·trac·tor

conj

in·stall

when

par

[137]

420 Thought for the Day

[55]

LESSON 

Principles

421 Word Ending -sume The word ending *-sume* is represented by *s-m.*

Spell: a-s-m, assume

assume	presume	assumed
resume	presumed	consumed
consume	presumably	consumer

422 Word Ending -sumption The word ending *-sumption* is represented by *s-m-shun.*

Spell: a-s-m-shun, assumption

assumption	resumption	consumption

423 Word Beginning Self- The word beginning *self-* is represented by a disjoined left *s.*

Spell: self-m-a-d, self-made

self-made	self-satisfied	self-supporting
self-assurance	self-reliant	selfish
self-confidence	self-defense	selfishness

424 Word Beginning Circum- The word beginning *circum-* is also represented by a disjoined left *s.*

Spell: circum-s-ten-s, circumstance

circumstance	circumstances	circumnavigate

Building Transcription Skills

425 PUNCTUATION PRACTICE ■ , and omitted

When two or more consecutive adjectives modify the same noun, they are separated by commas.

Enclosed is a stamped, addressed envelope.

However, the comma is not used if the first adjective modifies the combined idea of the second adjective plus the noun.

The book was bound in an attractive brown cloth.

◈ Note: You can quickly determine whether to insert a comma between two consecutive adjectives by mentally placing *and* between them. If the sentence makes good sense with *and* inserted between the adjectives, then the comma is used. For example, the first illustration would make good sense if it read:

Enclosed is a stamped and addressed envelope.

Each time this use of the comma occurs in the Reading and Writing Practice, it will be indicated thus in the shorthand: and o (,)

426 Business Vocabulary Builder

in excess of More than.

dynamic Having force or energy.

consumer One who buys or uses merchandise or services.

resumed Began again after an interruption.

Reading and Writing Practice

427 Brief-Form Review Letter

wom·en

conj (,)

ser (,) (,)

self-as·sur·ance

intro

conj

en·cour·ag·ing

ser

sit·u·a·tions

and o

am·bi·tious

par

[176]

428

and o

as

of·fer·ings

orig·i·nal·ly

intro

ex·cess

intro

and o

suc·cess

par

[208]

429

wom·an

when

poise

ser

par

ex·press

gra·cious·ly

dy·nam·ic

and o

and o

if

par

[138]

430

set·tled

ap

15

conj

in·ter·rupt

re·sump·tion

intro

and o

[123]

431

su·per·vi·sor

as

and o

skill·ful

per·son·al

[117]

DICTATION CHECK LIST

When you take dictation, do you—

■ **1** Make every effort to keep up with the dictator?

■ **2** Refer to your textbook whenever you are in doubt about the outline for a word or phrase?

■ **3** Insert periods and question marks in your shorthand notes?

■ **4** Make a real effort to observe good proportion as you write—making large circles large, small circles small, etc.?

■ **5** Do you write down the first column of your notebook and then down the second column?

LESSON

Principles

432 Word Ending -hood The word ending *-hood* is represented by a disjoined *d.*

Spell: m-a-n-hood, manhood

manhood	childhood	boyhood
neighborhood	parenthood	motherhood

433 Word Ending -ward The word ending *-ward* is also represented by a disjoined *d.*

Spell: o-n-ward, onward

onward	afterward	forward
backward	awkwardly	forwarded

434 Ul *Ul* is represented by *oo* when it precedes a forward or upward stroke.

Spell: re-s-ul-t, result

result	consult	adults
insult	consultation	culminate

435 Quantities and Amounts Here are a few more helpful devices for expressing quantities and amounts.

$600	8,000,000,000	several hundred
6,000,000	a dollar	4 pounds
$6,000,000	a million	4 feet

◈ Notice that the *m* for *million* is written beside the figure as a positive distinction between *million* and *hundred,* in which the *n* is written *underneath* the figure.

Building Transcription Skills

436 SPELLING FAMILIES

An effective device to improve your ability to spell is to study words in related groups, or spelling families, in which all the words contain the same spelling problem.

To get the most benefit from these spelling families, practice them in this way:

1 *Spell each word aloud, pausing slightly after each syllable.*
2 *Write the word once in longhand, spelling it aloud as you write it.*

Words in Which Silent E Is Dropped Before -ing

de·sir·ing	**guid·ing**	**pre·par·ing**
en·clos·ing	**hous·ing**	**sav·ing**
ex·am·in·ing	**in·creas·ing**	**su·per·vis·ing**
forc·ing	**man·u·fac·tur·ing**	**typ·ing**

You will find several of the words in this spelling family used in the Reading and Writing Practice of this lesson.

437 Business Vocabulary Builder

reservoirs Bodies of water collected and stored in natural or artificial lakes.

ultimately Finally.

incurred Ran into.

misgivings Doubts.

Reading and Writing Practice

438 Brief-Form Review Letter

thirsty

and o

par

135

quan·ti·ties

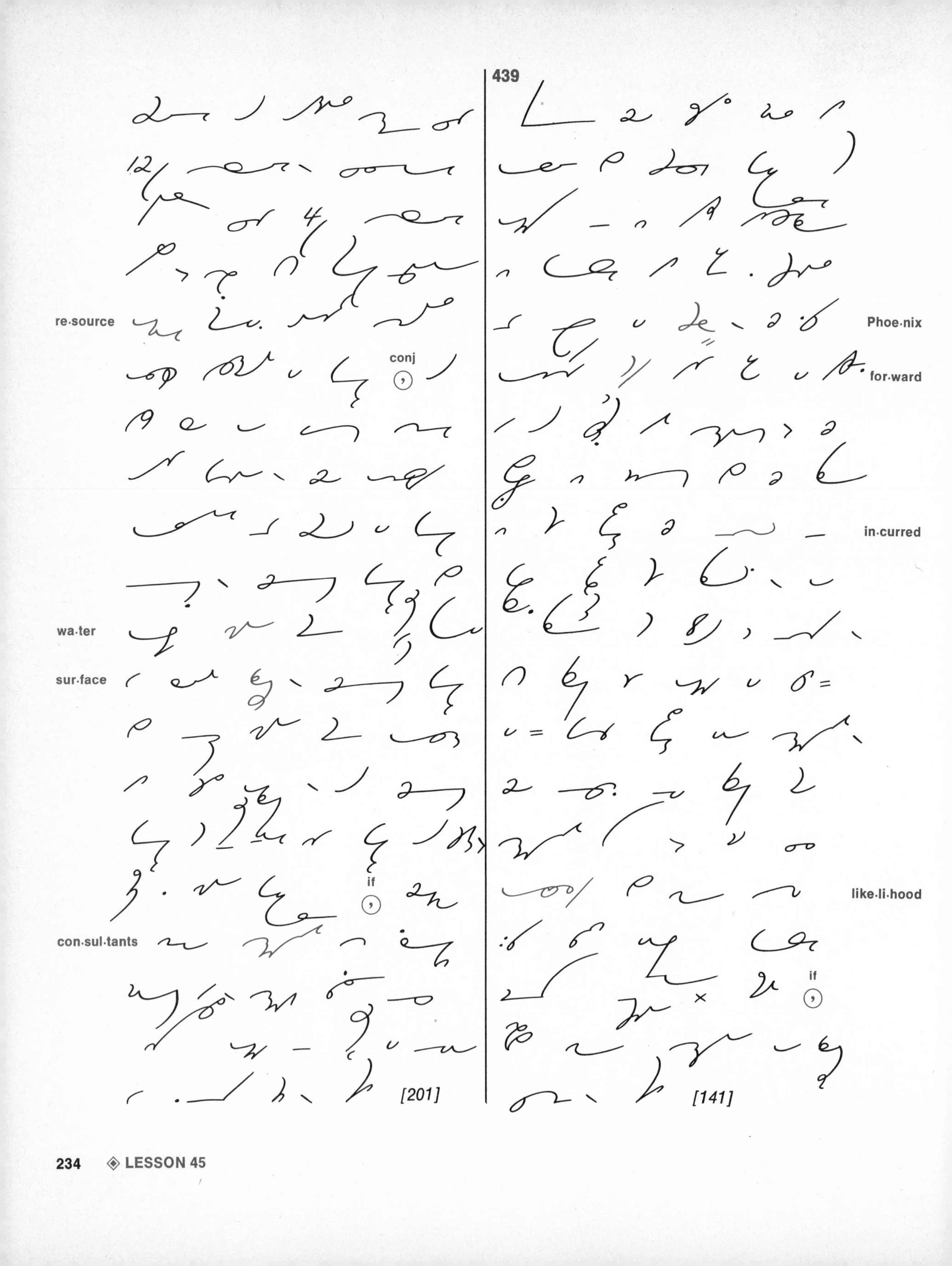

re·source

conj

wa·ter

sur·face

if

con·sul·tants

[201]

439

Phoe·nix

for·ward

in·curred

like·li·hood

if

[141]

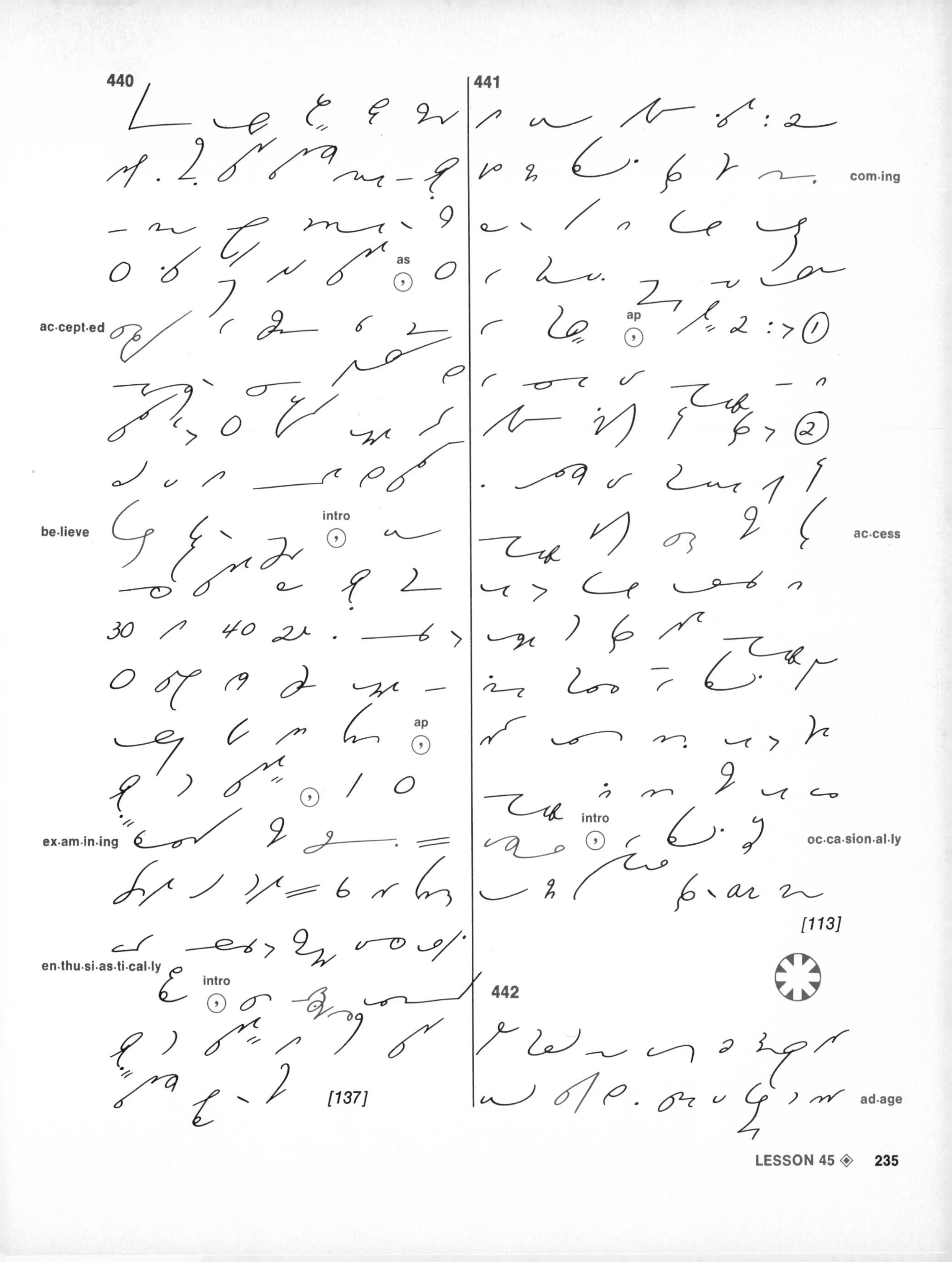

440

ac·cept·ed

as

be·lieve

intro

30 40

ap

ex·am·in·ing

en·thu·si·as·ti·cal·ly

intro

[137]

441

com·ing

ap

①

②

ac·cess

intro

oc·ca·sion·al·ly

[113]

442

ad·age

when

[158]

443

intro

ap

de·vice

chil·dren's

ser

un·in·ter·rupt·ed

sug·ges·tions

[97]

LESSON 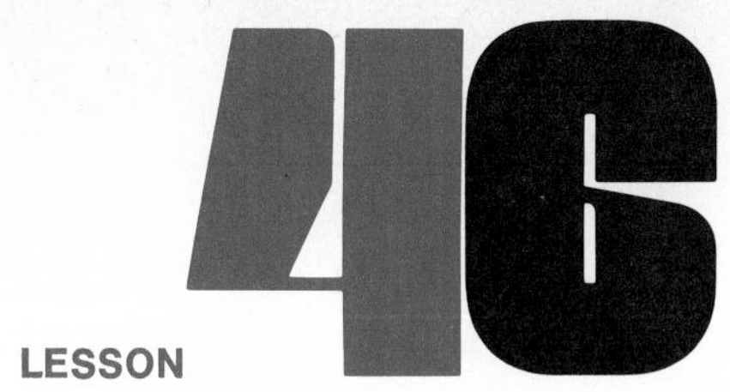

Principles

444 Word Ending -gram The word ending *-gram* is represented by a disjoined *gay.*

Spell: p-r-o-gram, program

program	cablegram	telegram
programmed	radiogram	diagrams

445 Word Beginning Electric The word beginning *electric* is represented by a disjoined *el.*

Spell: electric-l, electrical

electric	electric fan	electrical
electric light	electric motor	electrically

446 Word Beginning Electr- The word beginning *electr-* is also represented by a disjoined *el.*

Spell: electro-n-e-k, electronic

electronic	electroplate	electricity

447 Compounds Most compound words are formed by simply joining the outlines for the words that make up the compound. In some words, however, it is desirable to modify the outline for one of the words in order to obtain an easier joining.

anyhow	someone	within
anywhere	worthwhile	withstand
anybody	however	notwithstanding

448 Intersection Intersection, or the writing of one character through another, is sometimes useful for special phrases. This principle may be used when the constant repetition of certain combinations of words in your dictation makes it clearly worthwhile to form special outlines for them.

a.m.		vice versa	
p.m.		Chamber of Commerce	

Building Transcription Skills

449 SIMILAR-WORDS DRILL ■ it's; its

it's Contraction for *it is.*

A modern kitchen is not a luxury; *it's* a convenience.

its Possessive form of *it.*

Its operating efficiency will make cooking a delight.

450 Business Vocabulary Builder

majority stockholder The person who owns more than 50 percent of a company's stock.

practicable Feasible. (Do not confuse with *practical,* which means *useful.*)

thermostat An instrument used to regulate temperature.

Reading and Writing Practice

451 Brief-Form Review Letter

par

re·cent·ly

dif·fi·cul·ties

some·time (conj)

hand·some

ad·ver·tised

[174]

452

ac·quired

(ap)

pur·chased

ma·jor·i·ty (ap)

(par)

per·son·nel

pi·o·neer

ex·pan·sion

[171]

453

weath·er

as

clothes

an·nu·al

conj

1

elec·tric·i·ty

[178]

prac·ti·ca·ble

454

some·one

par

2

par

un·oc·cu·pied

when

intro

of·fered

lis·ten·ing

3

mod·ern

and o

it's

its

conj

show·room

par

for·ward

[172]

455

par

de·vel·op·ing

ser

ser

cat·e·go·ry

intro

ad·vice

intro

par

adopt

conj

su·pe·ri·or

[157]

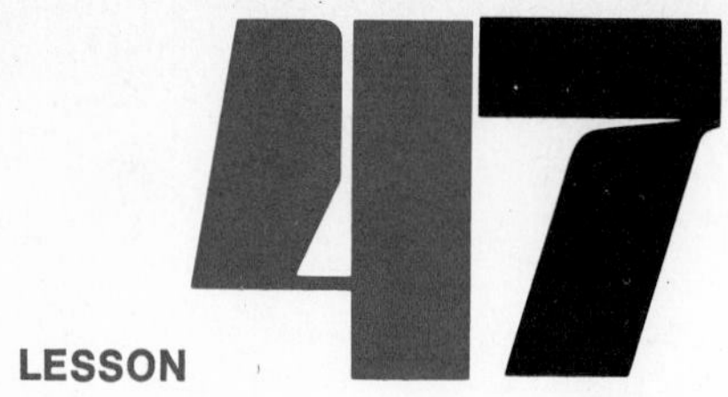

Principles

456 Geographical Expressions and Names In geographical expressions and proper names, the ending *-burg* is represented by *b;* the ending *-ville,* by *v;* the ending *-ington,* by a disjoined *ten* blend; the ending *-ingham,* by a disjoined *m.*

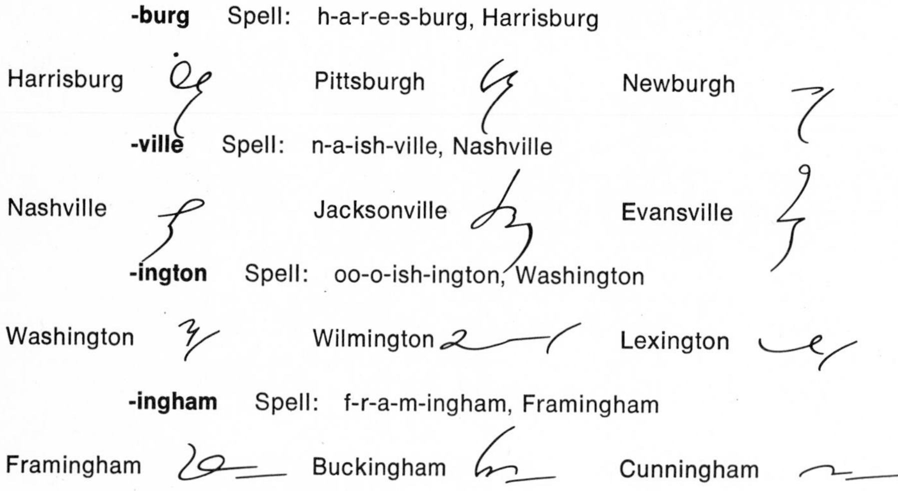

Building Transcription Skills

457 GRAMMAR CHECKUP

Most businessmen have a good command of the English language. Some rarely make an error in grammar. There are times, though, when even the best dictators will perhaps use a plural verb with a singular noun or use the objective case when they should have used the nominative. They usually know better, but in concentrating intently on expressing a thought or idea, they occasionally suffer a grammatical lapse.

It will be your job, as a stenographer or secretary, to catch these occasional errors in grammar and to correct them when you transcribe.

From time to time in the lessons ahead, you will be given an opportunity to brush up on some of the rules of grammar that are frequently violated.

GRAMMAR CHECKUP ■ subject and verb

A verb must agree with its subject in number.

Our president is looking forward to the pleasure of serving you.
Your canceled checks are mailed to you each month.

The inclusion of a phrase such as *in addition to, as well as,* or *along with* after the subject does not affect the number of the verb. If the subject is singular, use a singular verb; if the subject is plural, use a plural verb.

Our president, as well as the members of the staff, is looking forward to the pleasure of serving you.

Your canceled checks, along with your statement, are mailed to you each month.

458 Business Vocabulary Builder

mandatory Not to be avoided; obligatory.

durable Able to last.

availed Made use of.

Reading and Writing Practice

459 Brief-Form Review Letter

dis·play·ing

guest

per·son·al·ly

ap

ap

be·com·ing

[150]

460

intro ap

15 65 10

man·da·to·ry

suc·ces·sor

1971

conj

ef·fi·cient·ly

if

some·time 15

en·joyed 20

conj

[147]

461

par

au·tho·rize

intro

and o

per·son·al

if

ap·prov·al

[97]

462

su·per·in·ten·dents

equip·ment

when

prac·ti·cal

du·ra·ble

ser

[117]

463

conj

availed

en·ti·tling

com·pli·men·ta·ry

intro

gen·u·ine

par

intro

trav·el·ing

[150]

464

so·ror·i·ty

if

[153]

465

site 1800 intro

sym·bol

su·perb

its ser

ar·eas

when

for·ward

[87]

ap

SPELLING AND PUNCTUATION CHECK LIST

Are you careful to punctuate and spell correctly when—

- **1** You write your compositions in English?
- **2** Prepare papers for other classes?
- **3** Correspond with friends to whom you must write in longhand?

In short, are you making correct spelling and punctuation a habit in all the longhand writing or typing that you do?

RECALL

In Lesson 47 you studied the last of the new shorthand devices of Gregg Shorthand. In this lesson you will find an Accuracy Practice, a Recall Chart that reviews all the word-building principles of Gregg Shorthand, and a Reading and Writing Practice.

Accuracy Practice

466 Def

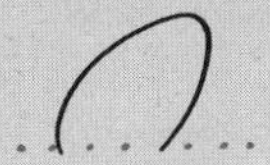

To write this stroke accurately:

a *Make it large, almost the full height of your notebook line.*

b *Make it narrow.*

c *Start and finish the stroke on the same level of writing, as indicated by the dotted line.*

practice drill

Divide, definite, defeat, devote, differ, endeavor

467 Ith **Ten** **Tem**

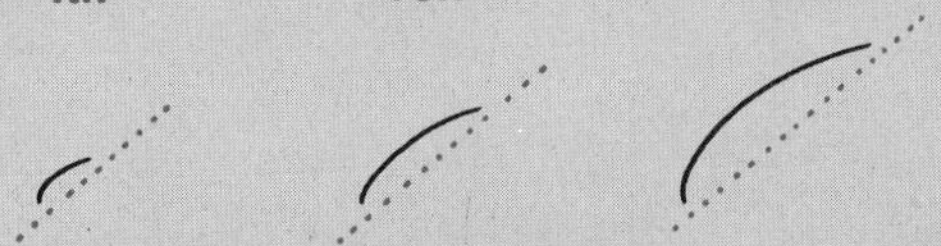

To write these strokes accurately:

a *Slant the strokes as indicated by the dotted lines.*

b *Make the* beginning *of the curves deep.*

c *Make the* tem *large, the* ith *small, and the* ten *about half the size of the* tem*.*

practice drill

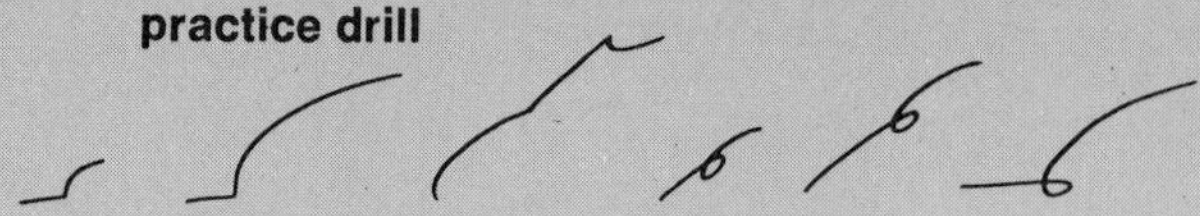

In the, in time, tender, teeth, detain, medium.

468 Recall Chart This chart contains one or more illustrations of every word building and phrasing principle of Gregg Shorthand.

WORDS

1
2
3
4
5
6
7
8
9
10
11
12
13
14

PHRASES

15
16
17

Building Transcription Skills

469 Business Vocabulary Builder

determination The mental power of deciding definitely and firmly.

trivial Of little importance.

apt Likely.

Reading and Writing Practice

470 Your Memory

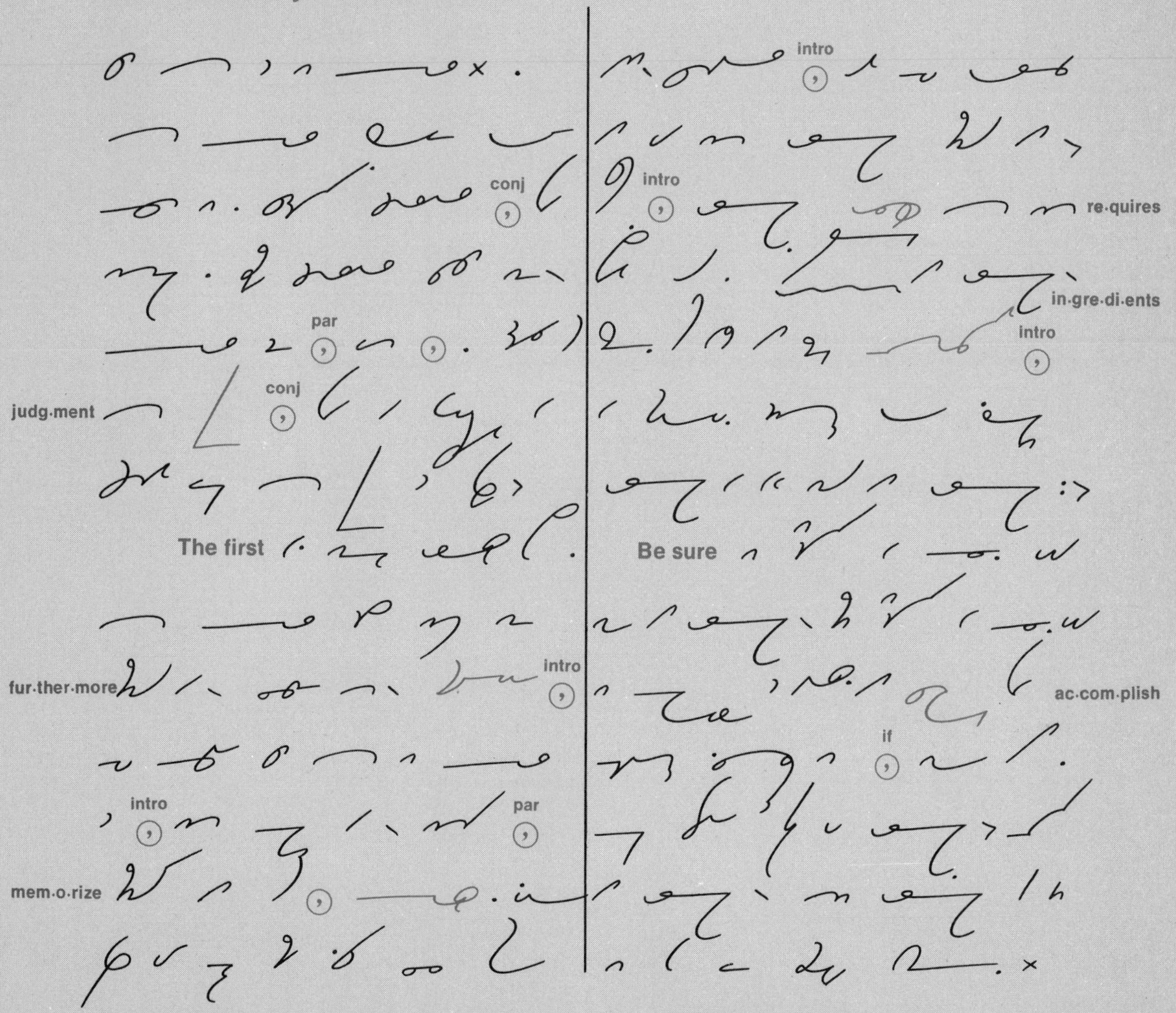

conj

par

judg·ment

conj

The first

fur·ther·more

intro

intro

par

mem·o·rize

intro

intro

re·quires

in·gre·di·ents

intro

Be sure

ac·com·plish

if

triv·i·al

apt

intro

par

2. Look

like·ly

intro

his·to·ry

conj

conj

5. Practice,

intro

ex·am·ple

phys·i·cal

and o

con·sis·tent

intro

ex·er·cise

won't

and o

conj

div·i·dends

[495]

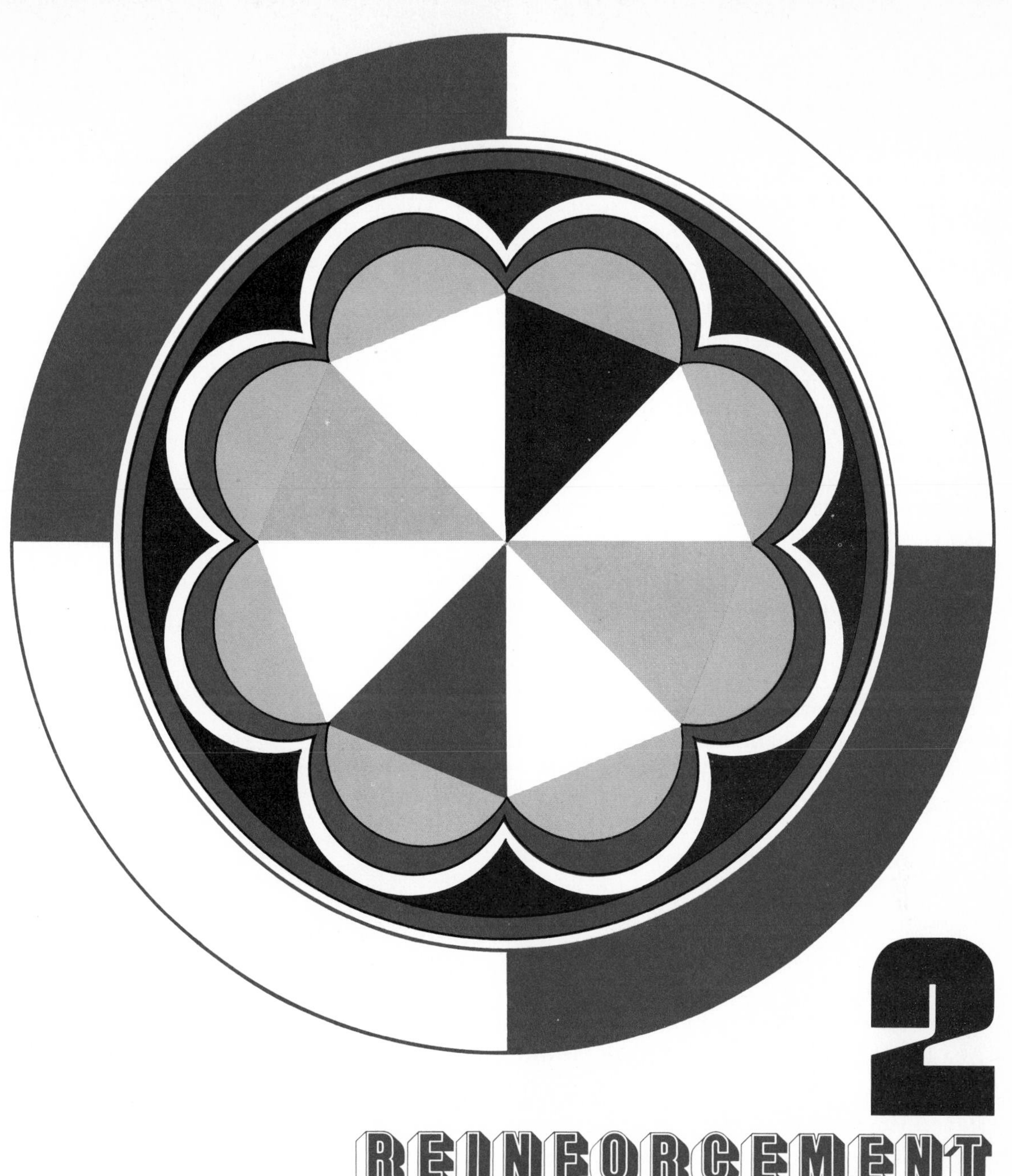

2
REINFORCEMENT

Chapter 9 Status and the Secretary

Today, more than ever, people are status-conscious. They select their clothes, their food, their houses, their recreation, and their friends with the hope that others will look with approval and admiration upon their good taste and their sophistication. Even the work that people do must have status—if not in *what* they do, certainly in what the job is *called*. Janitors want to be called *custodial managers* or *maintenance engineers*. The term *beauty operator* long ago gave way to the more sophisticated *beautician*. Many women object to the old term *housewife* and insist that they are really *homemakers*. Today's salesman is called a *service representative*, *sales consultant*, *product consultant*, or *sales engineer*.

The job of the secretary has increased in status over the years; yet the title has remained virtually unchanged. While the term *administrative assistant* is often used to identify a high-level secretarial position, it has been slow in gaining acceptance. The executive is responsible in large measure for this; he finds it difficult to refer to his assistant by any other name than *secretary*. But he certainly has no difficulty describing her status! The secretary is her boss's right arm. When the executive says "my secretary," he is, in effect, saying "the person who runs my office and my schedule." To find out the status of the secretary to an executive, you need only eavesdrop on the boss when the secretary is on vacation or at home ill. He is very likely to use such phrases as, "My secretary isn't here this week, and I have no idea where to find..." or "Would you mind calling again next week when my secretary returns? She knows what we decided, but I have forgotten..." or "I think I'll ask that client to wait another week until my secretary returns. She has all the facts."

Business would truly be paralyzed if the secretary were not on the job. The executive is helpless without her. He cannot retrieve needed materials from the files; he cannot get that important report ready because only his secretary knows where to get the facts;

he cannot schedule that meeting because he needs someone completely reliable to report the minutes.

Status is one of the reasons why secretaries enjoy their work so much. They know that they are on the firing line of executive decisions—that important reports, meetings, conferences, and decisions could not take place if they were not there to supply the information needed to "run the show."

With status, of course, go pleasant surroundings, good pay, security, and all the other hallmarks of the ideal position. If you want to feel needed, to make a valuable contribution to managerial performance, to sit in the front row of the drama of business—a drama that may affect the well-being and activities of thousands—become a secretary. There is no other job for a woman that has more status and that is more needed in the arena of the American economy.

And you don't have to sugarcoat the job by calling it something more dignified. The term *secretary* is fine just as it stands.

LESSON 49

Lesson 49 provides a thorough review of the shorthand principles you studied in Chapter 1.

471 BRIEF FORMS, DERIVATIVES, AND PHRASES

1 Is-his, will-well, have, Mr., but, Mrs., that, the, in-not.
2 It-at, willing, you-your, yours, can, cannot, are-hour-our, ours, I, with.
3 I will, I will not, in the, in that, with the, of the, I am, I have, is not.

Reading Practice

472

[64]

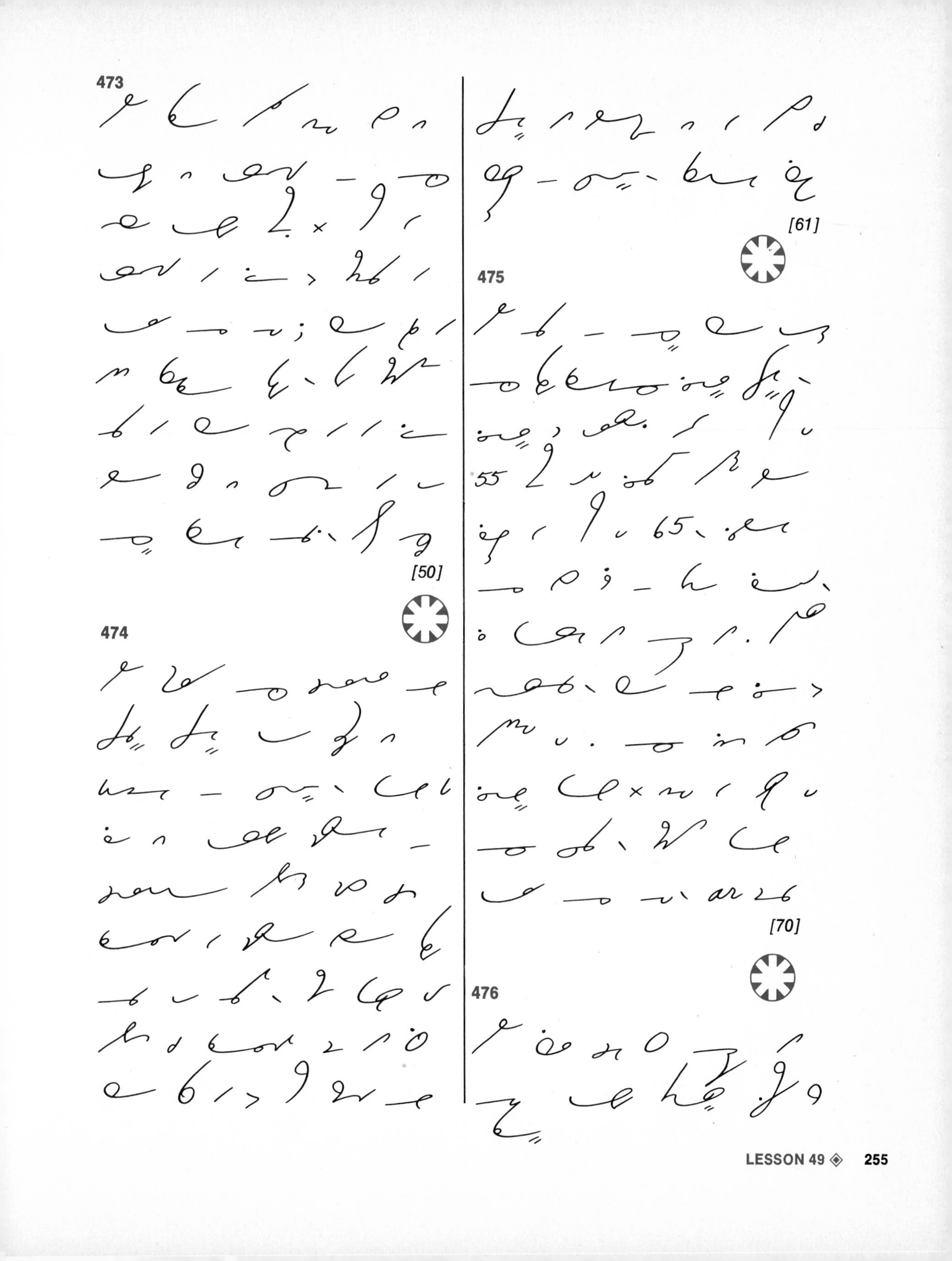

473

[50]

474

[61]

475

[70]

476

[110]

477

[74]

478

[110]

479

[71]

480

[77]

The practice material in Lesson 50 concentrates on the principles you studied in Chapter 2.

481 BRIEF FORMS, DERIVATIVES, AND PHRASES

1 Good, goods, and, this, there (their), would, be-by, being, put, putting, when.

2 Send, sending, sender, they, which, shall, from, should, could, was.

3 I would, I would not, I was, for the, for that, for this, this is, from them, when the, which is, I shall be.

482

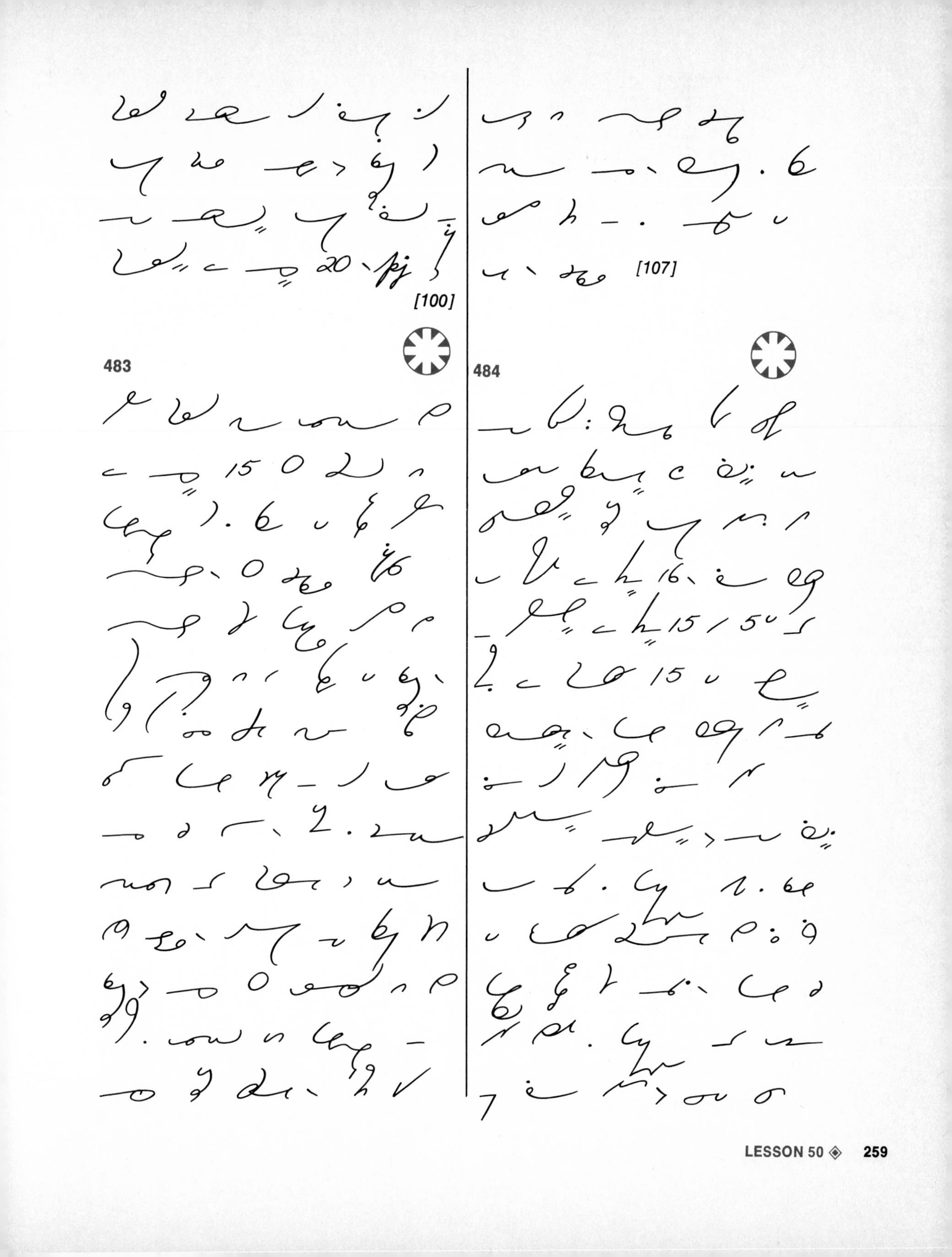

[100]

[107]

483

484

[110]

485

[109]

486

[76]

487

11:30

11:30

[145]

415-4122

[138]

488

LESSON 51

In this lesson you will review intensively the shorthand principles that you studied in Chapter 3.

489 BRIEF FORMS, DERIVATIVES, AND PHRASES

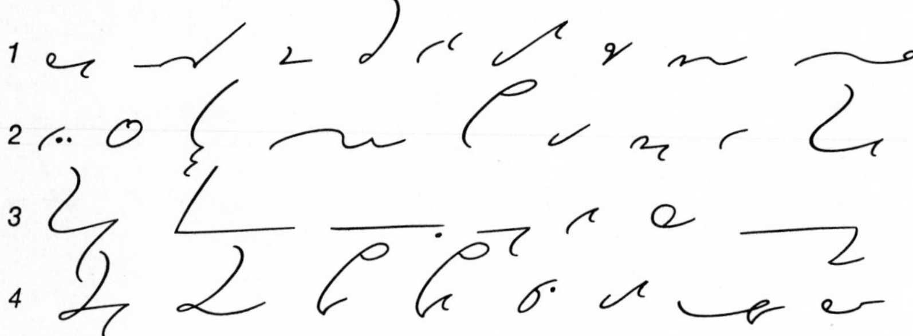

1 Years, enclosed, soon, very, thanks, orders, yesterday, worker, gladly.
2 Thinking, why, businesses, greater, about, what, once, than, values.
3 Valuable, gentlemen, morning, important-importance, those, where, manufacturer.
4 Very important, very well, about the, about those, I think, what is, less than, were not.

Building Transcription Skills

490 Business Vocabulary Builder

adjourn To end a meeting. (Do not confuse *adjourn* with *adjoin,* which means *to be close to.*)

rectify To correct.

Reading and Writing Practice

491

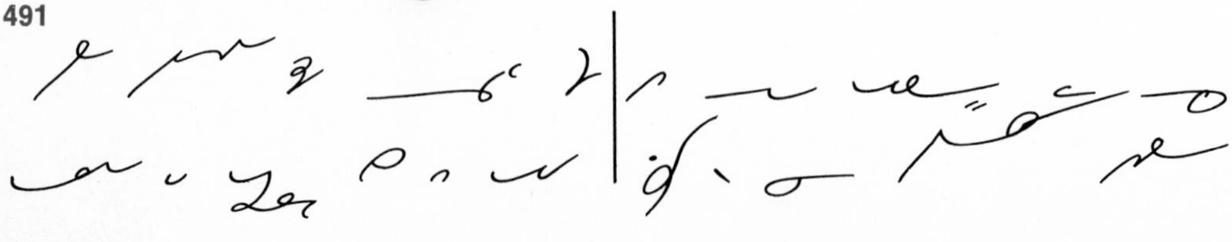

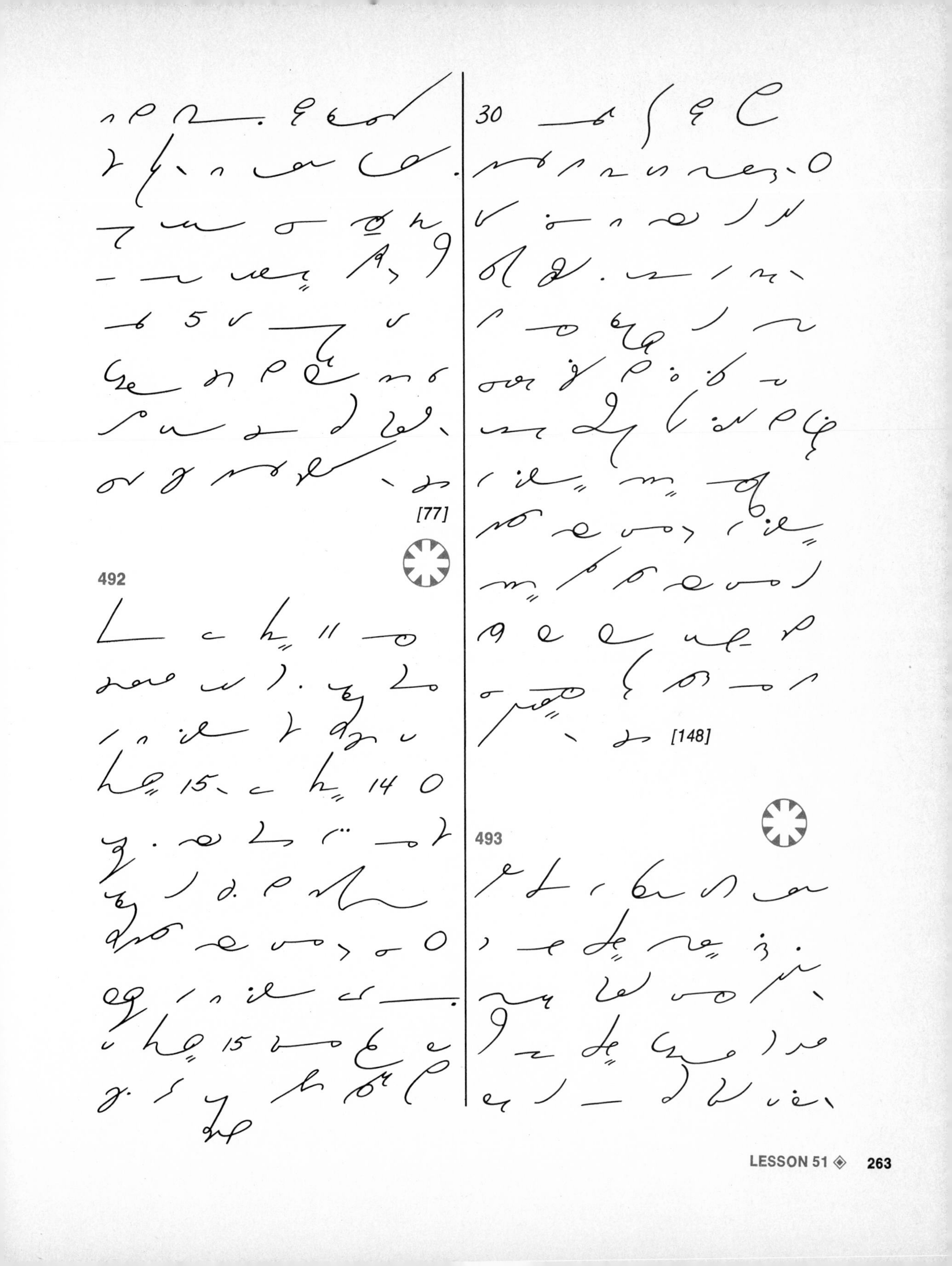

5

[77]

492

15 14

15

30

[148]

493

[124]

494

[94]

495

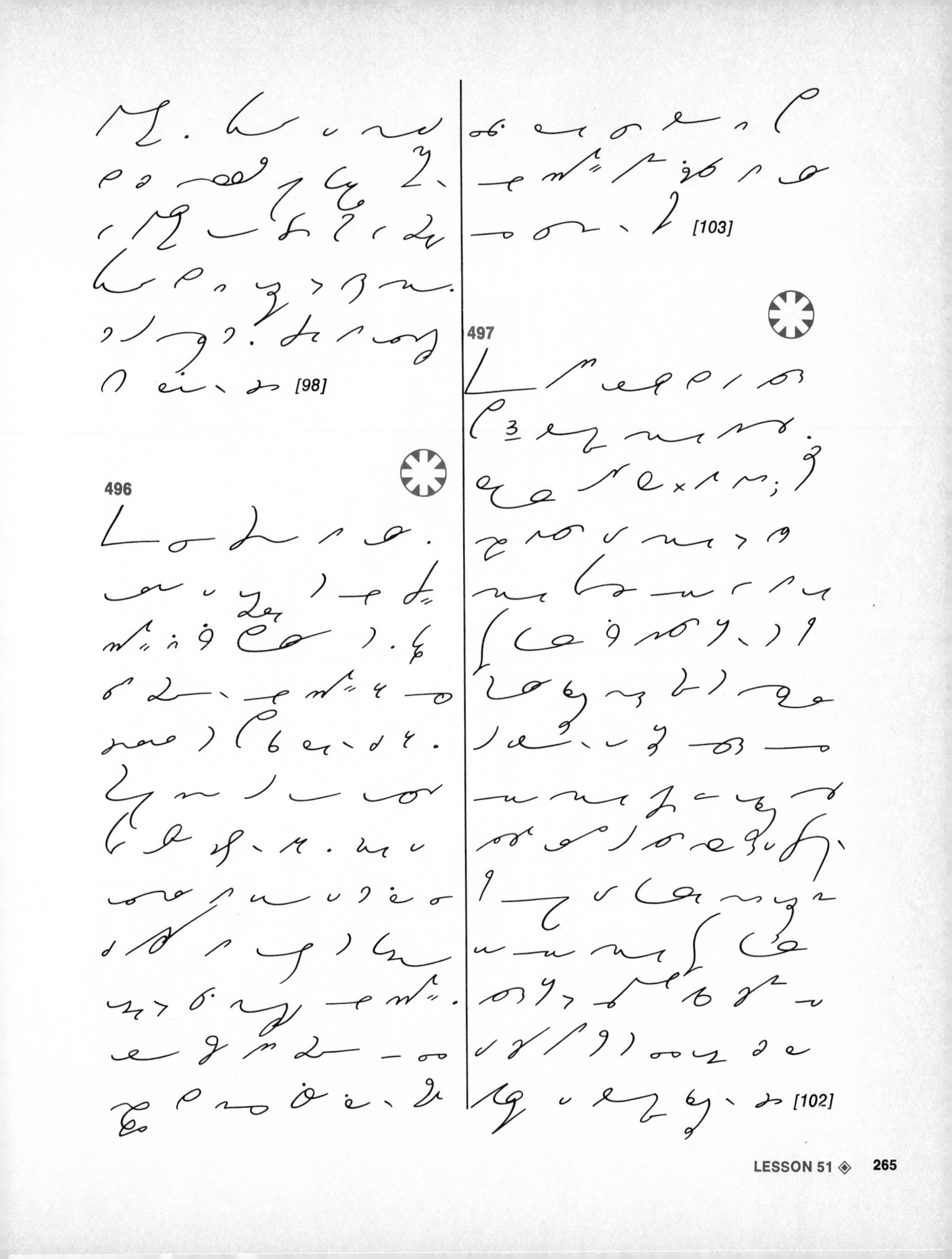

[98]

[103]

496

[102]

497

LESSON 

The practice material in this lesson concentrates on the shorthand principles you studied in Chapter 4.

498 BRIEF FORMS, DERIVATIVES, AND PHRASES

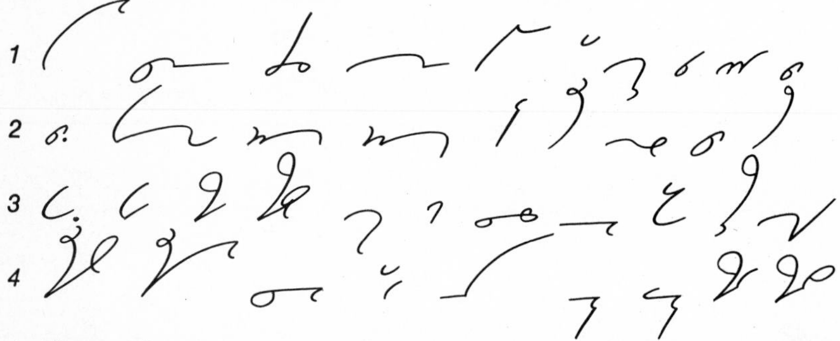

1 Times, acknowledgment, generally, gone, during, over, questions, yet, worth, use.

2 Using, bigger, suggest, suggestion, such, several, correspond-correspondence, how-out, ever-every.

3 Presenting, part, after, advertise, company, wish, immediately, must, opportunity, advantages, questioned.

4 Several days, several times, I must, over the, in time, in such, on such, after the, after that.

Building Transcription Skills

499 SPELLING FAMILIES ■ silent e dropped before -ment

Most words ending in *e* retain the *e* before the ending *-ment*.

ad·ver·tise·ment	**ar·range·ment**	**man·age·ment**
amuse·ment	**en·cour·age·ment**	**re·quire·ment**
an·nounce·ment	**en·gage·ment**	**state·ment**

but

ac·knowl·edg·ment	**judg·ment**	**ar·gu·ment**

500 Business Vocabulary Builder

consecutive Following one after the other.

conviction The state of being convinced or persuaded.

considerate Having a regard for the needs or feelings of others.

Reading and Writing Practice

501

an·nounc·ing

con·sec·u·tive

raise

judg·ment

[126]

502

equip·ment

thor·ough·ly

con·vic·tion

bro·chure

[109]

po·ten·tial

[130]

503

re·fer·ring

pre·par·ing

504

wast·ing

switch·ing

sur·prise

sur·vey

239-3752 [109]

505

ser·vice

man·age·ment

[104]

506

over·due

brought

Won't

ar·range·ments

ac·knowl·edg·ment

[134]

LESSON 

In this lesson you will obtain a thorough review of the shorthand principles you studied in Chapter 5.

507 BRIEF FORMS, DERIVATIVES, AND PHRASES

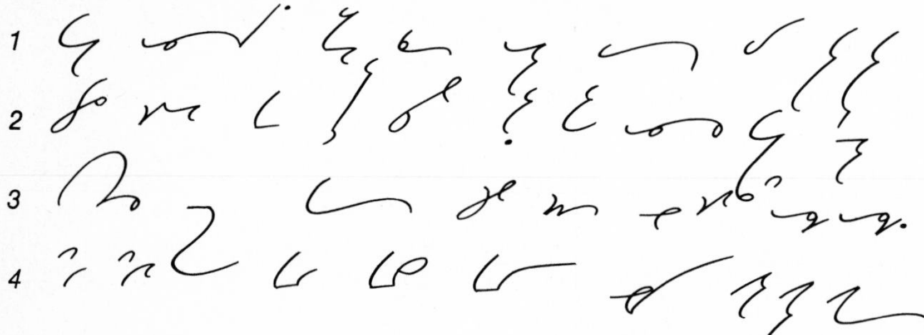

1 Purpose, regarding, opinions, circular, responsible, organization, ordinary, public, publish-publication.

2 Particularly, streets, upon, subjects, ideas, speaking, speaker, regularly, probably, newspaper.

3 Difficulty, envelope, progress, satisfy-satisfactory, success, next, states, under, request, requesting.

4 Under the, under those, upon the, upon that, upon them, next time, to speak, to publish, to progress.

Building Transcription Skills

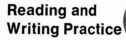

508 Business Vocabulary Builder

perplexing Confusing.

extensively Widely.

lapse Expire.

Reading and Writing Practice

509

manu·script

en·cour·ag·ing

ad·di·tion

ar·ea

[81]

511

ap·pre·ci·ate

prin·ci·ple

suc·cess·ful

[135]

510

en·gi·neers

edi·tion

lapse

prompt·ly

[127]

[137]

512

90

24

50

en·ve·lope

513

15

15

re·ceive

valu·able

[86]

514

ed·u·ca·tion

prompt

[114]

515

re·cent·ly

ac·cept·ed

trav·el·ing

[103]

516

sat·is·fac·to·ri·ly

212-4416

ef·fect

[96]

The practice material in Lesson 54 provides an intensive review of the principles you studied in Chapter 6.

517 BRIEF FORMS, DERIVATIVES, AND PHRASES

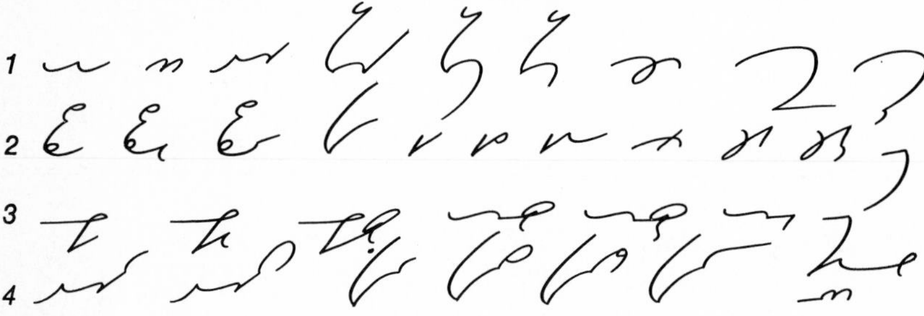

1 Railroad, world, throughout, objected, objective, objection, character, government, governs.

2 Experience, experiences, experienced, between, short, shortly, shorter, quantity, situation, situations, never.

3 Merchant, merchants, merchandising, recognize, recognizes, recognition, nevertheless.

4 Throughout the, throughout this, between the, between that, between these, between them, in the world.

Building Transcription Skills

518 SIMILAR-WORDS DRILL ■ their, there, they're

their Possessive form of *they.*

Some women make *their* own dresses.

there In or at that place.

He went *there* at my request.

they're Contraction for *they are.*

They're always ready to help you.

519

Business Vocabulary Builder

intricate Involved; complicated.

foresight The act of looking ahead.

shy away Timidly avoid.

Reading and Writing Practice

520

of·fer·ing

an·nu·al

in·tri·cate

Tech·ni·cal

ser

[143]

521

ap

ad

par

schedule

[104]

ser

character

ser

[149]

522

depressing

judgment

decorators

523

fuel

par

too

foresight

there

odor·less

par

con·trac·tor

[150]

524

their

they're

ser

par

am·a·teur

re·ceiv·ing

par

mod·ern

[114]

525

sched·ule

par

en·ve·lope

[73]

LESSON 55

In Lesson 55 you will review intensively the shorthand principles you studied in Chapter 7.

526 BRIEF-FORM DERIVATIVES AND PHRASES

1 Particularly, timely, partly, presently, gladly, probably, immediately, generally, ordinarily.

2 Greater, sooner, bigger, shorter, worker, manufacturer, speaker.

3 To progress, to part, to present, to speak, to publish, to put, to be, to have, to which, to value.

Building Transcription Skills

527 GRAMMAR CHECKUP ■ the infinitive

The infinitive is the form of the verb usually introduced by *to—to see, to be, to have, to do.*

Careful writers try to avoid "splitting" an infinitive, that is, inserting a word or phrase between *to* and the following word.

no

To properly do the job, you need better tools.

yes

To do the job properly, you need better tools.

no

He was told to carefully prepare the report.

yes

He was told to prepare the report carefully.

528 Business Vocabulary Builder

abuse (*noun*) Improper treatment or use.

inherited Received from someone at his death.

unwittingly Unintentionally.

Reading and Writing Practice

529

fre·quent

intro

sig·nif·i·cant

em·ploy·ees

intro

aris·en

cope

intro

if

[133]

530

as

in·sti·tu·tion

its

ex·pan·sion

intro

gen·er·ous

[139]

531

as

in·her·it·ed

par

trans·mit·ting

ti·tle

if

ef·fect

5 [105]

532

intro

ser

em·ploy·ee's

un·til

intro

[76]

533

1099

iden·ti·fy·ing

shown

if

[94]

534

al·though

intro

than

intro

wheth·er

won't

when

[96]

535

intro

ser

known

equiv·a·lent

as

re·quire·ments

if

[117]

The practice material in Lesson 56 concentrates on the principles you studied in Chapter 8.

536 BRIEF FORMS, DERIVATIVES, AND PHRASES

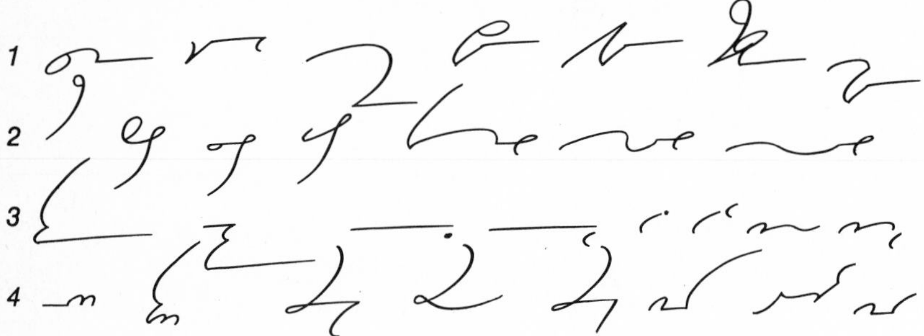

1 Acknowledgment, statements, government, apartment, department, advertisement, compartment.

2 Ever, wherever, whenever, whatever, bigness, greatness, gladness.

3 Businessmen, newspapermen, morning, mornings, thank, thanks, worker, workings.

4 In the world, business world, very important, very well, very much, one time, throughout the, one of the.

Building Transcription Skills

537 COMMON PREFIXES

Many words in the English language contain common prefixes. An understanding of the meanings of these prefixes will often give you a clue to the meaning of an unfamiliar word.

Perhaps you never heard of the word *superfluous.* However, if you know that *super* means *more than,* you will probably be able to figure out that *superfluous* means *more than enough.*

In each "Common Prefixes" exercise you will be given a common prefix, its meaning, and a list of words in which the prefix is used.

Read each definition carefully, and then study the illustrations that follow. A number of the illustrations are used in the Reading and Writing Practice.

COMMON PREFIXES ■ super-

super- over; more than

supervise To oversee.

supervisor One who oversees.

superior Over in rank; higher.

superfluous More than enough.

538 **Business Vocabulary Builder**

superb Supremely good.

unrewarding Unsatisfying.

highlight An outstanding event.

Reading and Writing Practice

539

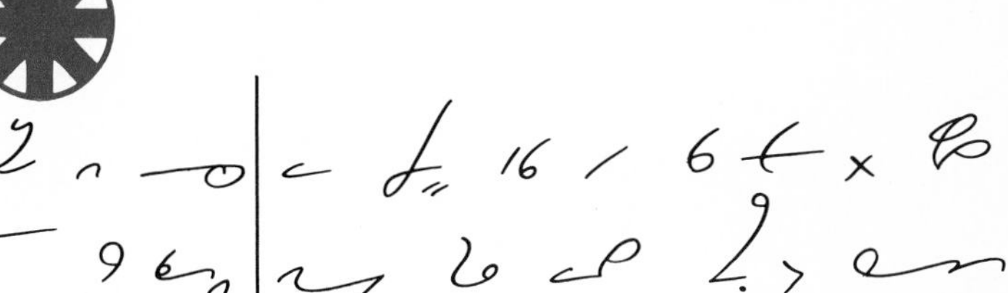

su·per·vi·sor

su·perb

ser

con·sum·er

intro

[121]

for·ward

540

par

conj

con·fi·dent

and o

worth·while

[84]

541

cal·cu·la·tors

when

intro

prop·er·ly

if

re·move

if

par

[157]

542

if

ser

re·ju·ve·nates

mod·ern·iz·ing

ser

cour·te·ous

when

[117]

intro

por·ta·ble

ser

weighs

par

[136]

543

if

re·lieve

and o

544

ap

intro

than

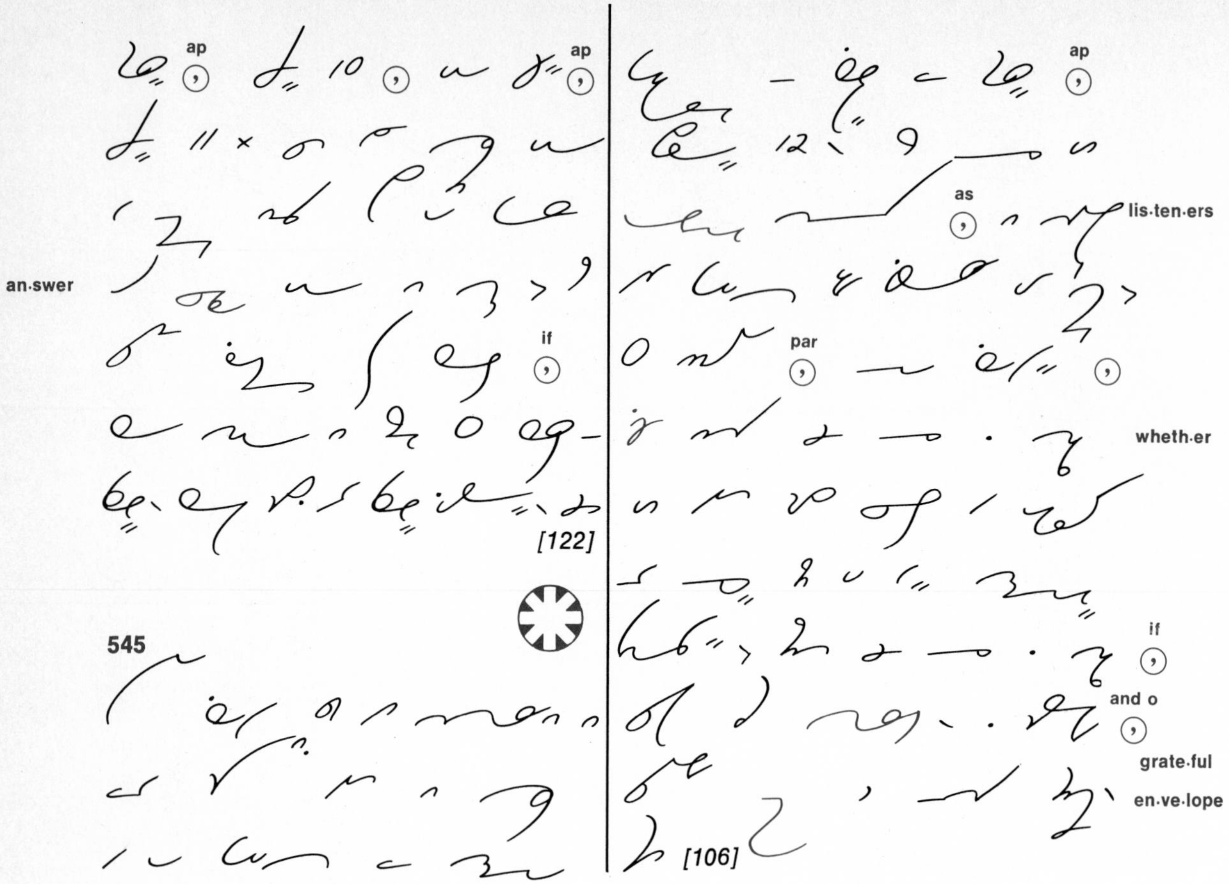

ap ap ap

lis·ten·ers
an·swer
if par

whet·her

[122]

545

if
and o
grate·ful
en·ve·lope

[106]

DID YOU KNOW THAT—

■ President Woodrow Wilson was an expert shorthand writer and that he drafted all his state papers in shorthand?

■ Samuel Pepys wrote his famous diary in shorthand? He wrote so legibly that students of literature had no difficulty making an accurate transcript of his notes.

■ George Bernard Shaw did all his composing in shorthand and then had his secretary transcribe his notes?

■ James F. Byrnes used his shorthand regularly while he was a Supreme Court justice, a Secretary of State, and the Governor of South Carolina?

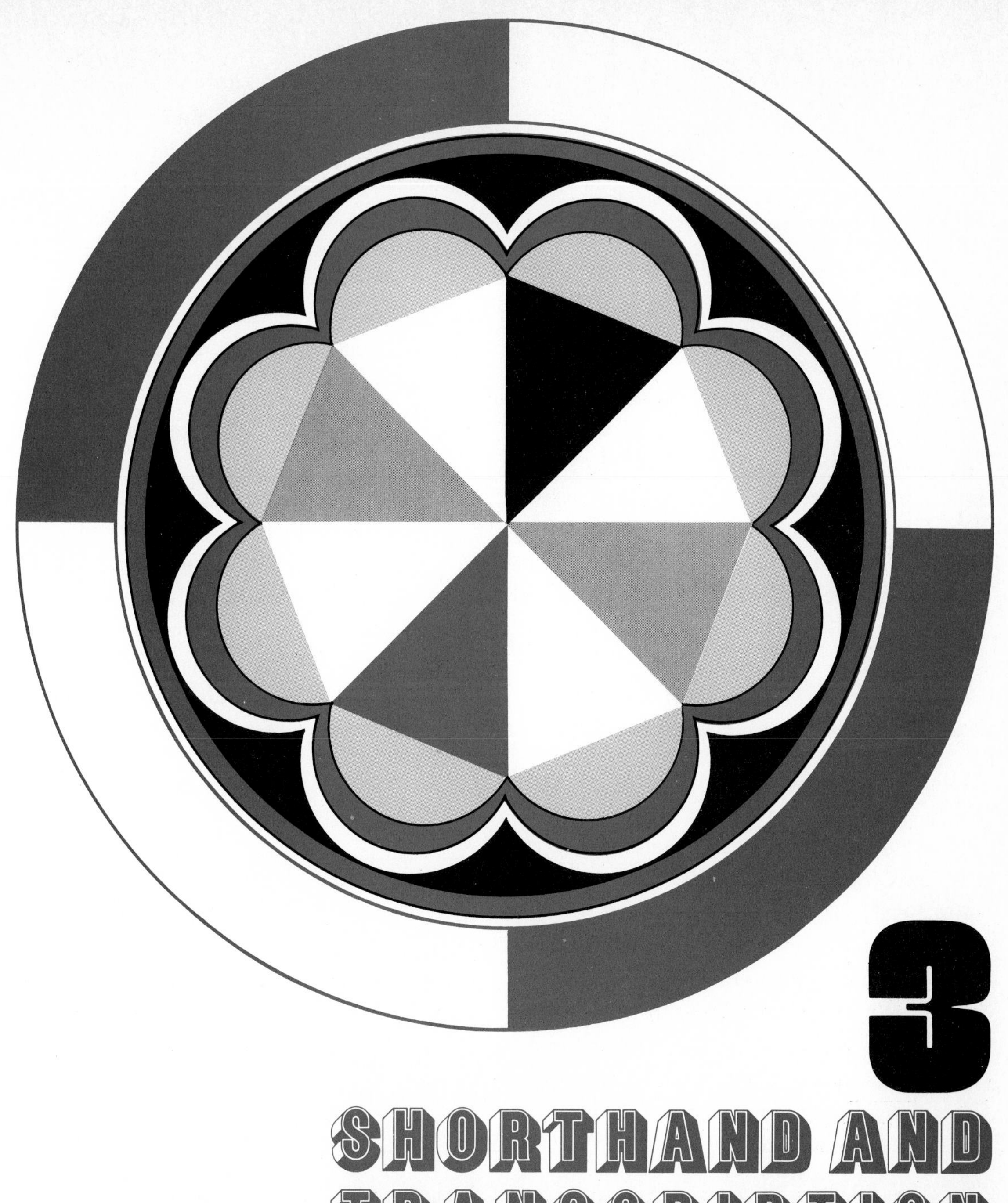

3

SHORTHAND AND TRANSCRIPTION SKILL BUILDING

Chapter 10 The Ideal Secretary

It is easy to list the qualifications the business employee should possess. He should be honest, dependable, intelligent, hardworking, friendly, cooperative, ambitious...But let's stop right there: *Any* favorable human attribute fits. Employers can reel off many traits they'd like to see in everyone they hire, but not a single boss really expects perfection. There are, however, four qualifications that the typical executive *insists* on for his secretary: excellent stenographic skill, good communication skill, poise, and good grooming.

EXCELLENT STENOGRAPHIC SKILL

"There is absolutely no substitute for good skills," the typical executive will tell you. By *skills* he means mainly shorthand, typewriting, and transcription skills. The secretary must be able to take his dictation at the rate the executive wants to give it without the plea, "You're going too fast for me." He expects her to transcribe her shorthand notes quickly and accurately on the typewriter. To do this, she needs a typing speed of at least 60 words a minute and a good knowledge of letter and report formats.

GOOD COMMUNICATION SKILL

It could be said that communication is the secretary's main job, for her duties involve conveying meaning, both through the written and the spoken word, and through her poise, manners, tact, and facial expressions. All are methods of communicating. As to the written word, the typical executive expects the secretary to be his editor. When he has dictated a letter, he may say, "You fix it up." That is, he wants her to put in the correct punctuation, paragraph the letter properly, correct errors in names, dates, figures, and word usage.

Many secretaries are expected to write simple letters, memorandums, and routine reports for their bosses. Letters include those that make travel or hotel reservations, acknowledge receipt of something, ask for something, follow up on an appointment or schedule, and thank someone for a favor. The secretary writes memorandums and reports to schedule and follow up on meetings, to report on progress, to review activities, and so on.

The secretary's voice is one of her most important assets. She greets callers, gives instructions to her employer's subordinates, communicates with other executives, and talks on the telephone to many people daily, both inside and outside the company. She may even be asked to talk before an audience.

POISE

To most people, poise means always looking cool, calm, and collected. However, poise means more than that. It includes knowing what to say to an irate customer who insists on tongue-lashing the boss (who doesn't want to be disturbed); how to explain tactfully why the executive is an hour late for an appointment with an out-of-town visitor; how to accept negative criticism from the boss even when she doesn't feel it is deserved; how to withold confidential information from those who are not authorized to obtain it, no matter how persistent they are. Poise is the reflection of a mature personality, of complete confidence in oneself. It is a quality that every top executive ranks high on his list of "musts."

GOOD GROOMING

Every executive has a right to expect that his secretary will always look her best on the job. Her appearance can reflect favorably or unfavorably on him. Of course, she must be immaculately clean from head to toe.

The smart secretary takes pride in herself, her job, and her boss; she never "lets herself go." This means daily attention to hair, nails, and complexion. It means getting sufficient rest so that she looks sharp and alert. And, of course, it means selecting clothing with great care and keeping it spotless and in good repair. Contrary to what some people believe, the secretary doesn't have to wear somber clothing. In fact, bright, tasteful colors are quite acceptable. What she must avoid is the extreme—the extreme in hair style and makeup, in clothing, and in accessories. The secretary who wants to look like the belle of the ball in the office is due for a rude awakening! But the secretary who puts it all together with good taste and good grooming is an asset to her boss and to the company.

LESSON 

The letters in Lesson 57 contain several hundred brief forms and derivatives. Because you have seen and written these brief forms many, many times, you should be able to read through the letters in this lesson with record speed!

Building Transcription Skills

546 SPELLING FAMILIES ■ -tion, -sion

Words Ending in -tion

ac·tion	**in·for·ma·tion**	**ques·tion**
ap·pli·ca·tion	**or·ga·ni·za·tion**	**rep·u·ta·tion**
col·lec·tion	**pro·tec·tion**	**sta·tion**
es·ti·ma·tion	**pub·li·ca·tion**	**sub·scrip·tion**

Words Ending in -sion

ap·pre·hen·sion	**di·vi·sion**	**pro·fes·sion**
col·li·sion	**oc·ca·sion**	**pro·vi·sion**
con·clu·sion	**per·mis·sion**	**ses·sion**
de·ci·sion	**per·sua·sion**	**tele·vi·sion**

547 Business Vocabulary Builder

extraordinary Exceptional; remarkable.

cope with Overcome problems and difficulties.

enviable Highly desirable.

Reading and Writing Practice 

548

ap

Mod·ern

curiosity

acknowledged

and o

offering

extraordinary

par

[141]

549

responsible

if

territory

ser

companies

enviable

if

intro

yours

request

30

30

12

110

10036

[187]

550

ques·tion·able

when

intro

[177]

cope

intro

ex·pe·ri·enced

551

ap

thefts

intro

dif·fi·cul·ties

conj

par

pre·cau·tions

sched·uled

valu·able

conj

ser

intro

when

conj

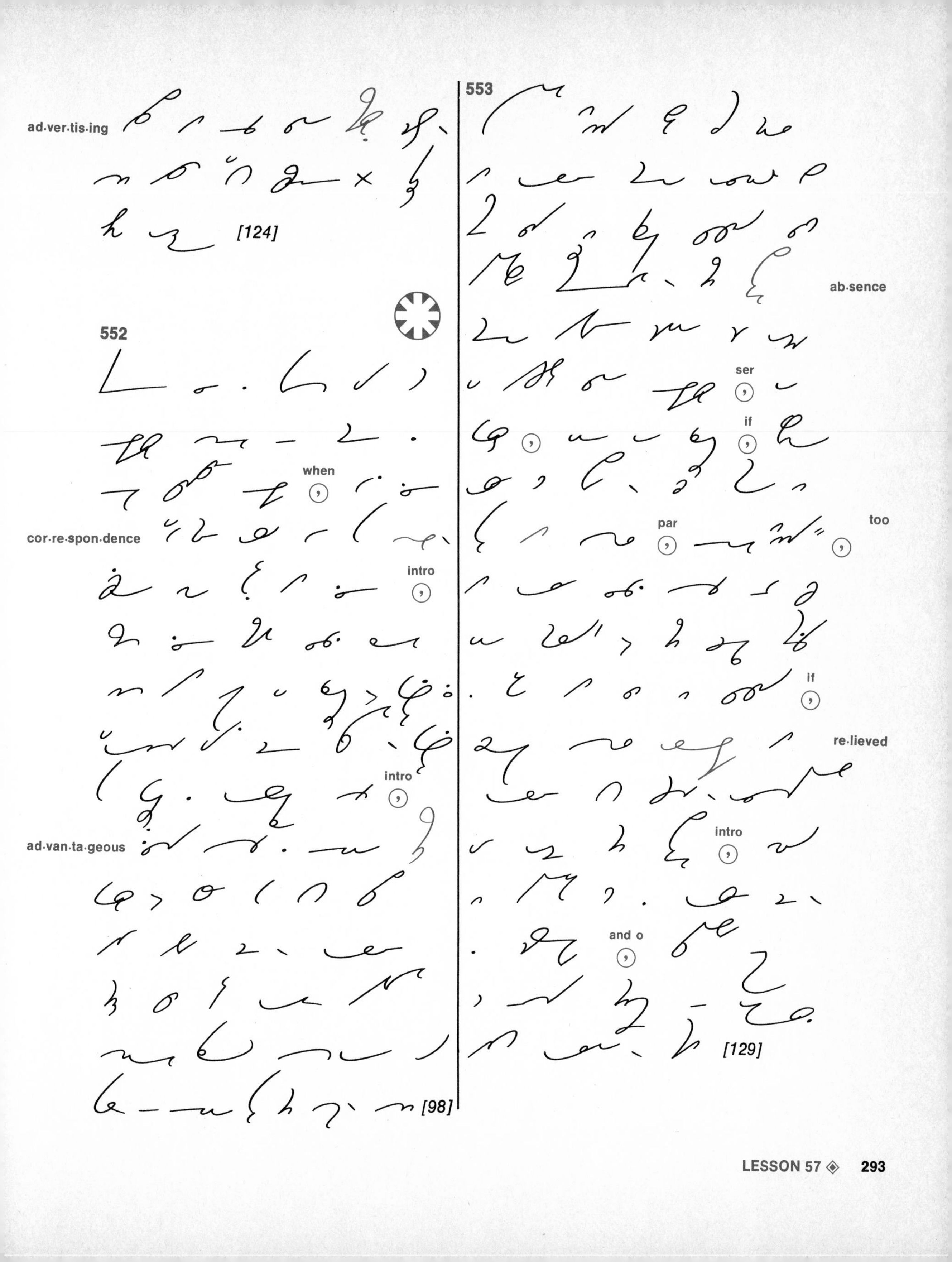

ad·ver·tis·ing

[124]

552

when

cor·re·spon·dence

intro

intro

ad·van·ta·geous

[98]

553

ab·sence

ser

if

par

too

if

re·lieved

intro

and o

[129]

554 Transcription Quiz In Lessons 31-56, you have been learning to apply nine rules for the correct use of the comma. In Lessons 57-69, you will have an opportunity to test your mastery of these rules through a Transcription Quiz—a letter in which no commas are indicated in the shorthand. It will be your job, as you copy the letter in shorthand in your notebook, to insert the commas in the proper places and to give the reasons why the commas are used. The shorthand in your notebook should resemble the following example:

At the head of each Transcription Quiz you will find the number and types of commas you should supply.

The correct punctuation of the following letter calls for 7 commas—1 comma as clause, 4 commas apposition, 2 commas parenthetical.

[121]

LESSON 58

Lesson 58 provides you with an opportunity to increase your skill in the use of the frequent phrases of Gregg Shorthand. The following letters are "packed" with phrases. Several illustrations of all the phrasing principles of Gregg Shorthand appear in the letters.

Building Transcription Skills

555 GRAMMAR CHECKUP ■ sentence structure

Parallel ideas should be expressed in parallel form.

no

I hope our relationship will be long, pleasant, and "of profit" to both of us.

yes

I hope our relationship will be long, pleasant, and "profitable" to both of us.

no

As soon as we receive the necessary information, your account will be opened and "we will ship your order."

yes

As soon as we receive the necessary information, your account will be opened and "your order will be shipped."

It is especially important to keep parallel all ideas in a tabulation.

no

Her main duties were:

1. *Taking dictation and transcribing*
2. *Answering the telephone*
3. *"To take care" of the files*

yes

Her main duties were:

1. *Taking dictation and transcribing*
2. *Answering the telephone*
3. *"Taking care" of the files*

556 **Business Vocabulary Builder**

replenishing Adding a new stock or supply to.

wardrobe All the articles of clothing belonging to one person.

gratifying Pleasing.

Reading and Writing Practice

557

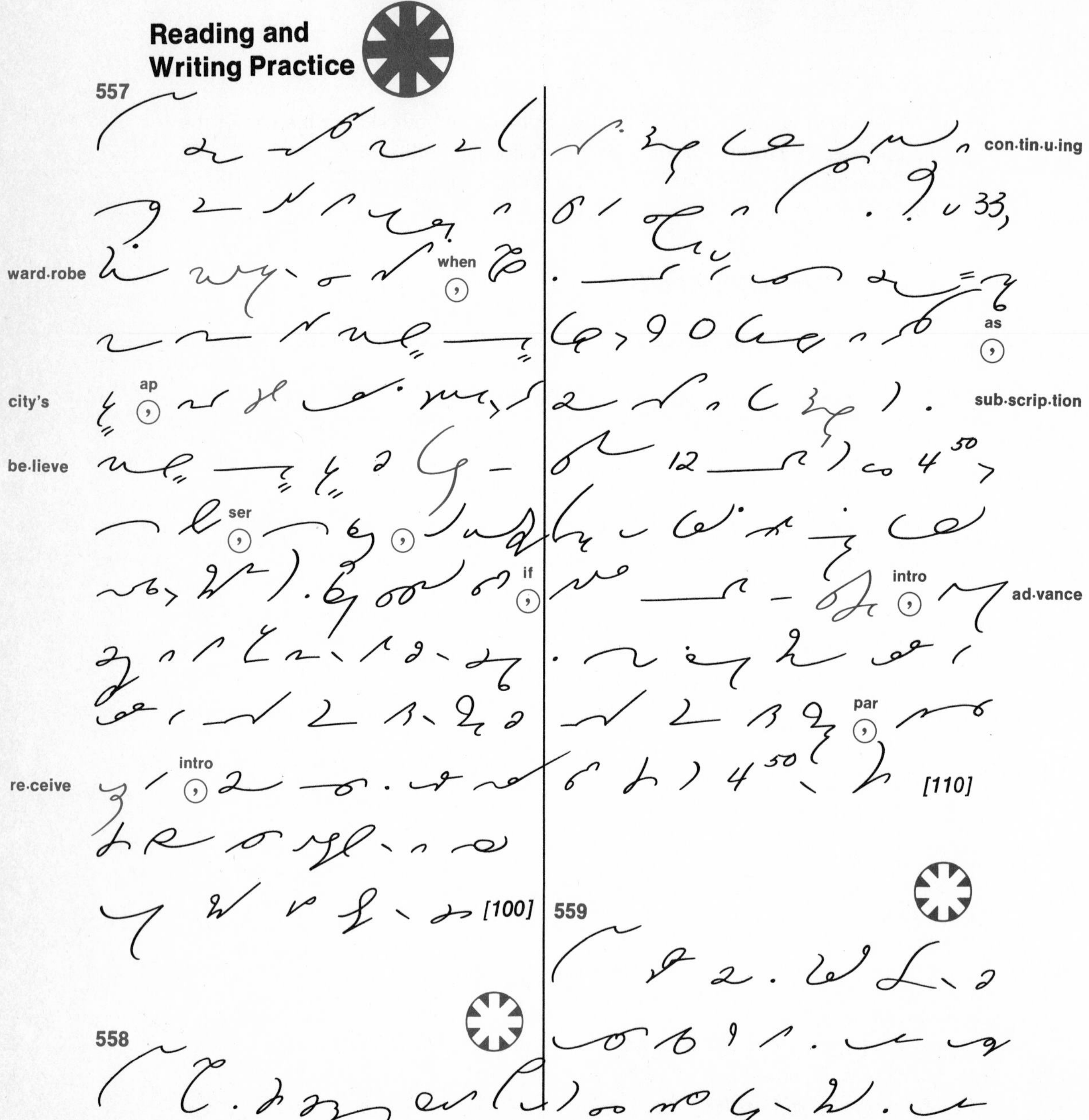

den·tal

ser

col·lege

if

debts

if

conj

in·di·vid·u·als

par

[104]

560

ste·reo

conj

ac·cept·ing

if

par

25/

re·ceive

[127]

561

18

18

10

18

mod·el

ex·haust·ed

conj

par

in·con·ve·nience

[99]

busi·ness

gra·ti·fy·ing

562

intro

par

par

[104]

563 Transcription Quiz To punctuate the following letter correctly, you must supply 5 commas—1 comma *and* omitted, 2 commas series, 2 commas parenthetical.

[127]

LESSON 

If any of the joined word beginnings are still a little hazy in your mind, here is a chance to fix them firmly in your mind. The letters in Lesson 59 have many illustrations of the joined word beginnings of Gregg Shorthand.

Building Transcription Skills

564 SPELLING FAMILIES ■ -ible, -able

A troublesome pair of endings for most stenographers and secretaries is *-ible, -able.* Unfortunately, there is no rule that enables us to determine when to use *-ible* and when to use *-able.* In most words in the English language the ending is spelled *-able.* However, it is spelled *-ible* in a sufficient number of words that you should think twice before you type an *i* or *a* before *-ble.*

Words Ending in -able

avail·able	**con·sid·er·able**	**re·li·able**
bear·able	**de·sir·able**	**suit·able**
ca·pa·ble	**mem·o·ra·ble**	**un·for·get·ta·ble**
com·fort·able	**ob·tain·able**	**un·rea·son·able**

Words Ending in -ible

ad·mis·si·ble	**im·pos·si·ble**	**pos·si·ble**
de·duct·ible	**in·cred·i·ble**	**re·spon·si·ble**
de·fen·si·ble	**leg·i·ble**	**sen·si·ble**
flex·i·ble	**plau·si·ble**	**ter·ri·ble**

565 Business Vocabulary Builder

survive Live through.

key personnel Employees who are vital to the successful operation of a business.

incredible Difficult to believe.

Reading and Writing Practice

566

re·open

intro

par

lose

if

when

de·scrip·tive

ap

[144]

567

re·ceiv·ing

can·celed

conj

intro

fur·ther

[97]

568

sub·scrip·tion

if

ar·eas 1985

and o

guide·lines

de·sir·able

conj

[127]

569

un·for·get·ta·ble ser

sights

heart

par fur·ther

[127]

570 10

in·ter·com·mu·ni·ca·tion

ser

over·head

lo·ca·tions

[104]

571 Transcription Quiz The correct punctuation of the following letters calls for 5 commas—4 commas apposition, 1 comma *as* clause.

[118]

LESSON 

Lesson 60 gives special attention to the joined word endings of Gregg Shorthand. The letters in the Reading and Writing Practice contain many illustrations of the joined word endings.

Building Transcription Skills

572 COMMON PREFIXES ■ pre-

pre- before; beforehand; in advance

preview An advance showing or viewing.

precaution A measure taken beforehand to prevent harm or to assure good.

preliminary Before the main business or action.

prediction An act of telling beforehand; a forecast.

573 Business Vocabulary Builder

potential Possible but not yet realized.

transferable Capable of being conveyed or shifted from one person to another.

via By way of.

Reading and Writing Practice

574

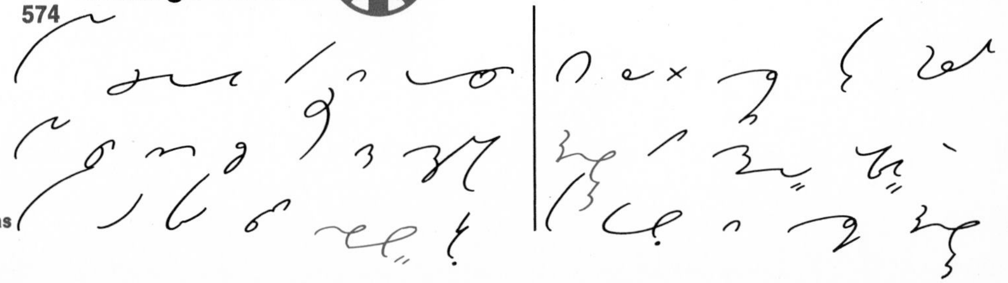

sub·scrip·tions

intro

Christ·mas

ac·tu·al·ly

ap

at·tached

ef·fi·cient

and o

par

shop·ping

[141]

575

po·ten·tial

conj

choose

intro

sub·scribe

ser

en·ve·lope

intro

fam·i·ly's

[131]

576

intro

equip·ment

fa·vor·able

intro

intro

filled

ser

when

wel·come

[131]

577

an·nu·al

15 ser 16 17

of·fer·ing

intro

pre·ferred

intro

13 14

13 14 [134]

578

when

ex·change

re·cy·cle

if

di·rec·to·ry

en·vi·ron·ment

intro

intro

[95]

579

ap

pol·lu·tion

conj

to·mor·row's

re·gard·less

[113]

580 Transcription Quiz The correct punctuation of the following letter calls for 5 commas—1 comma *as* clause, 2 commas introductory, 2 commas parenthetical.

As you copy the Transcription Quiz in your notebook, be sure to insert the necessary commas at the proper points and to indicate the reason for the punctuation.

[131]

LESSON 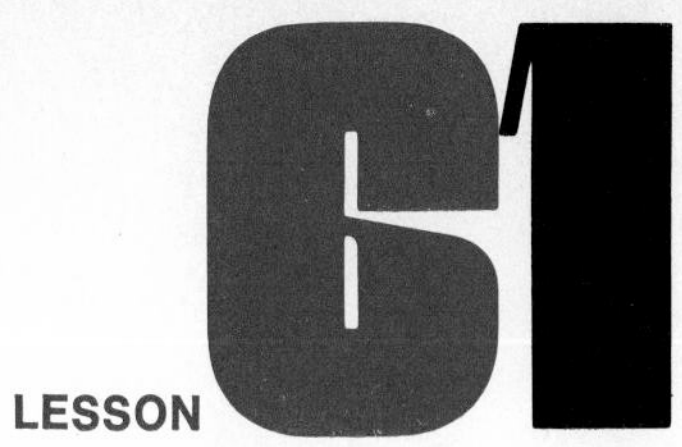

Disjoined word beginnings are given intensive treatment in Lesson 61. The letters in the Reading and Writing Practice contain many illustrations of the disjoined word beginnings in Gregg Shorthand.

Building Transcription Skills

581 GRAMMAR CHECKUP ■ comparisons

The comparative degree of an adjective or adverb is used when reference is made to two objects; the superlative degree is used when reference is made to more than two objects.

comparative

Of the two boys, Jim is the taller.

Which boy is more efficient, Jim or Harry?

Is Mr. Smith or Mr. Green better qualified to do the job?

superlative

Of the three boys, Jim is the tallest.

Which of the boys is the most efficient, Jim, Harry, or John?

Is Mr. Smith, Mr. Green, or Mr. Brown best qualified to do the job?

582 Business Vocabulary Builder

diligent Industrious; done with painstaking effort.

interior appointments The furnishings and equipment on the inside of a car.

transatlantic Across the Atlantic Ocean.

Reading and Writing Practice

583

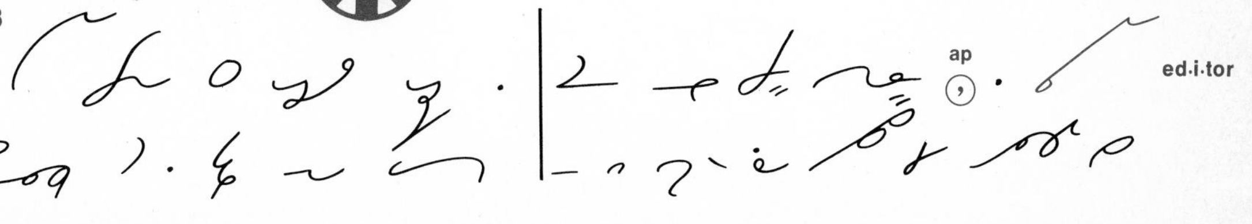

ap

ed·i·tor

trans·por·ta·tion

conj

intro

par

en·ve·lope

and o

[124]

584

ap

ap·plied

conj

su·per·vi·sor

intro

ar·ea

trans·ferred

conj

[168]

585

Ro·mance

ap

30=

intro

re·ac·tion

[112]

586

par

in·ter·state

hon·ored

than

[89]

587

ser

intro

ar·ti·cles

and o

de·scribes

ad·vance·ments

ser

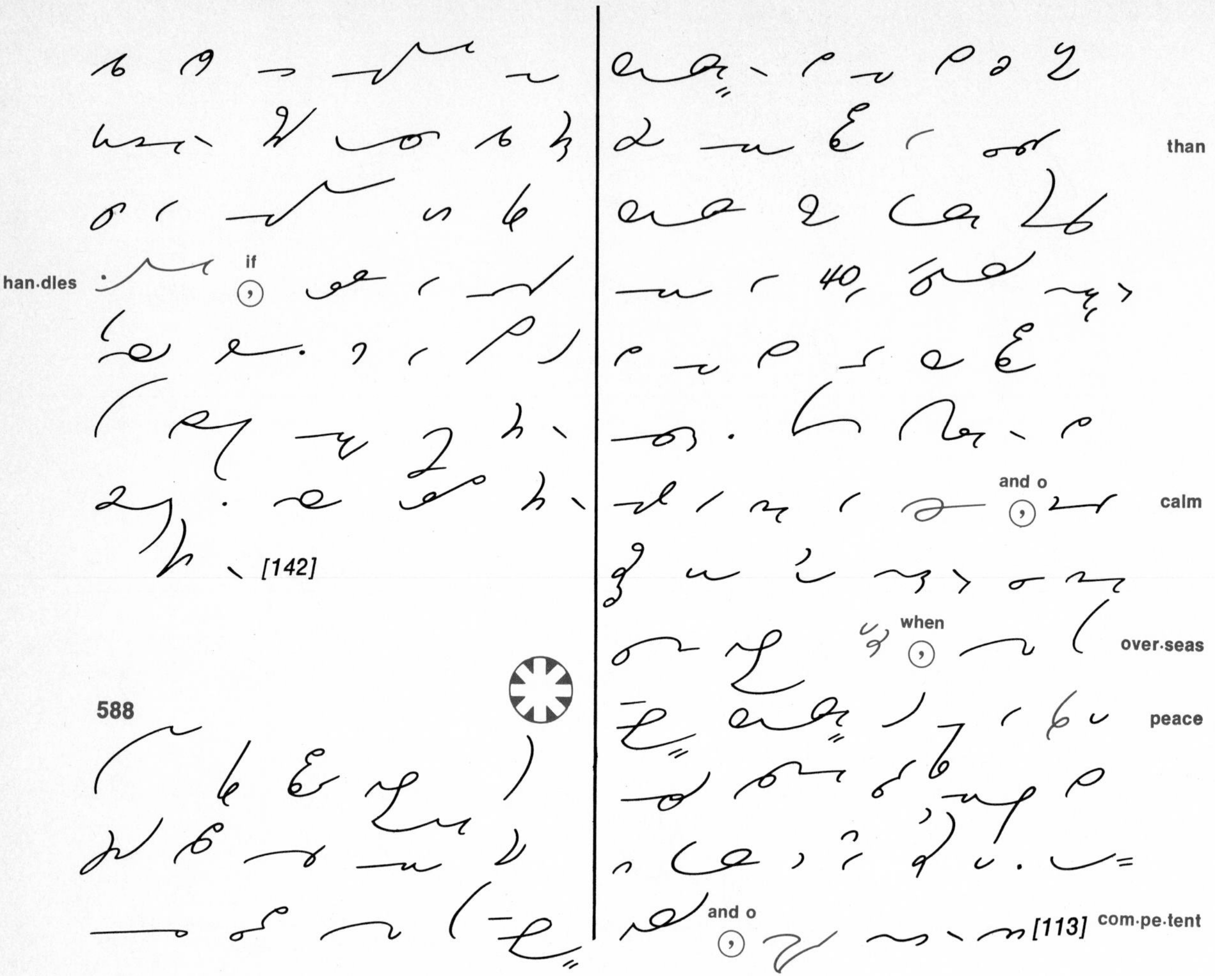

589 Transcription Quiz To punctuate the followng letter correctly, you must supply 4 commas—1 comma *if* clause, 2 commas parenthetical, 1 comma *and* omitted.

[76]

LESSON 62

In this lesson you will brush up on the disjoined word endings of Gregg Shorthand. All the disjoined word endings are used several times in the Reading and Writing Practice.

Building Transcription Skills

590 SIMILAR-WORDS DRILL ■ loss, lose, loose

loss (*noun*) That which one is deprived of.

He suffered a *loss* through theft.

lose (*verb*) To be deprived of.

I know that you do not want to *lose* your paintings.

loose Unattached; not fastened.

We are forwarding to you our *loose*-leaf booklet.

591 Business Vocabulary Builder

excerpt A passage copied from something, such as a book, record, or letter.

diminishing Lessening.

facility Ease.

conserved Saved.

Reading and Writing Practice

592

when

12

Tech·ni·cal

1960

150

par

com·mit·tee

if

coun·sel·or

[138]

593

ex·cerpt

de·vel·op·ing

and o

par

self-con·fi·dence

[157]

594

fu·el

conj

di·min·ish·ing

intro

com·mer·cial

ser

intro

re·mod·el·ing

intro

like·li·hood

[162]

595

graph·ic

ser

tu·ition

screen

wom·en

if

than

par

ab·sorb·ing

[121]

596

ser

con·ve·nient

phys·i·cal

[103]

597 Transcription Quiz The following letter requires 4 commas—2 commas parenthetical, 1 comma introductory, 1 comma *if* clause.

[125]

One of the major reasons why Gregg Shorthand can be written so rapidly and fluently is its blends—single strokes that represent two or more sounds. In the Reading and Writing Practice of this lesson you will find many words and phrases that employ these blends.

Building Transcription Skills

598 COMMON PREFIXES ■ co-

co- with, together, jointly

cooperative Working together.

cooperation The act of working together.

coordinate To bring together.

coeducation Joint education, especially the education of boys and girls at the same school.

599 Business Vocabulary Builder

commitments Promises to do something.

primary First in order of importance.

honorarium A payment given to a professional person for services for which fees are not required.

Reading and Writing Practice

600

ap

em·ploy·ees'

when

ac·cept

as

com·mit·ments

oc·curred

intro

shown

par

[125]

601

ecol·o·gy

lis·tened

intro

yours

conj

intro

intro

[97]

602

and o

suc·cess·ful
ad·he·sive

drug·store

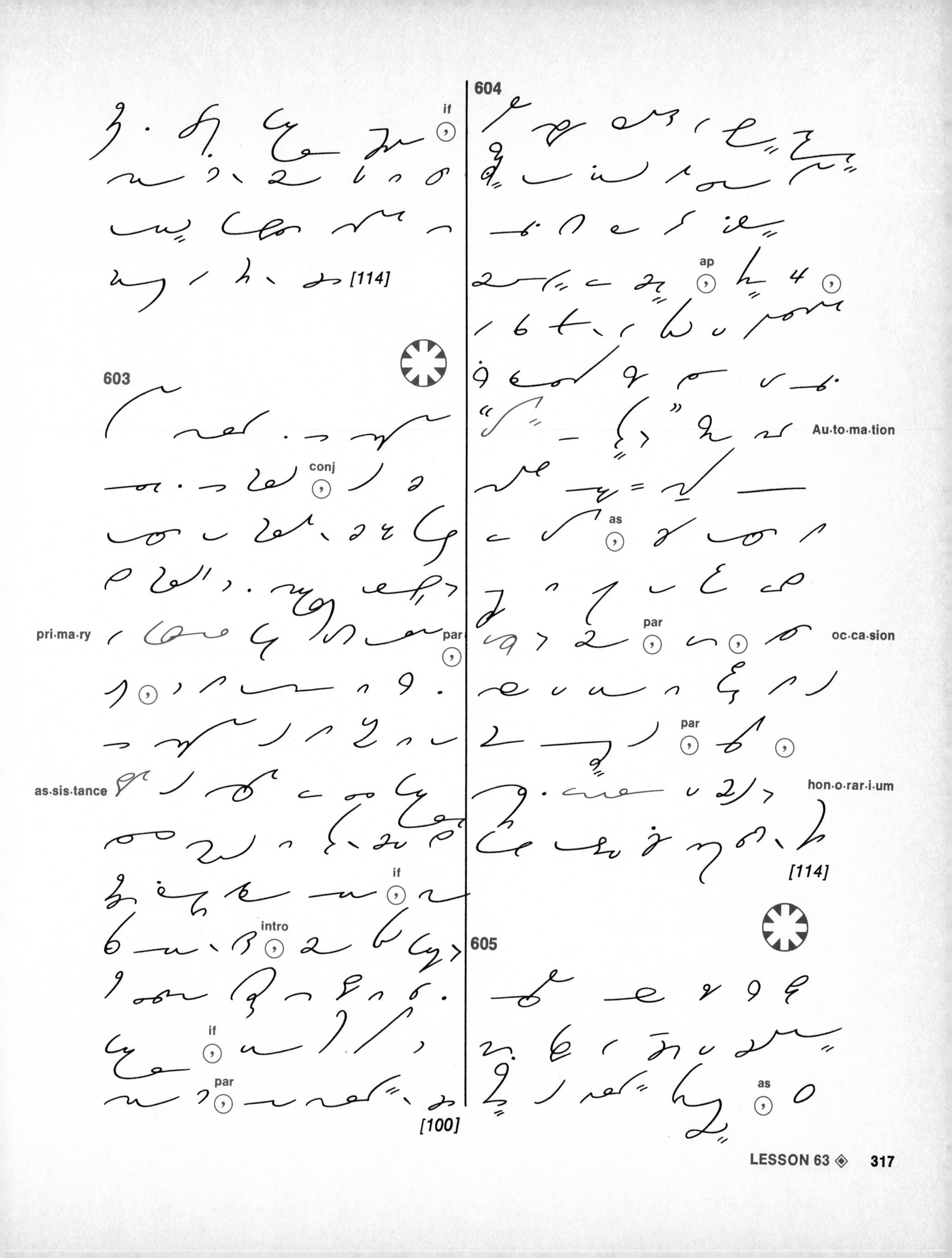

if

[114]

603

conj

pri·ma·ry

par

as·sis·tance

if

intro

if

par

[100]

604

ap

Au·to·ma·tion

as

par

oc·ca·sion

par

hon·o·rar·i·um

[114]

605

as

ac·ci·dent

traf·fic

par

[134]

606 Transcription Quiz The following letter requires 7 commas to be punctuated correctly—2 commas *and* omitted, 1 comma introductory, 2 commas series, 2 commas parenthetical.

Remember to indicate each comma in your shorthand notes and to give the reason for its use.

[107]

LESSON 64

As you learned during the early stages of your study of Gregg Shorthand, unnecessary vowels are omitted in some words to help us gain fluency in writing without sacrificing legibility. In the Reading and Writing Practice of this lesson you will find many illustrations of words from which unnecessary vowels are omitted.

Building Transcription Skills

607 SPELLING FAMILIES ■ -ary, -ery, -ory

Words Ending in -ary

an·ni·ver·sa·ry	el·e·men·ta·ry	pri·ma·ry
com·pli·men·ta·ry	glos·sa·ry	sec·ond·ary
con·trary	itin·er·ary	sec·re·tary
cus·tom·ary	li·brary	tem·po·rary
dic·tio·nary	nec·es·sary	vo·cab·u·lary

Words Ending in -ery

bind·ery	ma·chine·ry	re·cov·ery
de·liv·ery	mas·tery	re·fin·ery
dis·cov·ery	mys·tery	sce·nery
gro·cery	que·ry	sta·tio·nery

Words Ending in -ory

de·pos·i·to·ry	fac·to·ry	man·da·to·ry
di·rec·to·ry	his·to·ry	sat·is·fac·to·ry
ex·ec·u·to·ry	in·tro·duc·to·ry	ter·ri·to·ry
ex·plan·a·to·ry	in·ven·to·ry	vic·to·ry

608

Business Vocabulary Builder

hearty Expressed with warm feeling. (Do not confuse *hearty* with *hardy*, which means *rugged, strong*.)

induce To persuade.

middleman An agent between the producer of goods and a retailer or consumer.

Reading and Writing Practice

609

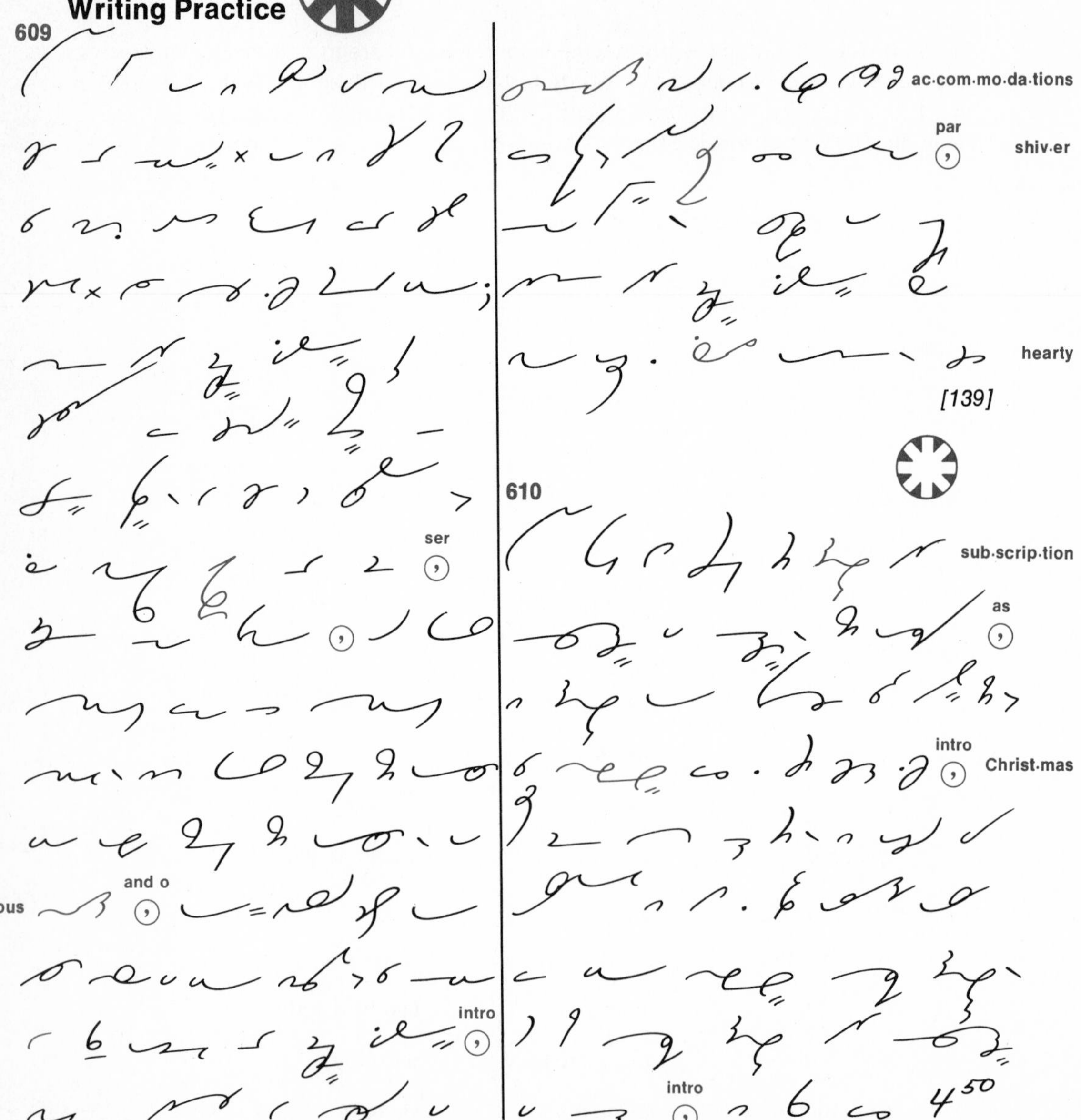

pe·ri·od·i·cal

intro

ide·al

par

[155]

611

wel·com·ing

ap

1970

intro

in·duce

[106]

612

when

cu·ri·ous

intro

mys·tery

32

cour·te·ous

par

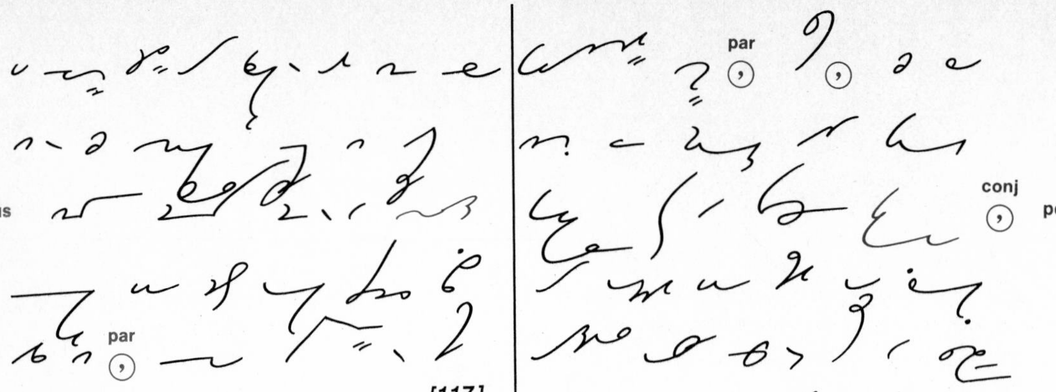

[117]

613

be·gin·ning

conj

par

conj

pop·u·lar

waste

if

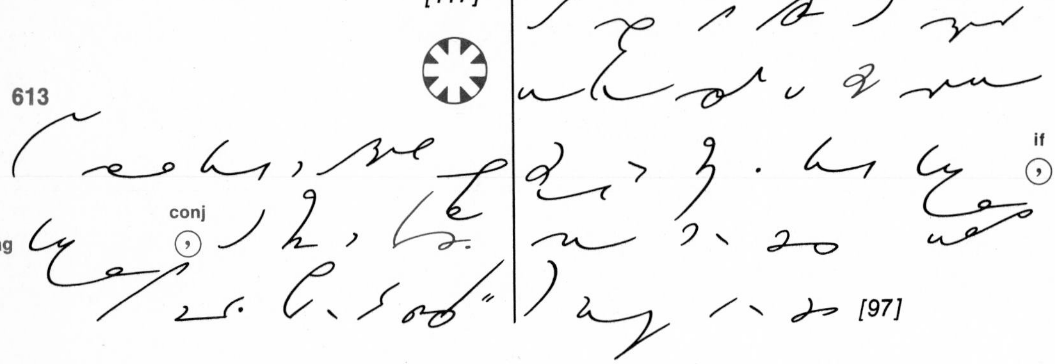

[97]

614 Transcription Quiz In the following letter you must supply 4 commas to punctuate it correctly—3 commas introductory, 1 comma *if* clause.

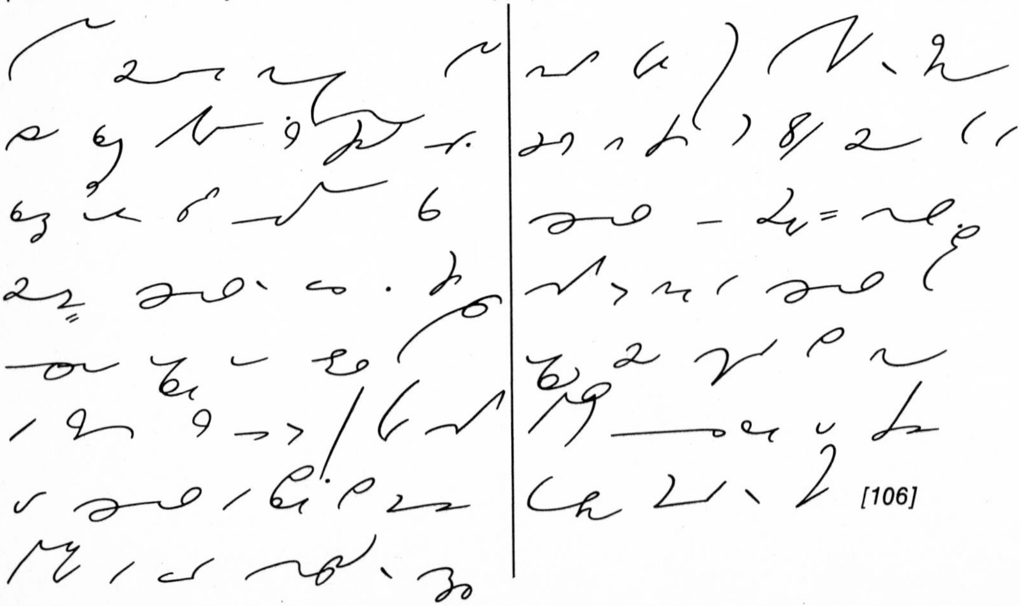

[106]

LESSON 65

There will be times on the job when you will have to take dictation that contains numbers. Because of the importance of accuracy in transcribing numbers, always take special care in writing numbers in your shorthand notes. The letters in the Reading and Writing Practice of this lesson will help you fix in your mind the devices in Gregg Shorthand for expressing numbers and quantities.

Building Transcription Skills

615 SIMILAR-WORDS DRILL ■ county, country

county A political division of a state.

Our plant will be located in Rensselaer *County,* near Troy, New York.

country A nation.

Our *country* produces more aluminum than any other country.

616 Business Vocabulary Builder

anticipate Look forward to; expect.

proceed Go ahead. (Do not confuse *proceed* with *precede,* which means *come before.*)

recourse A turning to for help.

Reading and Writing Practice

617

50-50

than

quan·ti·ty

ex·am·ples

Re·al·i·ties

ap

an·tic·i·pate

yours

par

[144]

[148]

618

619

fur·nish·ing

cat·a·log

intro

sug·ges·tion

intro

as

intro

if

con·se·quent·ly

intro

intro

intro

pro·ceed

conj

[230]

620

as

ap·prov·al

ap

Coun·ty

ap

grate·ful

when

mod·ern

coun·try

neigh·bors

intro

ac·quaint·ed

conj

for·ward

[166]

621

ear·marked

par

gen·er·os·i·ty

intro

ex·ceed

[69]

622 Transcription Quiz For you to supply: 3 commas—1 comma introductory, 2 commas series.

[134]

LESSON 

This lesson provides another opportunity to test your knowledge of the brief forms of Gregg Shorthand. In the Reading and Writing Practice there are hundreds of brief forms and derivatives.

Building Transcription Skills

623 COMMON PREFIXES ■ un-

un- not

unhappy Not happy; sad.

unsatisfied Not content.

uncertain Not sure.

unsolicited Not asked for; voluntary.

624 Business Vocabulary Builder

paralyzing (*adjective*) Powerless.

versatile Capable of doing many things.

Reading and Writing Practice

625

as

cor·re·spon·dent

conj

sat·is·fied

intro

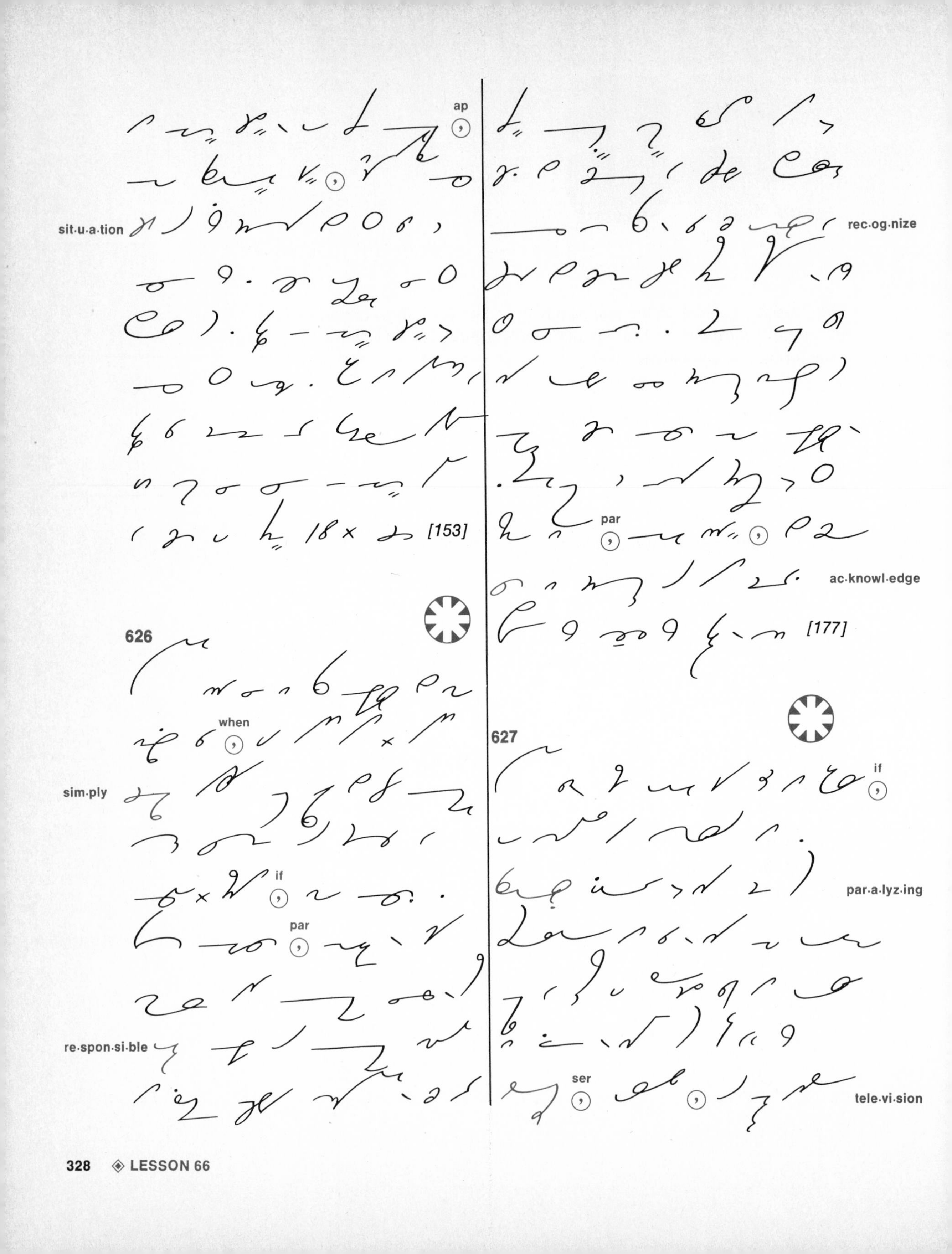

ap

sit·u·a·tion

[153]

626

when

sim·ply

if

par

re·spon·si·ble

rec·og·nize

par

ac·knowl·edge

[177]

627

if

par·a·lyz·ing

ser

tele·vi·sion

conj

their

en·ter·prise

[127]

628

re·ferred

as

par

touch

par

sim·i·lar

[110]

629

li·brary

par

re·ceive

com·pli·men·ta·ry

par

intro

25,

con·ve·nience

[111]

630

when

taste·ful·ly

and o

intro

shab·by

if

com·ple·ment

161-1118

[153]

631 Transcription Quiz For you to supply: 5 commas—1 comma *when* clause, 1 comma *and* omitted, 2 commas series, 1 comma conjunction.

[106]

Lesson 67 provides you another opportunity to sharpen your phrasing skill. The letters in the Reading and Writing Practice contain several illustrations of all the phrasing principles of Gregg Shorthand.

Building Transcription Skills

632 GRAMMAR CHECKUP ■ verbs—with "one of"

1 In most cases, the expression *one of* takes a singular verb, which agrees with the subject *one.*

One *of the men on the staff* is *ill.*
One *of our typewriters* does *not work.*

2 When *one of* is part of an expression such as *one of those who* or *one of the things that,* the verb following is usually plural, to agree with the plural object of the preposition *of.*

He solved one of the problems *that* have *been annoying businessmen for years.*
He is one of the men *who* drive *to work.*

633 Business Vocabulary Builder

reverses Changes in fortune from better to worse; setbacks.

undue Excessive. (Do not confuse *undue* with *undo,* which means *to cancel.*)

complimentary Flattering. (Do not confuse *complimentary* with *complementary,* which means *filling out* or *completing.*)

stationery Such items as paper, envelopes, pencils, etc. (Do not confuse *stationery* with *stationary,* which means *remaining in one place.*)

Reading and Writing Practice

634

im·prove·ments

par

intro

if

ad·van·tage

pleasure

par

[137]

635

as

prompt·ness

intro

de·vel·op·ments

af·fect·ed

sim·i·lar

non·pay·ment

intro

par

conj

if

ap·pre·ci·ate

[126]

636

ap 18

ar·ea

par

intro

par

per·ma·nent

in·ter·rupt intro

5

intro

ap 25

un·due [134]

637

un·der·take

intro

equip.ment

18

if

con·ve·nient

[141]

638

par

ex·pe·ri·enced

ac·cus·tomed

urg·ing

and o

de·pend·able

par

if

[99]

639 Transcription Quiz For you to supply: 4 commas—2 commas introductory, 2 commas parenthetical.

[144]

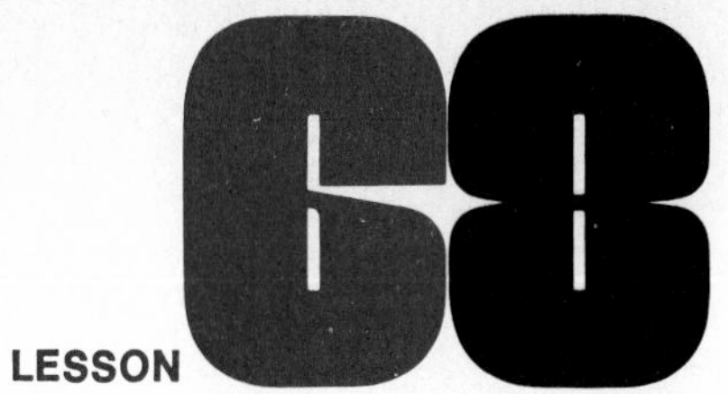

LESSON 68

Lesson 68 contains a general review of the major principles of Gregg Shorthand.

Building Transcription Skills

640 SIMILAR-WORDS DRILL ■ due, do

due Owing; payable.

You must pay your bills when they are *due.*

do To carry out; to perform.

I cannot *do* the work in the time I have been given.

641

Business Vocabulary Builder	
resemblance	Similarity.
decor	The decorative style of a room or home.
apprehensive	Fearful.

Reading and Writing Practice

642

ap

Chi·ca·go

re·signed

par

re·sem·blance

de·cor

de·scribes

ser

rea·sons

when

intro

in·ter·view

392-

6877

conj

Eu·ro·pe·an

intro

[139]

[125]

643

644

as

if

res·i·dents

sat·is·fy·ing

and o

conj

intro

de·vel·op·ing

intro

at·trac·tive

les·sons

when

prac·tic·ing

intro

par

[120]

ap

645

intro

[158]

for·get·ting

intro

646

if

op·por·tu·ni·ties

ap

par

par

ac·ci·dent

conj

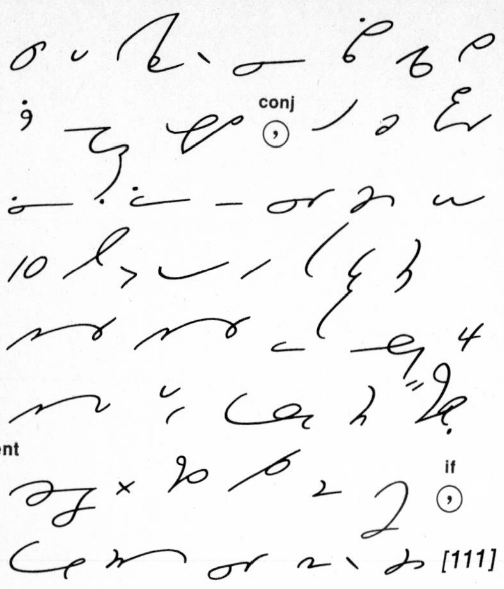

conj

par

won't

due

con·ve·nient

if

[111]

par

[83]

647

648 **Transcription Quiz** For you to supply: 4 commas—2 commas parenthetical, 1 comma conjunction, 1 comma *and* omitted.

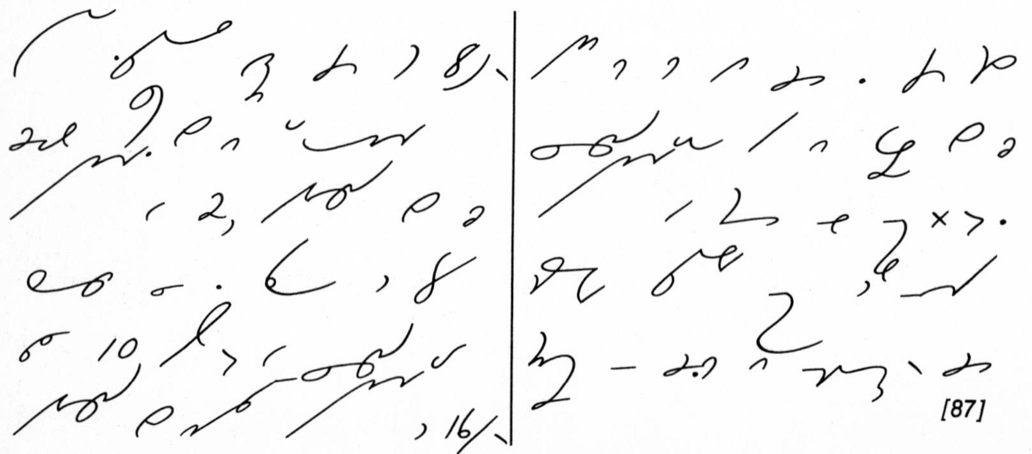

[87]

LESSON 69

Lesson 69, like Lesson 68, contains a general review of the major principles of Gregg Shorthand.

Building Transcription Skills

649 COMMON PREFIXES ■ re-

re- again

reorder To order again.

reconsider To take up again.

reconfirm To assure again.

replenish To fill or supply again.

repeat To say again.

650 Business Vocabulary Builder

eligible Qualified for. (Do not confuse *eligible* with *legible,* which means *able to be read.*)

waive Dispense with.

capacity The position in which one functions.

Reading and Writing Practice

651

re·ceived

ap

intro

when

wal·let

intro

intro

han·dle

flight

conj

when

re·act

par

oc·ca·sion

when

if

[144]

[118]

653

652

skid·ding

if

el·i·gi·ble

cope

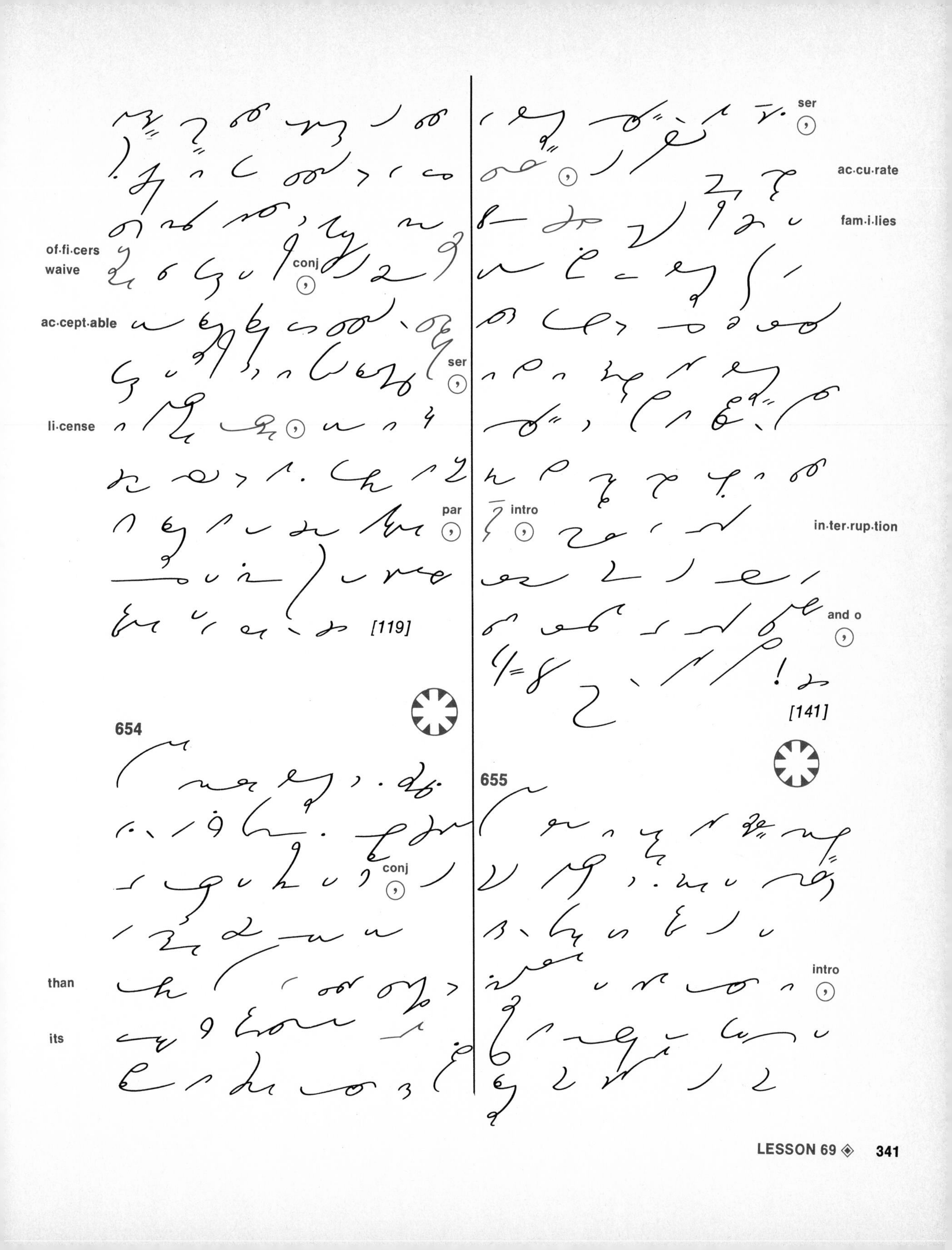

of·fi·cers
waive
conj
ac·cept·able
ser
li·cense
par
[119]

654

conj
than
its

ser
ac·cu·rate
fam·i·lies
intro
in·ter·rup·tion
and o
[141]

655

intro

com·mu·ni·ty

en·cour·ag·ing

par

too

par

[123]

656

adapt

ap

intro

ap

di·rec·tor

par

for·ward

[91]

657 Transcription Quiz For you to supply: 5 commas—1 comma conjunction, 1 comma *when* clause, 1 comma *and* omitted, 2 commas parenthetical.

[116]

LESSON 70

You will find the articles in Lesson 70 interesting and enlightening.

Building Transcription Skills

658 SPELLING FAMILIES ■ -ious, -eous

Words Ending in -ious

con·scious	**gra·cious**	**pre·vi·ous**
cu·ri·ous	**in·ge·nious**	**se·ri·ous**
de·li·cious	**ju·di·cious**	**stu·di·ous**
de·vi·ous	**ob·vi·ous**	**te·dious**
en·vi·ous	**pre·cious**	**var·i·ous**

Words Ending in -eous

ad·van·ta·geous	**er·ro·ne·ous**	**out·ra·geous**
cou·ra·geous	**hid·eous**	**si·mul·ta·neous**
cour·te·ous	**mis·cel·la·neous**	**spon·ta·ne·ous**

659 Business Vocabulary Builder

erroneously Incorrectly.

judiciously Wisely.

passive Not active.

Reading and Writing Practice

Reading Scoreboard Now that you are on the last lesson, you are no doubt very much interested in your final shorthand reading rate. If you have followed the practice suggestions you received early in the course, your shorthand reading rate at this time should be a source of pride to you.

To get a real picture of how much your shorthand reading rate has increased with practice, compare it with your reading rate in Lesson 18, the first time you measured it.

Lesson 70 contains 459 words	
If you read Lesson 70 in	your reading rate is
9 minutes	**50 words a minute**
10 minutes	**45 words a minute**
12 minutes	**40 words a minute**
13 minutes	**35 words a minute**
15 minutes	**30 words a minute**
18 minutes	**25 words a minute**

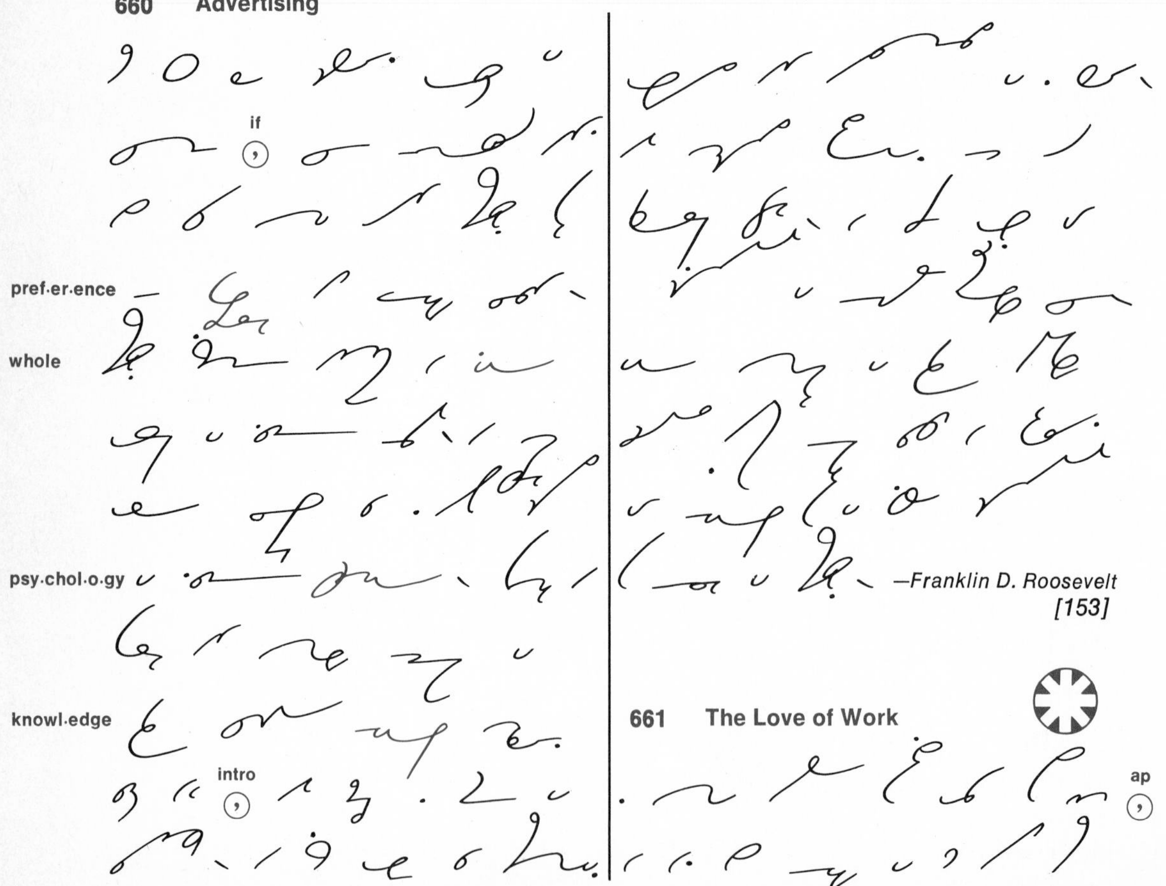

intro

er·ro·ne·ous·ly

be·lieve

par

usu·al·ly

ser

ju·di·cious·ly

pas·sive

busy

If you will

if

if

dis·tinc·tion

par

wheth·er

purge

Every kind

te·dious

par

sour

when

pres·tige

spurs

[306]

APPENDIX

States

The abbreviations in parentheses are those recommended by the Post Office Department.

Alabama [AL]

Alaska [AK]

Arizona [AZ]

Arkansas [AR]

California [CA]

Colorado [CO]

Connecticut [CT]

Delaware [DE]

Florida [FL]

Georgia [GA]

Hawaii [HI]

Idaho [ID]

Illinois [IL]

Indiana [IN]

Iowa [IA]

Kansas [KS]

Kentucky [KY]

Louisiana [LA]

Maine [ME]

Maryland [MD]

Massachusetts [MA]

Michigan [MI]

Minnesota [MN]

Mississippi [MS]

Missouri [MO]

Montana [MT]

Nebraska [NE]

Nevada [NV]

New Hampshire [NH]

New Jersey [NJ]

New Mexico [NM]

New York [NY]

North Carolina [NC]

North Dakota [ND]

Ohio [OH]

Oklahoma [OK]

Oregon [OR]

Pennsylvania [PA]

Rhode Island [RI]

South Carolina [SC]

South Dakota [SD]

Tennessee [TN]

Texas [TX]

Utah [UT]

[Vermont VT]

Virginia [VA]

Washington [WA]

West Virginia [WV]

Wisconsin [WI]

Wyoming [WY]

Principal Cities of the United States

Akron
Albany
Atlanta
Baltimore
Birmingham
Boston
Bridgeport
Buffalo
Cambridge
Camden
Canton
Charlotte
Chattanooga
Chicago
Cincinnati
Cleveland
Columbus
Dallas
Dayton

Denver
Des Moines
Detroit
Duluth
Elizabeth
Erie
Fall River
Flint
Fort Wayne
Fort Worth
Gary
Grand Rapids
Hartford
Houston
Indianapolis
Jacksonville
Jersey City
Kansas City
Knoxville

Long Beach
Los Angeles
Louisville
Lowell
Memphis
Miami
Milwaukee
Minneapolis
Nashville
Newark
New Bedford
New Haven
New Orleans
New York
Norfolk
Oakland
Oklahoma City
Omaha
Paterson

Peoria
Philadelphia
Pittsburgh
Portland
Providence
Reading
Richmond
Rochester
Sacramento
St. Louis
St. Paul

Salt Lake City
San Antonio
San Diego
San Francisco
Scranton
Seattle
Somerville
South Bend
Spokane
Springfield
Syracuse

Tacoma
Tampa
Toledo
Trenton
Tulsa
Utica
Washington
Wichita
Wilmington
Worcester
Yonkers

Common Geographical Abbreviations

America
American
United States

England
English
Great Britain

Canada
Canadian
Puerto Rico

Index of Gregg Shorthand

In order to facilitate finding, this Index has been divided into six main sections—Alphabetic Characters, Brief Forms, General, Phrasing, Word Beginnings, Word Endings.

The first figure refers to the lesson; the second refers to the paragraph.

INDEX OF BRIEF FORMS

The first figure refers to the lesson; the second to the paragraph.

INDEX OF BUILDING TRANSCRIPTION SKILLS

The first figure refers to the lesson; the second figure to the paragraph.

COMMON PREFIXES

GRAMMAR CHECKUP

PUNCTUATION PRACTICE —COMMAS

SIMILAR WORDS

SPELLING FAMILIES

Frequently Used Phrases

of Gregg Shorthand

	A	B	C	D	E	F	G
1							
2							
3							
4							
5							
6							
7							
8							
9							
10							
11							
12							
13							
14							
15							
16							
17							
18							
19							